D1188475

Loving Men
for All the Right Reasons

Loving Men
for All the
Right Reasons

Yehuda Nir, M.D.
Bonnie Maslin, Ph.D.

THE DIAL PRESS
NEW YORK

Published by
The Dial Press
1 Dag Hammarskjold Plaza
New York, New York 10017

Copyright © 1982 by Yehuda Nir and Bonnie Maslin

All rights reserved.

Manufactured in the United States of America
First printing
Design by Karin Batten

Library of Congress Cataloging in Publication Data

Nir, Yehuda, 1930–
Loving men for all the right reasons.

1. Love—Case studies. 2. Interpersonal
relations—Case studies. 3. Problem family—Case
studies. I. Maslin, Bonnie. II. Title.
BF575.L8N56   646.7′7   81–12440
ISBN 0–385–27209–X   AACR2

To François Truffaut
&
Adele H

Contents

Loving Men
for All the Right Reasons

Intimacy

There is an important principle involved here. Namely, that intimacy should be a goal of relationships, and the capacity to achieve it is central to a person's well-being.

There is no value judgment being made that intimacy must be achieved through marriage or that this particular form of partnership is a necessary prerequisite for the development of important emotional bonds between man and woman. Although marriage, in and of itself, does not automatically guarantee intimacy, it is our conviction that "there can be no intimacy without some exclusivity."*

Intimacy is possible only when a relationship has a durable foundation. Casual connections just don't provide this. Becoming involved with a man is an experience, not an event. Whether your man is

Husband
Lover
Friend
Consort
Mate

* Virginia Adams, "Erikson Sees Psychological Danger in Trend of Having Fewer Children," *The New York Times*, August 4, 1979, p. 17.

Suitor
Partner
Roommate
Cohabitant

the key to happiness is in making a serious commitment to that other person. With this sense of purpose you can learn to love for all the right reasons.

   It seems that some things remain the same no matter how rapidly the world changes. We all want to love and to feel loved. We all want to have that feeling of caring and belonging, of being close to someone, of being in someone's thoughts—of being remembered. There is nothing more joyous than knowing you are special to someone and that someone is special to you.

   The need to love, to belong, and to feel connected reflects a very central aspect of our lives, of our being human. This need to be intimate with another person is deep-seated. We arrive in the world helpless and dependent on others for food, care, attention, security, and love. This helpless condition is crucial to our emotional growth. We are vulnerable as children, and it is only through our parents that we begin to form ourselves and negotiate a course through life. Ironically, it is through this sense of helplessness that we begin to develop the feeling of being valued by another human, and of our valuing others. Out of this simple fact of our nature emerges the need to be loved. Once established, it accompanies us through the rest of our days.

   This type of belonging, of sharing intimacies, affects our emotional state and health. Clearly attachment and commitment are central to happiness and our sense of well-being. For most women it means finding "the right guy," or "that special person," and it involves intimacy with a romantic partner. Not finding the right partner leaves one feeling detached and not needed—in a word, lonely. (That is not to say this is what one must feel. It is simply what most women report as their response to the situation.)

In our adult lives each one of us attempts to find our own way of experiencing intimacy. Beginning with our parents and families, intimate relationships shift to friends and romantic involvements with men. Casual acquaintances, romantic infatuations, one-night stands, living together, marriage, the building of families—only some of these relationships are truly gratifying. Only some fulfill our basic needs for intimacy and commitment. Others just fulfill a small aspect of our needs for sex and superficial companionship.

The way a woman relates to a man she regards as a potential partner is not a series of accidental events. Everything reflects her personality, her character, her nature—from the type of man she gets involved with to how the relationship proceeds. How she chooses a man, whom she finds appealing (her "type"), who turns her on, who has that something special—all are part of her style. How she behaves on a date, the sex they have (or don't have), how she treats a man, the attitudes and role she assumes toward him—all are aspects of that lovestyle. For some women their style brings them the intimate commitment they ultimately seek. However, a woman who wants a deep relationship and fails repeatedly to develop one is caught by her style. She reaches out to a man she wants and fails to connect. The pain it can bring—the intense sense of loneliness when what she desires and what she has are at odds—is great. In her disappointment she may not recognize that it is probably her own behavioral pattern and not necessarily men who have caused her this great unhappiness.

If a woman's lovestyle is unsuccessful, her attempt to become comfortably close to a man can be fraught with seemingly endless complications. Instead of love, acceptance, and closeness there are rejection, exploitation, misunderstanding, hostility, and anger. The only way to cope with this is to confront the pattern of behavior and to try to change it.

WHAT IS A LOVESTYLE?

A lovestyle is a way of relating that leads to a bond with another person. It is an approach to love. A successful lovestyle means being able to relate to a man in a spontaneous way by coming into a relationship with basic trust and being open to the experience with all its facets, good and bad. It means delaying judgments, criticisms, and premature conclusions about both the positive and negative sides of the man with whom you will share yourself. It means taking the whole person into consideration.

Seeing your role in the ups and downs of the relationship is essential to a successful lovestyle. Honest exchange must replace the fear of being taken advantage of, and a sense of thoughtful acceptance needs to displace a desire to change or remold the man. This ability to relate sensitively, realistically, and openly to a man does not come easily to anyone, but it can come from laying to rest the fears and conflicts we carry around with us from our earliest, formative relationships. Reflect—stop and think—before you cast blame.

Ironically, a successful lovestyle means having no predictable pattern in the way you respond to a man. Each man is different, as is each experience with him. To be able to establish true commitment you must be able to adapt to this everchanging person (just as he, also, must adapt to you). Rigidity and predictability are what doom a relationship. Flexibility, adaptability, true freedom, are the hallmarks of success in love. Conversely, an unsuccessful lovestyle is a self-defeating pattern marked by inflexible behavior. It consists of unwitting reenactments of earlier patterns. Each man is recast in the image of someone from the past. Such unconscious repetitions of past scenarios usually doom a relationship before it has a chance. Instead of enabling a woman to confront another human and realistically evaluate him, the pattern dictates an automatic response, reflecting her distortions and preconceived notions. Instead of each encounter with a man marking the beginning of an experience with a specific individual, a preexisting set of feelings about men is activated. Onto him are projected the impressions of what he must be. The real relationship becomes muddled. He doesn't have a chance to be a real, live person and, instead, is relegated to playing out his role in a predestined drama.

Imagine a cocktail party where the host introduces a woman to a famous actor. Awed by her stereotype of what a famous actor is—"too important to talk to me"—she finds herself nervous and unable to have even a simple social conversation. She walks away dejected, confirmed in her view that this important man didn't really want to talk to her.

What happened? Her preconceived notion has made her fail to respond to the actual situation. Instead of seeing him as a real person, she automatically responds to him with her own preconceived image of what he must be, not what he is. She reenacts her own scenario and succeeds in transforming reality to verify once again that she was right all along. Though she suffers disappointment, this woman avoids facing the unknown, the anxiety of dealing with this "important man." She manages to walk away from the situation sure of her perception of him and of famous men in general. Unfortunately her security and equilibrium are maintained at a great price. Her pattern has cut her off from a potentially pleasurable experience, from what might have been interesting and even fun.

In love, unwitting repetition of patterns reduces a man to a one-dimensional character. A man is replaced by a caricature. A woman who has an unsuccessful lovestyle is bound by a pattern of behavior. She is absolutely sure in thirty

seconds either that a man is for her or that he is not her
"type." This predisposition allows him to sweep her off her
feet, or it allows her to dismiss him without a second
thought. There is no room for the natural evolution, for the
real growth, of a relationship. When things go wrong, she
will only blame him, never taking responsibility for her contribution to the situation. All men are the same—the right
guy, the unattainable guy, or the wrong guy. They fit preconceived notions. Unfortunately, so do the relationships
that develop.

In the past, society made decisions for the individual fe-
male. Women had to get married, and early. It may have
been an arranged marriage or one dictated by social pressure, the only way to leave home or the only acceptable
way to have sex, but without question marriage was the
preeminently desirable state. Today the pressures and the
directives are gone. There is a new reality to being single.
And it is now more difficult than ever to find a partner.

The new freedom has had a major effect upon people's
attitudes toward personal relationships. The very matrix of
society has altered, since many people remain single these
days. The acceptance of the single parent, the changing role
of women, the more progressive attitudes toward sex, abortion, longer life expectancy—these are just a few contribut-
ing factors to the growing number of unattached women.

Many of the social changes that serve to create the "single society" are welcome signs of progress. However, the
dissolution of mores and the lack of structure they entail
make life more trying. The net effect of this radically
changed social climate is that more and more women have
discovered that, with the social pressure off, they cannot find
a partner—a frightening revelation, difficult to cope with.

Each individual woman who desires a mate must now work at finding a partner without much assistance.

Getting connected is entirely up to you, for society has ceased to be the major resource for creating partnerships. Looking your best, being educated, having a career—all suddenly take on new meaning. But even having the right look, the proper schooling, and a good job are not enough. What is important is to understand your relationship to men: Why do you choose the men you do? What do you look for and what do you end up with? In short, what is your lovestyle, your pattern of interrelating. Recognizing your lovestyle is critical in this new kind of search for intimacy and commitment.

An unsuccessful pattern of relating can lead to great disappointment with a seemingly endless succession of men who never meet your wants. But perhaps the most troublesome thing about the unsuccessful pattern is the enormous difficulty in even recognizing it. It is always the other person's pattern that we can recognize with ease. It seems strikingly obvious in others. "Oh, Robin, she always gets involved with married men—men she knows damn well are solidly married and not going to leave their wives for her." "Rachel, you know her. She's only attracted to those SOBs. The nastier they are, the more she's turned on."

Recognizing someone else's self-defeating behavior carries with it a tacit comment: "Look, don't you see what you're doing? Don't you understand that there's something off about the way your life's proceeding?"

Recognition means a critical view of behavior that implies things are wrong and in need of change. But it's natural to resist change. Why do we struggle to keep our modes—however inadequate—intact? We do this because they are familiar and predictable, they are what we know best, and anything that threatens what we feel comfortable with creates anxiety. It is this threat of anxiety, this uneasiness, that prevents us from viewing ourselves with the same critical eye with which we view others.

Every human being is critically influenced by roots, up-bringing. Like many living things, we are subject to the impact of environment. By the time you leave home, at eigh-teen years of age, you've spent some 6,500 days (158,000 hours or 9.5 million minutes), a quarter of your life, associ-ated with your family. A TV commercial of one minute's duration is expected to, and does in fact, influence your be-havior as you choose one product over another because you've been familiarized with it and impressed by the tele-vised endorsement. Imagine, then, the impact of millions of such exposures on your behavior. And, of course, you've had millions of exposures as you've grown up. The sheer amount of time spent with family must make an indelible impact on your behavior. There is no way of avoiding the fact that relatives, especially parents, are key figures in one's life. Whatever your feelings toward them, from adoration to hatred, their influence is undeniable. It affects you when you seek or choose a partner. Accepting this notion does not mean blaming current difficulties in relating to men on past experiences. Rather it means becoming self-aware and ac-knowledging the factors that determine your psychological makeup.

Our goal is to provide you with a key with which to suc-cessfully understand your past and free yourself from your current problems. One word of caution: Feeling victimized by your past, feeling sorry for yourself, doesn't make for change. Mastering your life means gaining insight and under-standing and taking responsibility for your relationships. And that's exactly what you must do.

Eileen

Eileen is a woman caught in a self-defeating lovestyle. Eileen's affair with her boss, a doctor, was at a standstill. She still loved him as much as ever. But, although he said he cared, she had begun to doubt his feelings for her. As far as she was concerned, their affair had reached an end; continuing would be useless and painful. After all, in the beginning of their love affair he had promised to leave his wife, and now, three years later, he was no closer to separating than he had been in those first weeks. It was hard to believe things had gone on this long. Dick confided in her about his failing marriage; he was deeply unhappy. He reached out to her, and she could not turn him down. He really needed her. Yet in all this time he had made no concrete change in his marital situation. Even his moving out and sleeping in the waiting room of his medical suite was short-lived. One week of guilt and anxiety about the children and he was back home again.

At first Eileen was patient with his excuses. Being one of his nurses, she knew how incredibly busy he was. Then there was the settlement his wife would demand. As an M.D. he would have to give away a small fortune. And with his recent move to new offices money was tight. He simply couldn't make it if big alimony payments were involved.

Eileen did a slow burn as she waited for him to leave his wife, Judy. However, she knew he felt more for her than he had ever felt for Judy, and knowing this made the waiting bearable at least. He loved her; they had a great relationship and fantastic sex, something Judy had denied him since their youngest child had been born. Eileen was always turned on and loved sex with him anytime and anywhere, although on occasion she was afraid someone would catch them in the office or recognize them coming out of a downtown motel.

His canceling her birthday trip to the Bahamas because of Judy's brother's wedding finally made her decide to end their relationship. Dick pleaded that he couldn't miss it. This was too much for Eileen. She couldn't endure postponing another important event in her life or spending it alone. She couldn't stand losing out to Judy once again. She was through. The thought of missing Dick filled her with sadness, but she was also bitter. "You just can't trust a married man. He'll tell you he loves you but *never* leave his wife." All those standard warnings swirled in her brain. She thought about Jason, a former lover who had sworn he was through with his wife but a year into their affair got his wife pregnant. Eileen was beginning to believe those women's magazine articles: Married men *are* bad news. Dick would be the last one she'd ever get mixed up with. That was a promise. She'd never let him lead her on again.

What really happened?

Eileen was full of self-recrimination for dating a man who had no potential for her—for making a mistake. However, what she failed to recognize was that she was not simply making a mistake, but repeating one. Feeling victimized by Dick, Eileen hadn't seen that she had allowed her self-destructive pattern of behavior free rein. She hadn't recalled that she had been disappointed once before by a man who wouldn't leave his wife. Instead she allowed herself to be deluded into thinking (despite many indications to the contrary) that Dick would leave his wife and family for her. Once more she had set herself up to fail.

DISCERNING THE PATTERN

In the vast majority of unfulfilling relationships, such as Eileen's, a predictable sequence can be discerned. Though highly individual, this pattern conforms to a universal model. No matter what the personal elements are, human behavior follows some fundamental principles, which determine everyone's behavior. The idea of an underlying principle does not take away from the uniqueness of each one of us; it only highlights what is predictably human in all of us.

Not all women evidence predictable patterns of relating. That is quite true. Personal maturity and flexibility can allow for fulfillment in love. For many others, like Eileen, however, a relationship falls victim to a cycle without true satisfaction.

What is this cycle? It begins with a *wish*.

Eileen wanted to be involved with and to marry a man. This is her recognized, conscious feeling, her *wish*. However, Eileen is not aware that this wish is influenced by an unrecognized, unconscious *need*: to share a man with another woman. Startling? Certainly. But true. Unaware of this motive, she finds a man who satisfies her need to share rather than her wish to marry. This is why Eileen exercises *poor judgment*; this is why, despite her wish to marry, she becomes involved with a man who will never become totally committed to her. Eileen's judgment is poor because her unconscious need to share her man, not her conscious wish to marry, determines her *choice* of a partner in her relationships.

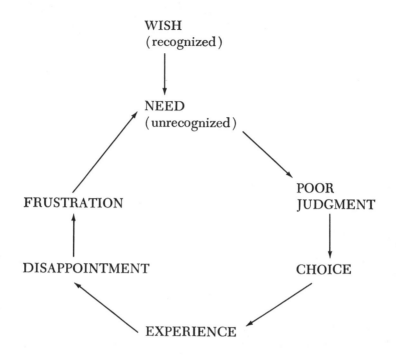

WISH
(recognized)

NEED
(unrecognized)

POOR
JUDGMENT

FRUSTRATION

DISAPPOINTMENT   CHOICE

EXPERIENCE

The trouble begins here because she chooses without identifying the fact that she has unsuccessfully used this same approach before. Why is this unsuccessful? Why does poor judgment prevail? Because deep down, it is more important for Eileen to satisfy her need than to fulfill her wish. For Eileen the need to share Dick with another woman has priority over her wish to marry.

Experience with Dick repeatedly indicates he will not leave his wife. This arrangement satisfies Eileen's need. In contrast, Eileen's wish is being met with repeated *disappointments*. Eventually the relationship becomes a source of *frustration* for her wish. Eileen's conscious wish is not being satisfied. Angry and hurt, she ends the affair. Her wish to have someone continues unfulfilled. Her unconscious need—unrecognized and unacknowledged—stays buried inside, left to reassert itself in her next love affair. Eileen has come full circle, ready to begin again.

A relationship cannot work on this basis. Intimacy and commitment are not possible when need and wish are at cross-purposes.

Since Eileen wishes to marry, she exhibits poor judgment when allowing herself to have a three-year affair with Dick. Married and with children, he is also a busy doctor burdened with many financial responsibilities and commitments —hardly a likely candidate for making Eileen's wish come true. Yet, the great irony is that—as far as her unconscious need to share a man is concerned—Dick is a *perfect* choice. This is the paradox. For Eileen's wish, Dick is a poor choice. But for her need he couldn't be more suitable. Such is the power of an unconscious need. When unresolved and unacknowledged, it acts as a major factor in relationships. A woman is attracted by and drawn to a man who fits her need.

Where does this need come from? Why does it exert such an influence? The answers to this may lie in Eileen's early life.

Her earliest years had been happy and relatively carefree. The oldest of three children, she had had a loving relationship with her parents, but as a teenager she began to argue and fight with her mother. At thirteen it seemed as if her mother had changed overnight: Strict rules about curfews, dating, and friends suddenly became important. A relatively calm household turned into a battleground as her life became a misery. Eileen's father assumed the role of intermediary and tried vainly to restore peace. It didn't work. He always ended up caught in the middle, accused by both of taking the other's side. If he seemed to support Eileen, her mother became enraged, apparently jealous of the closeness between them and furious at his desertion of his parental role. When Eileen felt both of them were united against her, she would stalk out of the house, disappearing for hours and sometimes overnight.

In her calmer moments Eileen often regretted her behavior, especially toward her father. Whereas her mother was largely impossible to deal with, she knew her father was really very kind and concerned. He was only appeasing her mother. In a way, Eileen felt sorry for him. Sometimes she found herself thinking that theirs wasn't really a happy marriage, that he just kept it going for the sake of her and her brothers. When she turned seventeen, the situation at home was still very tense and uncomfortable. Eileen left for nursing school. It was the only way of getting out of the mess at home.

What relevance does this have to her current situation? How does this influence Eileen's relationships with men? How does this relate to her need?

Eileen's relationships with her parents developed into the model for her future relationships with men. Because of her miserable family life, her mother's strongly decrying her sexual awakening at puberty, the only way Eileen can respond to men is when they, like her father, are caught between two women. This relationship of a jealous rivalry over a man is the style she is accustomed to. When Eileen becomes involved with men, her lovestyle provides her with a kind of continual reenactment of her unfinished family business. In a sense Eileen's development is fixed—arrested—at this stage. Why? Eileen's family never allowed her to move beyond them. They never freed her from family ties or supported her being involved with boys her age. Instead they kept all her emotions tied up in their family struggles.

Not being able to resolve her family conflict and having only run away from it to nursing school, Eileen knows just one way of dealing with men: the pattern her family forced upon her, namely, two women fighting for one man's attention, love, support. She continues to have the unconscious need to share a man with another woman. Though this style of relating never brings Eileen fulfillment, there is a catch to it. It does bring her something. In exchange for the pain she gains safety, a very special sort of safety. As painful as this pattern may be, it is predictable. And it is familiar. It is what she knows best: a triangle of two women and one man. This is why Eileen is attracted to Dick. She responds to Dick because he fits into her view of the world, of man-woman relations. He confirms her sense of what relationships are like. In choosing Dick, Eileen can avoid the anxiety and the fear of the unfamiliar that she would encounter if she were to become involved with a truly available man.

Though it may be clear to the objective observer, what Eileen misses is that Dick was chosen because of this need. Ultimately he was chosen for all the wrong reasons.

Unable to see her unsuccessful pattern, Eileen remains in the dark as to why she cannot find the "right man." Instead of taking responsibility for her situation, she regards herself as a victim, a woman taken advantage of by a married man. Finally, left alone on her birthday, she breaks up with Dick, unaware of her contribution to the relationship and that she will no doubt repeat her unsuccessful pattern again and again, for the next man in her life will surely be a man she shares with another woman.

FOUR STEPS FOR SELF-CONFRONTATION

Eileen's pattern is only one of twelve patterns we will investigate, and no doubt there are additional patterns and variations that may apply to your own situation. In each case, the woman is caught up in a self-defeating cycle that keeps her from achieving the intimacy she seeks. For Eileen, or for any woman who finds herself in a similar predicament, there are four necessary steps to confront the problem—the

EILEEN'S CYCLE

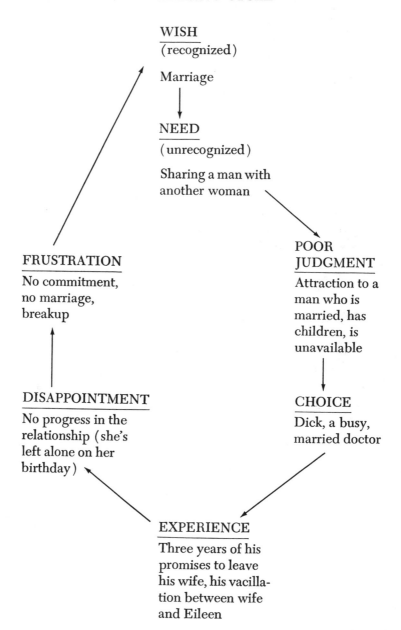

WISH
(recognized)

Marriage

NEED
(unrecognized)

Sharing a man with
another woman

POOR
JUDGMENT

Attraction to a
man who is
married, has
children, is
unavailable

FRUSTRATION

No commitment,
no marriage,
breakup

DISAPPOINTMENT

No progress in the
relationship (she's
left alone on her
birthday)

CHOICE

Dick, a busy,
married doctor

EXPERIENCE

Three years of his
promises to leave
his wife, his vacilla-
tion between wife
and Eileen

first steps toward climbing out of the rut of your cycle. What you must do first is:

1. Acknowledge that you have a problem finding the right man.
2. Accept the responsibility for your pattern, the repetitive quality of your behavior, such as affairs with married men or with men seriously involved with other women.
3. Understand how your need contributes to an unsuccessful lovestyle.
4. Find the sources of your need.

These steps are difficult and complex. But they are necessary. Only after this process of self-confrontation can you begin to work on the next step, which is change.

How do we help you accomplish this self-confrontation?

Step 1 *Acknowledging That You Have a Problem*

In buying this book you have made an important statement. You are honestly willing to acknowledge frustration. Things have reached a point where you feel you might use some help. You've gotten all the advice you've wanted and more. It didn't work. So you are seeking to understand yourself better, to get out of your rut. Buying this book means that you are open to self-exploration, to introspection.

But maybe you're not sure if you really have a problem; your friends seem to have the same complaints about men, and anyway everybody's entitled to a mistake or two. Still, do you have a problem?

You've tried hard to meet Mr. Right, but it hasn't happened.

When you see people in love, you say, "Damn, I'm really missing something."

You have men in your life you like but can't make "it" happen.

Your timing is off.

Your relationship is filled with tension, struggle, games.

You like your man but don't love him.

You love your man but don't like him.

Your relationships don't grow, they stagnate.

You constantly tell yourself, "If only circumstances were right, things would work out."

You find yourself thinking "I'm not ready to get serious and settle down."

You're afraid a serious commitment would mean giving up too much.

You sometimes feel the chase is too much of a hassle, that being alone or with girl friends is easier.

When it comes to sex, you can't get it together.

You think a change of scene (new job, new city) would improve your social life.

Men never turn out to be as good as they first seem.

You continue to ignore a man's reputation or your friends' criticism.

You pick men very different from yourself.

The way you feel toward a man is different from the way you act toward him. There's a difference between what you say and what you do in a relationship.

You delay making decisions about a man.

Maybe you'll never get married. It just isn't for you; it's not in the cards.

If any of these statements reflects your concerns, your frame of mind, and the state of your love life, this book will help you. It's for you.

Step 2 *Accepting Responsibility for Your Pattern*

The experiences of other women may enable you to see the repetitive and predictable pattern in your own behavior with men, the lovestyle that traps you into unsuccessful relationships. Presented in the following chapters are the most troublesome and universal patterns of unsuccessful relationships.

In each instance the underlying pattern will be discerned, permitting you an opportunity to observe another woman's behavior with men and from this recognize her particular problem. And perhaps your own. You may well find a pattern that mirrors your own. It may vary somewhat from your experiences, but a chord of recognition may sound, a light flash, a smile cross your face, as you read about a lovestyle that resembles yours and you exclaim, "It sounds like me."

Still, reactions are not always so immediate. Perhaps you will struggle for a while, saying, "This has nothing to do with me." This feeling may mean that you are not ready to look, to confront, to learn more about yourself. In which case, stop and put the book on the shelf. Your frustration, discomfort, and unhappiness are not yet acute enough to make you take the plunge. Look at it again after your next unsuccessful relationship comes to an end.

However, if you are ready to continue, you can begin to recognize the predictable patterns that run through your relationships. You will begin to see the lovestyle that is specifically yours. Comparing yourself with the women in this book, matching up your lovestyle with theirs, gives you a chance to step back and gain perspective on yourself. You become an observer of your own behavior, which is a critical shift from being a passive participant in a cycle. You become active, taking your life in hand. You are on your way to changing helplessness into control.

Once you become an observer of your own behavior, you begin to function within a new, mature, and highly sophisticated psychological framework. The act of seeing yourself allows you to consider the role you play in your difficulties and to see how unsuccessful relationships that repeat themselves are no accident but the legacy of a pattern.

Like a critic at the theater, you must learn to remove yourself from the action and watch carefully, analytically, at a distance from the characters; this permits you to give an honest and impartial evaluation of all members of the cast. No one should be given preferential treatment. As an objective observer consider the personalities, feelings, and motivations of everyone who is involved, including yourself. This capacity for independent analysis is what you must work to develop.

It's not an easy task to use this technique on yourself, to be both participant and observer of your own actions and motives. It challenges your preconceived notions, your past. It challenges the rationalizations you've been developing and using for years and even your basic ideas about men. Basically it demands that you see your relationships as those who are objective see them. It means looking into a mirror, seeing a true reflection, and then taking responsibility for what you see. And that is one of the hardest things all of us must eventually do if we are to direct our own lives.

It is especially difficult if until now you've gone along from experience to experience, from lover to lover, feeling that events in your life were accidental, unrelated. If you dismissed things, ascribing them to luck, fate, chance, timing, chemistry, divine intervention, circumstances, or whatever else. But finding yourself and your situation on these pages will make all those seemingly unrelated pieces fit into a whole pattern. You cannot get off the hook. You have identified that you have a pattern of interpersonal behavior, that you have an unsuccessful lovestyle for which you must assume responsibility.

What exactly do you look for in order to identify your own pattern? Experiences that repeat themselves. Start by recalling the names of men you've dated over the years. No one is unimportant enough to be omitted. What did your lovers have in common? What has been repeated in your encounters?

Start with appearance. What about their looks? Do you go for a certain "type"? What about dress? Preppy or casual? Profession? Age? Background? Religion? Class? Level of success? Any common denominators?

Take out your old photos. Put their pictures side by side. This may tell you something words can't. How available were each of these men (married, divorced, with or without children, mama's boys, confirmed bachelors, widowed, living with another woman, bisexual)? Now analyze the relationships. How did each begin (intense, accidental, planned, on the rebound)? What were your first reactions? What was the pace of the relationship? How long did it last? What went wrong? Whose fault was it? How did it end? How were you treated and how did you treat him? What were the problem areas (money, time, other women, work, communication)? How was sex?

Can you detect similarities in the kind of men you've gone with? What was the emotional tone of your times together (fun, superficial, casual, angry, tense, relaxed, argumentative, boring, dead, noncommittal)? How did friends and family react to each man? Were the same criticisms or praises voiced each time? What were your afterthoughts about him? "Why did I let it go on?" "I thought I knew him." "I lost a good thing."

These are not all the questions you can ask yourself, but beginning with these, compare and contrast your experiences until you can tease out the trends, the themes . . . the pattern.

Once you've initiated the process, you have the basics for comparing yourself with other women.

Not everyone's love life is in trouble. You may sense that every relationship you have had was in fact different and unique. That each experience was one of a kind. That each had its satisfactions. That each man was a friend with whom you shared a different stage of your life. In comparing the men in your life, if you feel you are in a process of moving forward, growing, learning more about yourself and what you want and need out of life and love, then you have a comfortable style of relating to men, which at some point will lead to a lasting and gratifying tie with a man you love.

If you have uncovered a pattern, then progressing from recognizing it to discovering the underlying need that keeps it in motion is complex. It is a process of finding the driving force behind your behavior. The more experience you have at learning to connect need and pattern, the easier it will be. Each chapter gives you the opportunity for this experience. In some ways this book is a teaching machine. Making the connection between wish and need will reinforce your own skill.

It is important to think of this as the beginning of a process. Using the help of friends who may be more objective or consulting a professional whose training is aimed at developing this expertise are other ways of getting there.

It is possible to reject what is being proposed here, to refuse the notion that any of this applies. So be cautious. Admittedly, the lovestyles in the chapters that follow will not be exactly the same as yours. In fact, you might very well see yourself in several cases or only identify with a few elements in one. However, be assured. If you are alone, unattached, and unhappy about it, the pattern of your intimate relations is here somewhere waiting for you to find it, confront it, and change it. Don't turn away.

Step 3   *Understanding How Your Need Contributes to an Unsuccessful Lovestyle*

By becoming an observer of your behavior, by being able to recognize your own pattern, you set the stage for the next important step in changing your lovestyle. Once you have established how you relate to men, you are ready to ask why you behave the way you do. What is the need that keeps your unsuccessful love cycle spinning?

Ironically, despite the seemingly endless variety of ways that unattached women relate to men, there are really a limited number of lovestyles. In love, as in drama, despite the countless plays that have been written, there are really only a certain number of basic plot elements, of which the rest are variations.

Each lovestyle reflects a specific need and how that need maintains the unsuccessful cycle. Find your lovestyle and you will come to understand your need. How? Pattern and need are inextricably linked. Our studies have shown that lovestyles are the conscious expression of an unconscious need. Once you acknowledge your pattern, you will know and be able to confront your unconscious need.

For example, look at Eileen's situation. If Eileen were to take responsibility for her behavior and acknowledge that her patterns of involvement always include married men, she would learn to understand her need, her unconscious need, to share a man. By asking herself the right questions about her relationships and really thinking out the answers, Eileen would discern the need that creates her pattern. Questions like the following:

Have you dated many married men?

(The wife is the third person in the relationship. With a wife around, no man is totally available. He's by definition a shared property.)

Do men you date struggle over you and another woman, their mothers, daughters, the memories of their deceased wives?

(A wife is not the only "other woman" in a man's life. A mama's boy might be closer to mom than to any girl friend.

A possessive daughter may not let her father out of her reach, and a recent widower may not be ready to start a new life.)

You continue with a guy even if you know he's involved with another woman.

(A woman who doesn't give up must be getting satisfaction out of a triangular relationship. She is sharing.)

Have you been disappointed by men who miss special moments with you because of someone else in their lives?

(These disappointments are the signal that you're a secret sharer. It means you are losing out to someone and tolerating it. A sure indication of your competitive streak.)

Do you enjoy competing for a man?

(Competition turns a sharer on. Competing's the game, not winning.)

Do you think you're better than his other woman? You have better sex with him; he spends more money on you; he spends more time with you.

(Remember, if you're scoring in the visitor's column, there's always a home team.)

You may be jealous but don't mind the space you get when he's with the other woman.

(Saying you need space may be a fancy rationalization for not feeling you can handle a total commitment, a total person.)

Your relationship has highs and lows. It's an emotional seesaw; you do a lot of fighting and making up.

(This is common if you have a need to share. The excitement comes from shifting from almost losing him to nearly winning him.)

Your relationships are often secret, maintained on the sly, hidden from people.

(Sharers get turned on by the clandestine, by the possibility of discovery.)

Your relationships are of necessity part-time—limited to certain hours, days, places.

(Relationships with such boundaries simply mean that someone else is with him on the "days off" from your relationship. You may not want to confront it, but it signifies a need to share.)

Step 4   *Finding the Sources of Your Need*

Once you connect your lovestyle to your need, each chapter will also give you the chance to understand where this need came from. This is the next step in the struggle to break an unsuccessful pattern: finding the source of the need in your past and then understanding the power it exerts over your behavior with men in the present. A need has its roots in the past, usually in early relationships. For better or worse, no matter how we protest, there's continuity in our lives, especially our love lives. Only by understanding this link, this connection between need and personal history, can you begin to change. Only by understanding that the need is connected to the unfinished business of the past can you attempt to alter your behavior. By finding a connection between past and present, you gain control over behavior.

Eileen's need to share a man was the product of her continuing conflict with her mother during her turbulent adolescence and the role her father played in this period of her life. Eileen never managed to leave her conflicts back in the past, where they belonged. Instead of settling this conflict with her family, she merely interrupted it by running off to nursing school, and it remained a central part of her psychological makeup for years.

By asking herself the right questions about her past, Eileen would discover the roots of her need, the sources of the pattern she's now a slave to. Questions like:

Did you feel your mother didn't like you when you were growing up?

(Bad feelings between mother and daughter can create an emotional distance that can make them rivals rather than allies, and this feeling may be generalized and come to play with other women later in life.)

Did your parents disagree about how to raise you? Even argue over it?

(Being permitted to feel at the center of a parental relationship can make a girl sense that she has permission to come between two adults, which she then repeats in her love affairs.)

Did you feel your father was on your side?

(This creates an emotionally charged atmosphere in which father and daughter stand against mother. It's this sense of "having" her father that sets the stage for battling against other women through a man.)

When your father agreed with your mother, it was only to appease her; he didn't really mean it.

(This is the beginning of the feeling "I'm really better than mother, I'm more liked." It lays the groundwork for those endless comparisons with the "other woman" in adulthood.)

Was your mother jealous of your social life?

(Rivalrous feelings with your mother are carried over into feelings toward other women. Mother's jealousy subtly introduces the issue of sexual competitiveness.)

Did you think your father could have been happier with another woman?

(This feeling underscores the sense that Dad is unhappy with Mom and there's room for someone else. As an adult the girl becomes that "someone else" for the man in her life —the "other woman.")

As a young girl did you ever fight over a boy?

(As an adult the fighting continues, but in a more sophisticated way.)

Did you disapprove of your brother's girl friends?

(This is another form of disguised competition for a male.)

Did you ever wonder about whom your father cared for more, you or your mother?

(This is the "little girl's" view that Daddy is positioned between mother and daughter and that competing for position is absolutely central to male/female relationships.)

Were you always trying to be number one in school? With friends?

(The competitive streak often carries into other childhood activities.)

Your father was close to you, shared secrets with you, treated you as "special."

(A father can make a daughter feel she is more important than his wife. A grown woman's love life may be an attempt to restore that feeling of being the chosen central person.)

OVERCOMING RESISTANCE TO CHANGE

Now that you have begun to face the underlying factors behind your need, you must try to break your pattern.

Knowing the forces that have caused you to repeat your unproductive routine, you now must try to counter them.

This is difficult and demanding. Why is it so traumatic to give up these old ways, to relinquish your old need? How bad can it be to change? After all, your pattern offers no solution, no real satisfaction. Why, then, do you keep it? Why do you perpetuate it?

You hang on to your lovestyle because it does offer something, a very basic and fundamental feeling—security. Unfortunately, it's the wrong kind. However unfulfilling your relationships have been, they have been predictable: your world is kept stable, reliable, and consistent. As in all things, you create security by searching for confirmation of yourself, your attitudes, your opinions, your feelings. You accept information that supports your view. Information that does not fit your view of your life and the people in it is not acknowledged. You will keep the surroundings familiar at all costs. This need for security through predictability is a powerful force. And it has its origins far back in our younger days.

All children are vulnerable. Faced with total dependence on others and unable to understand the world, they are easily frightened and overwhelmed by the unfamiliar, the unpredictable. Early on, people learn to thwart or reduce these anxious feelings by screening out things they cannot cope with. In this way, by keeping only to the familiar and avoiding change, anxiety is kept at bay. This early search for certainty remains an important part of your life. When you become an adult, it offers you a constant reference point in, and control over, an otherwise ever-changing world. Even as an adult you carry a fear of being vulnerable. Always sensitive to that early fear, always afraid of the anxiety of the unknown, you are unlikely to give up old behavior with ease. So, as painful as your unsuccessful lovestyle may be, at least it's a refuge from the anxiety of change.

Take Eileen. Her abortive relationships with married men

kept her in familiar territory. Through her adolescent struggles with her mother, she painfully learned to be expert in relating to a man caught between two women. From that time on, she saw women as jealous, in angry competition with one another, and she saw men as but pawns in this contest. And it was this distortion that Eileen brought to her adult relationships by transferring it to men in her life. In one form or another, she has replayed this sequence in all her love relationships. The familiar pattern draws her into her lovestyle.

Never learning to relate in other ways, Eileen was left with few resources to cope with men differently. She had never had the chance to relate to a man who could be hers, and only hers. In the meantime, the prospect of an actually available man is so overwhelming that she unconsciously avoids the possibility of such an involvement. Although her relationships don't ever work out and are a source of disappointment, Eileen is attracted to the least disturbing course— namely, disappointing but predictable relationships.

This drive to reduce anxiety and make ourselves secure exerts a very forceful pull. Often, we are obsessed with protecting ourselves from anxiety rather than trying to remain open to new experiences. With this attitude of "safety first," our decisions, our actions—our relationships—suffer. This is the price we pay for having a kind of control over our lives. With this control there are no surprises and nothing to throw us off balance. No risks. No chances. Security! This is the big trade-off. We gain security and control by giving up curiosity, flexibility, freedom, and the happiness of truly gratifying relationships. Given the emotional safety that this security provides, it takes real courage to abandon your pattern, to hold your need at bay and to attempt to change.

The move to give up familiar styles of behavior, acknowledge your need, face the conflicts that underlie them, and open yourself to those experiences you have steadfastly avoided is a complicated matter. Not only must you summon up the courage to explore new feelings, but in doing so you must relinquish long-standing and ingrained ways of maintaining your personal emotional security. Is it any wonder, then, that there is so much resistance to such a change?

Change doesn't happen spontaneously. There must be pressure, stress, for it to occur, and this goes hand in hand with understanding and insight into your own personal lovestyle patterns.

By questioning your behavior you provide the pressure for change. And, yes, we want you to feel conflicted about your preexisting notions about yourself and the men you've been involved with. Though we hope to stir up this conflict, we will also help you find a remedy in more gratifying relationships. We can equip you with the means, but you must be willing to make the effort.

Finding your personal lovestyle will force you to give up the excuses, the blame, and the apologies for your failed relationships. You can't get away with the self-indulgent, cozy cop-out of feeling sorry for yourself. You must effect change.

It's hard work being responsible for your own behavior. You have to carry the weight of yourself on your own shoulders. You have to look in the mirror and see your true reflection. Though this sounds harsh, we can safely urge this action for a good reason. Experience shows us that what you see in the mirror may offer you a pleasant surprise. What you imagine and fear about yourself is always worse than the reality of what you are. Although initially you might feel embarrassed or ashamed by the knowledge you gain about yourself, be assured that if you are valiant enough to look at yourself honestly, you can learn to like what you see. Give yourself a chance.

Breaking rigid patterns and becoming more adaptable has another advantage. Others will react to you differently. People will respond in kind to your being free and genuine.

When you are caught up in your own patterns, you are likely to attract others who are also victims of their own rigid cycles. Becoming more authentic means finding people who are a true joy to be with.

THREE STEPS FOR UNLEARNING THE PATTERN

In order to change you must unlearn old ways of responding to men and relearn new ones instead. Unlearning involves moving in new directions.

Until now the focus has been on analyzing your present love life and past experience.

In large measure, personal growth depends on making sense of your behavior. Self-awareness brings the potential for change. Creating this potential is the goal of the four steps we discussed earlier. Yet no matter what its meaning, an unsuccessful lovestyle is habitual, automatic. You can make every effort to understand it, but unless you can interrupt it, change is unlikely. The following steps are aimed at using the insight you've gained to disrupt your pattern:

1. Memorize your need.
2. Use your understanding of your need to reflect on the men in your life.
3. Become sensitive to anything about a man who turns you on, that even remotely resembles or relates to your need.

Step 1   *Memorizing Your Need*

The awareness of your need must reverberate through your thinking so that whether you are working or taking a bath or out on a date, you are continuously conscious of it. It should become your personal obsession, never being allowed to slip back into the recesses of your unconscious mind. The more you think about it, the less likely you are to act it out. Keep your need in view. Write it down.

My need is . . .

Place reminders of your need in strategic locations relevant to your pattern. Eileen could use one in her locker at work; she would face it every morning before she faces her married boss. The makeup case she takes to the motel so she can put herself back together after her "lunch hour" could be the right location. On her calendar near her birthday, Christmas, New Year's—on all the days she would invariably lose out to a wife—her need to share a man should be clearly posted.

Self-consciousness is a way of helping to put the brakes on your behavior. Remind yourself whenever and wherever possible.

Paste a need reminder to your mirror. Jot it down on a note card and slip it into your pocketbook. Talk to your best friend about it. Work on it until your understanding of your need is firmly planted in your mind and heart. Once you're sure that you have a secure hold on it, it's time to make the next move.

Step 2   *Reflecting on the Men in Your Life*

All those males—your friends, relatives, lovers, idols, the man of your dreams. Think about these men and see if your need has affected your feelings toward them.

Is your need in some way the motivation behind your different involvements with men? Is it the common denominator in all your relationships?

How do you know if it is the theme running through your relations with men? How do you go about finding this out? Suppose you suspect that, like Eileen, you have a need to share a man. How do you confirm it?

List all the men you care for or have cared for in various ways. Alongside each name, write anything about the relationship that might have to do with your lovestyle. For example, Eileen's relationship analysis might look something like this:

Brother-in-law Jack
He thinks Eileen is great and sometimes teases her sister, saying, "If I'd met Eileen first, I would have married her."

Uncle Wayne
He always compares Eileen with his daughter, Janice. His usual comment: "Why can't you be like your cousin Eileen?"

Mr. Scranton, eleventh-grade teacher
His wife was the school nurse. "I could never see what a man like Mr. Scranton could see in that witch."

Mr. MacKenzie, Eileen's best friend Mary's father
He was Eileen's confidant, someone she could always talk to, even though Mary and he were never that close.

Looking over her list and comments, it becomes clear that whenever Eileen cared for a man, she found herself competing with another woman for his affection, whether vying with a sister, her cousin, the school nurse, her best friend.

Analyzing the important male relationships in your life will give you a chance to evaluate the role your need plays. This sort of analysis is crucial. It will dramatically reinforce your understanding of the pervasiveness and power of your need.

Once you know and fully understand your need, you must produce your own list and conduct your own investigation.

Don't forget any man who may have been important to you. Lover, boss, colleague, coach, friend, acquaintance, doctor, teacher, politician—all must come under scrutiny.

Step 3   *Becoming Hypersensitive to Things You Like Because of Your Need*

After you've analyzed your need and how it has influenced your past, you must come to grips with how it dominates your present. For example, what should Eileen be alert to? What kind of situations should warn her of the fact that her need is in operation?

Eileen should be asking herself, "Is this man in any subtle or disguised way part of a three-way relationship?" What are some kinds of sharing relationships, besides married men, that warn her of her need taking over?

> Men separated, recently divorced, or involved in custody disputes
> Recent widowers who talk about their wives a lot
> Single men who have just ended a long-term affair
> Guys who insist on dating other women
> Men who advocate a *ménage à trois*
> Sons still living with their mothers

Obviously when confronted with this group, you can see that looming behind each category may be the specter of another woman. Each intimates a great potential for a sharing relationship. You must catch yourself in the act of sharing, of responding to your need. Every casual encounter in a bar, every date, every man attractive to you, must be "checked out." When you become aware of the fact that a man is associated with your need, end the relationship. Your insight into yourself and into your need—not your gut reaction—must dictate your behavior with men if you are to end the cycle.

Let's suppose Eileen has reached a point where she could hold herself in check. Where once she wouldn't have given more thought to her first encounter with a man than to decide if the chemistry was right, she now proceeds with caution. She carries around a checklist. As soon as she feels attracted, she checks to see if the primary force behind the attraction is a need to share.

Often it makes Eileen feel calculating, as if she were putting brakes on her emotions. This is exactly how it should feel, since the aim is to replace automatic action with thoughtful self-awareness.

Eileen met Pierre at a friend's party. Even across the room he seemed interesting; staid looking in a dark suit. Eileen knew he was a diplomat. Cornering her friend, she pumped her for information. The most eligible bachelor in the French delegation, no live-in girl friend, a date that night who was just a friend—Eileen felt she knew enough so she could give in to her attraction.

That evening was followed by another, more intimate one. But plans for another date didn't go quite as smoothly. Pierre's secretary called: He was back in Paris on short notice. Eileen's disappointment was blunted by the understanding that only the most pressing sort of business would have made for such a hasty departure.

As it happened, government business wasn't the matter at hand. A phone call about the health of Pierre's mother had prompted the trip. Once he returned, Pierre explained that he was the only one his mother had. In fact this trip had made him realize the problems of the distance between them.

"Fortunately it was just influenza. But she's a delicate woman. As soon as she's up to it, she'll be coming here. After all, with my staff at the embassy and all the extra room, it's not necessary for the separation," he explained.

Eileen's initial reaction was sympathetic, but as she heard the details of the "influenza," she felt herself growing irritated. "Here I am thinking he's off conquering the diplomatic world and he's holding his genteel mother's hand." In due course Mama arrived. Pierre was apologetic but unavailable for days. For Eileen it was a week of being alone that had a painful familiarity. It flashed: She was sharing. But this time the other woman she was losing out to was Mother. Eileen would never have considered it possible.

Pierre was handsome, charming, impressive—yet not for her. It took every emotional reserve she had, but the next time he called, there was a short conversation. It ended with Eileen saying, "Pierre, I don't find happiness for myself when a man I want to be with is deeply attached to another woman. I've learned I don't want to share a man."

Eileen couldn't be sure Pierre would understand, so she made it clear that she simply wasn't going to continue their relationship. Pierre's assurances that he'd have more time for her when Mother settled in left Eileen unconvinced. The call was their last contact.

A note of warning: An honest awareness of your need will be painful. It's not a comforting or pleasant thing to discover how much your need controls your life and your choice of men. You will feel embarrassed and foolish. You will be disappointed and feel at odds with yourself. You thought you were smarter, that your choices were rational. Don't despair. This is the common feeling all women have when they catch themselves in the act. As unpleasant as this confrontation with your lovestyle is, as difficult as it is to go against your apparent instincts—the pull of your need—it is the critical prerequisite for changing. Unless you're ready to intercept your need-determined relationships by severing your ties to the men who satisfy your need but leave you unfulfilled, you *cannot* change.

TAKING RESPONSIBILITY

One consequence of a woman's unsuccessful lovestyle is that she is likely to find herself involved with men who are caught in their own pattern, their own unsuccessful lovestyle. Eileen, who needs to share a man, finds Dick, who seems unable to make up his mind between the two women in his life. Her pattern draws her to a man whose pattern meshes with her own. There is a kind of psychological fit between their styles, one that makes it unlikely that there can be sufficient change within the relationship for growth to take place. Staying with a man who fits your need and working toward intimacy with him would require an enormous effort from each person. It would depend on both people feeling the same degree of unhappiness and being ready to, and motivated to, confront their needs at the same moment.

Though it is technically possible, this perfect timing just doesn't usually happen. This is why a woman struggling with her own lovestyle must end or stay away from relationships with a man who fits her need.

Avoiding these men does not suggest that your problem lies with them or is somehow their fault. Rather, this avoidance rests on the understanding that men are not enemies, just people struggling with the same complexities of life as you.

This realization can make it clearer why breaking out of a pattern is so difficult. The men now in your life do not support your efforts. They are unwittingly pushing you back into acting out your need. They are in no position to help you change. If, for example, Eileen were able to say to Dick, "I don't want to spend my life sharing you; I'm ready to love you in a total way and I expect that from you," it's unlikely that Dick would respond with similar insights about himself. His reaction might more likely be:

I just need more time
I'm not ready
I can't do it to the kids
But you know I really love you, not my wife
We have such good times together
Let's just keep what we have

Not ready for change, Dick works to keep the status quo.
This is a kind of emotional seduction, a pull that is hard to
resist. Eileen has strong feelings for Dick, after all, even if
they are rooted in her need.

Were Eileen to continue asserting herself, it is probable
that the relationship would end. Pressed to change, Dick
would not be capable of it. His possible reaction: "I guess
this means it's over." Giving up your need means giving up
him. Implied in this statement is that you will be responsible
for ending the relationship.

Contrast this with the way Eileen actually ended her relationship with Dick. She was angry, frustrated, but she could
blame him. Though hurt, she could seal herself up in anger
against Dick and against all men. If, on the other hand, she

were to relinquish her *need,* she would have to face the loss
squarely; she would be forced to take responsibility for the
outcome of her love life. It is no wonder giving up your need
is a complicated task. You are pretty much on your own; the
men in your life can't help you in this process. This book
can.

GETTING INVOLVED WITH A MAN WHO DOESN'T FIT THE PATTERN

So far you've been analyzing your lovestyle and patterns.
Now it's time to act. It's time to stop your old behavior and
start anew by developing another kind of approach to men.

You now must make a conscious decision to get involved with a man who doesn't fit your unconscious need. How do you go about it? Begin a relationship with an unlikely candidate—with a man who doesn't excite you but is acceptable as a friend. If no one is currently around, dig someone up who you may have thought was okay, nice enough, but rejected in the past because you felt no vibrations.

Your goal is to get to know this person as you would any friend. Delay judgments and criticism, suspend your tendency toward premature conclusions, replace your constant evaluation of your relationship with openness. Relate to the whole person. Don't accept or reject him for any one phrase or action. Don't blame, don't complain; examine your role in the relationship.

Nowhere is it more important to suspend your judgments than with sex. Learn that sexual understanding, like any other aspect of a relationship, takes time. Give it the time it needs. Don't dismiss the person because he is not your alleged "type."

The results of this deliberate and well-thought-out attempt to fight your need will not be dramatic. However, the frustration, the insecurity, will all slowly be displaced by understanding. Without the drama of your need chasing your wish, there will be the possibility of a mature relationship, the one you have always desired.

Eileen found herself increasingly more sensitive to her need, more able to catch herself in the act of slipping back into her pattern.

Where did this leave her? It left her for a while in the awkward position of relinquishing choices based on her need but not yet sure of how to develop new, open, and mature relationships.

But for Eileen there was no turning back: She was a

woman on the verge of controlling her own life. Though it was sometimes an unnerving feeling, there was something too important to let it go, to let it be undone.

Armed with insight, Eileen set out in a deliberate and thoughtful way to know a man, not just share him.

Buddy was an intern at her new hospital job. There was nothing especially exciting about him, and Eileen in the past would never have given him a second glance, but Buddy liked her and asked her out. So Eileen, critical of her tendency to ignore men who didn't turn her on, went against her impulse to dismiss him and worked on keeping an open mind. She accepted, not thinking that sparks would fly but with the idea that she would get to know him as a person. She'd give him (and herself) a chance.

Dating him several times without a burning desire to be with him, she recognized it as unfair, even ridiculous, to expect to have important feelings for a person over the short run. The first time they went out for dinner there was a lot of talk about medicine and hospital gossip. Eileen had a pleasant, not great, time. At home she wondered if she would see him again. But thinking about their evening and her need, she realized that it was one of her first Saturday night dates in months (Dick could never manage to leave his wife on weekends) and the first time she hadn't chosen a restaurant just so she wouldn't be seen by people she knew. This awareness forced Eileen to question if what she really missed with Buddy was the tension of sharing. Maybe pleasant feelings were a real beginning. Still, she was unsure of how she should respond to him. Deep down, Eileen welcomed Buddy's statement that since night duty left him exhausted and he would be studying for exams the next couple of weeks, he would have to curtail his social life.

This worked out better than Eileen could have anticipated. They spent time together at the hospital, Eileen free from the pressure of having to say no or yes to him. Free from having to work on a romance, free to see him as a potential friend.

Eileen began to have warm feelings for Buddy. She even switched to weekend night duty. Of all the things she could do or people she could be with, being with Buddy, who was on call, seemed the best thing to do.

Once Buddy's exams were over, he asked Eileen out again. It would be wonderful to declare that in several months of dating, Eileen grew to love him. It would be a happy, but a not altogether honest, ending. In fact Eileen is still seeing Buddy. Still learning about herself. Still grappling with new and different feelings. Most critically she is developing a different set of expectations about men and about loving. She's working toward loving a man, this time for all the right reasons.

In each chapter to come, a relationship will be described, followed by an analysis of the lovestyle pattern and the need that maintain the cycle.

Caution: You might find something that shocks or dismays you. But no matter what the nature of your reaction, you will have the opportunity for self-confrontation and growth. It may not be painless, but it is rewarding.

3

Vanessa

At thirty Vanessa is a long way from her small hometown in southern Minnesota. She had always wanted to leave Hagersville to be an actress, and now, running from one New York audition to another, Vanessa feels she is living her dream of succeeding in her craft, her last stage appearance having received respectable reviews. If not for the fact that she had a short affair with her director, Vanessa would really feel a sense of triumph. She could kick herself for not having been able to resist. Though she had promised herself she would not end up in bed with the guy, damn it, it never failed to happen. She just couldn't say no. There must be something wrong with her, she thinks. The idea that she must be a whore races through her mind. These thoughts depress her a lot: Even back in Minnesota this was a problem. Vanessa wishes she could erase some of her sexual encounters—those times in grade school, especially, when she and her cousin had fooled around.

What bothers Vanessa is that she likes sex. She loves a man's body and always falls for the well-built type, especially if beneath the masculine and strong exterior is a tender soul, a guy who after a wild screw still wants to hold and

stroke her gently. This is the kind Vanessa's a sucker for. It
feels so good then. If only she could avoid that morning-
after guilt trip. "I go to bed to make love and get up feeling
that I fucked." It's as if in all those years of her Sunday
school classes, Reverend MacIntyre's "nonsense" catches up
with her those mornings.

Vanessa loves the city. She never felt comfortable back in
Hagersville, despite the fact that her family had lived there
for generations. She felt like a misfit. She was determined to
leave eventually but has never been exactly sure why she
needed to or how she'd go about it. Vanessa cannot pinpoint
this feeling but thinks it may have a lot to do with how
miserable she used to feel about her dad's drinking. The only
escape from the tension at home was school. Cheerleading
practice and drama club helped lengthen the day away from
home.

This is what saved her then and gave her a chance to
make it in New York. Now, with her coterie of theater
friends, she feels at home. She finds herself especially comfortable with gay friends who don't hassle her.

Things have worked out well in the eight years she's been
in New York, although it could have been better as far as
men are concerned. Her relationships, especially the long-
term affairs, left a lot to be desired. Take Michael, for example. Though she is into a serious relationship with Shawn,
it doesn't stop her from talking to Michael, and sometimes
more.

She and Michael are still on good terms, but they certainly aren't as intense as they were a little over a year ago.
That spring's weekend jaunt to the Kentucky Derby was
nothing less than spectacular. A private jet, dinner with the
governor, a box at the track, a fancy dress ball—she basked
in Michael's importance. He told her that he loved her, and
it seemed she had everything. When three weeks had passed
and Michael hadn't even called or responded to her messages, she couldn't believe what was happening. "It blew my

mind." After spending days thinking it was something she had said or done, Vanessa flew into a rage every time she thought of him and vowed she'd never speak to him again. But then in the face of two dozen long-stemmed roses and a call from Michael's press agent that he'd like to meet her for dinner, all her anger melted away.

For the whole year afterward Michael flew in and out of town, and Vanessa's life, calling her when the mood struck him. Things came to a head this past winter. In making plans for a Christmas party at her home, Vanessa asked Michael to make sure he would be in town that week. She was startled by his refusal and his excuse that he planned to spend the holiday skiing in Aspen. Vanessa's insistence didn't make a dent. That was it. Hurt and disappointed, Vanessa broke with Michael.

Shawn seemed a welcome relief from Michael's games. He lived in New York and wasn't trotting around the globe. She knew he was an important investment banker, yet one wouldn't have guessed from meeting him that he wielded a lot of influence in the financial world and was quoted often in *The Wall Street Journal*. The fact that he was divorced, unlike Michael, the jet-set bachelor, made her feel that with Shawn there was potential for a future together.

His conservative exterior gave no hint of how wild Shawn could be in bed. A night with him meant little if any sleep. The next day she would drag herself around in a pleasant stupor. Six months passed and nothing changed. The problem was how little time they had together. Shawn often worked from eight in the morning until ten at night. The nights they spent together were just not enough. As committed as she was to acting, it didn't seem as demanding or absorbing as Shawn's career. Coming second to his work irritated her. When her old flame Michael called in July, she didn't hang up. Maybe, she reasoned, she had been too harsh with Michael. Maybe some of their difficulties were her fault.

DISCERNING THE PATTERN

Vanessa's wish is to feel wanted and secure in a relationship. This is a feeling she recognizes. What she is not aware of is her need. Her need is to *win* a strong man away from an obsession that keeps him from her. This is her pattern. She needs to possess a driven man. Unaware of the need, she expects that her affairs, which begin with great intensity, will grow into lasting relationships. However, Vanessa's relationships never reach that happy ending. She chooses men who are so absorbed by their pursuit of power and their work that, while they may regard her as lovely and good to be with, she is clearly a peripheral element in their lives— not unimportant but not first. Michael is a self-interested swinger caught up in his single-minded pursuit of the "good life." It takes precedence over all else, including Vanessa. Shawn, while more reserved than Michael, is also a man possessed. His power broking and his work are the central pursuits of his life, not Vanessa. Though both care a great deal for her, they cannot give her the prominent place in their lives that she so needs. Vanessa's experience with her men is a series of peaks and descents. Seeing that other things come first for them, she takes this as a personal rejection. Disappointment follows these repeated experiences until, after a time, it becomes apparent that things are not moving toward that all-encompassing love she seeks. Frustrated, Vanessa never satisfies her wish. Unfulfilled, and unaware of her contribution to this cycle, she returns to square one in the game and begins looking for another man who will be totally taken with her and thereby bring her the happiness that still eludes her. She begins anew with the conviction that next time it will come out all right.

VANESSA'S CYCLE

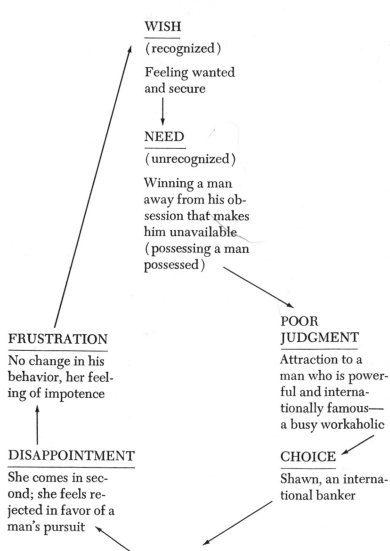

WISH

(recognized)

Feeling wanted
and secure

NEED

(unrecognized)

Winning a man
away from his ob-
session that makes
him unavailable
(possessing a man
possessed)

POOR JUDGMENT

Attraction to a
man who is power-
ful and interna-
tionally famous—
a busy workaholic

FRUSTRATION

No change in his
behavior, her feel-
ing of impotence

DISAPPOINTMENT

She comes in sec-
ond; she feels re-
jected in favor of a
man's pursuit

CHOICE

Shawn, an interna-
tional banker

EXPERIENCE

Six months of
fruitless competi-
tion for his time

Where does Vanessa's problem originate? Why is her need to make a man give up his obsessive interest, and be available to her, so powerful? How did this unhappy pattern arise? Why does an attractive, talented, intelligent young actress in a city filled with thousands of potential "Mr. Rights" always end up with the wrong guy?

Vanessa comes from a family haunted by her father's drinking. The center of her stormy and unpredictable life at home was her father. As she recently explained, "We would freeze in our tracks when the doorbell rang after five P.M. Had Dad not bothered with his keys, or was he too drunk to find them? Would he walk in or stagger in? Sometimes Mother would shrink into a corner and cry as my brothers dragged Dad upstairs. Other times she'd take over, directing us like a traffic cop and chewing Dad out for being a "no-good bum."

Not all the memories are bad. "When Dad was on the wagon, there wasn't a better guy in the whole world." Vanessa wasn't the only one who felt this way. "It seems like yesterday when Dad ran for state assemblyman. Four whole months of campaigning and never a drop of liquor on his breath. And the house crammed with important people. The mayor himself at dinner, blowing smoke rings for my entertainment." How hurt and disappointed she was when, after his narrow defeat, he lapsed. Vanessa pleaded with him to stop. As always, it was to no avail. There would be arguments between her parents, no work for father, debts, even physical abuse for Vanessa and her brothers.

In trying to make sense of what was taking place, Vanessa found herself angry at her father, blaming him for the weakness that drew him back to alcohol, or else she would be annoyed with her mother for not being a help to him. "If Mother were really behind him," she would think, "Dad wouldn't do these things."

At her lowest moments Vanessa was sure she herself was responsible. "If only I were a better child," she'd think, "he wouldn't drink." With all the confusion at home, Reverend MacIntyre's sermons were a relief. He always knew what was right and wrong. The hard work of learning acting also took Vanessa's mind off her unhappy home life. Having memorized and practiced her roles, she welcomed putting herself in the hands of her competent director.

Vanessa's relationship with her father became the prototype for her adult relationships with men. He was a potentially successful man whose drinking problem made him unavailable to her. Yet Vanessa knew he could be different: sober, prominent, powerful, wonderful. This made her feel that if she could get him to change and give up alcohol, he would be the constant and good father she longed for and knew he could be. This relationship to her father is actually present in all her adult involvements. She invariably becomes enamored of powerful men who are not totally available to her because of their absorption in their own interests.

Ironically, these men, who first seem so different from her father, inevitably leave her feeling rejected, as he had. They just have different motives. What Vanessa fails to see is that, just as her father had put alcohol before his concern for her, the men she chooses put a higher priority on their various ambitions than they do on her companionship. Like her father's drinking, their other main drives and concerns come first.

For a time in a relationship Vanessa, rather than accepting a man's style of life, wages a battle to change his priorities. She is, in effect, repeating her fruitless attempt to alter her father's behavior. She had no impact then, and she feels the impotent rage of having no impact now.

Sex plays a special part in this. In bed with a man she can

feel, at least temporarily, that he's totally involved with her, that she is first in his life. When the physical closeness does not translate into a relationship where she remains as central out of bed as she was in it, she feels bitterly disappointed and cheap. Once more she has failed to change and hold a man. She has been relegated to second place.

Learning from the Present

Do any significant elements in Vanessa's relationship sound like yours?

Do you tend to look for rich, important, famous, or prominent men?

(These are the signals that throw your need into operation. The chances are that men like this may well be men with all-absorbing pursuits. For you this means all systems "go.")

Do you find yourself very turned on by a man's prestige or authority but then become annoyed when it interferes with your relationship?

(This is the double bind of your love life. You want him powerful and compliant, tough and tender, at the same time. This is the struggle built into your relationships before they start.)

Do you make few of the decisions in the relationship? Does it always seem to be on his terms? And do you have to fit into his schedule?

(A woman with your pattern is always "reacting" to the man in her life. You're out to win over a man; yet, in fact, you put yourself at his mercy. This contradiction makes you feel powerless and irritated.)

Do you vacillate between blaming yourself and blaming him for things not going right?

(Feeling that you aren't getting what you want and need from a man and being unsure of whose fault it is, is a recurring feeling.)

Have you ever been left alone by a man on a holiday or other special time?

(Being left like this is a sign that something else holds more importance for your man than you do. This brings pain and often fury. The message is, you have not displaced his obsession.)

Do you enjoy sex but feel cheapened by it afterward?

(Without realizing it, you use sex as a way of deluding yourself into thinking a man is all yours. Your fantasy is if you turn him on enough, you can hook him. In bed you're putting your self-worth to a test. When it doesn't work, it's no wonder you feel bad.)

Do you feel a man is more important for your fulfillment than your career or social position?

(In your pattern a man is placed as a first priority, and other things follow. The irony is that the men you choose do the opposite. Career first, you second.)

Do you value financial security highly?

(You want to be sure of a man. For you money is a symbol of security; the hope is that if a man can provide security in one area of life, he can do it in all areas.)

Do you prefer men who know their own minds?

(Though you may fight it, hate it, decry it, you would never go for a man without a strong character, opinions, point of view.)

Do you feel you have little leverage in the relationship?

(Feeling powerless, as if you didn't have an equal say or even any say at all, is a position you find yourself in frequently.)

Do you compete with his work?

(You can be sure that if your pattern is to win a man from his obsession, you are in neck-and-neck competition with another activity, usually work.)

Do you think you're going to change him?

(Though you can rationally say to yourself he's too set in his ways to change, you cherish the secret fantasy that he will do it—for you.)

Are you persistent? Do you refuse to give up, despite many failed attempts to change him?

(Going back for more is a hallmark of this pattern. Your relationships are punctuated with breakups and reconciliations. You start in again as if this time you were really going to have things your way.)

Do you find yourself dating workaholics?

(Men with addictive habits, such as work, are your fatal attraction. With you he's going to kick it, you're thinking.)

Do you ever think that your man would be great if only . . . ?

(This is a common refrain. If only he weren't a selfless physician, a driven businessman, a crusading lawyer, things would be better. There's the tacit and unrealistic demand that a man give up the core of his personality. There's an inability to acknowledge the fact that a man is a package deal.)

Are you disappointed when great sex doesn't translate into a great relationship, when the hold you have over him in bed doesn't carry over?

(Only with physical contact can you feel sure of a man. Once he's out of your arms, you're plunged into uncertainty.)

Do you find yourself vacillating between wanting a man and wishing they would all disappear from the face of the earth?

(Your dissatisfactions mount until you explode [or implode] with frustration. Once the air clears, you're ready for more. Your style is to pile up grievances, create a confrontation, and start in again.)

Are you most comfortable with gay men?

(With these men you can totally relax. By their declared sexual preference for men, they eliminate the arena for your struggle. You can just be friends.)

Learning from the Past

Was your father's behavior erratic or unpredictable like that of a gambler, drug addict, abuser, or womanizer?

(The aftereffect of such an unpredictable childhood is often a struggle for emotional stability. For you it can only come when a man gives up other involvements. Your battle to be number one is a drive to get this from men, as you wished you could have from Father.)

Was your father an alcoholic or a heavy drinker?

(An addicted father can create chaos for a child, who feels, "Sometimes he loves me, sometimes he does not." The sense that there is a powerful outside force that keeps a father from being totally available is the same feeling that is resurrected in your struggle against a man's obsession.)

As a child did you find yourself totally absorbed in school and other activities outside your family—theater, dance, music, studies, church?

(This was the great escape. Unfortunately you did have to go home. As an adult no matter how absorbed you become in any activity, you are drawn back into frustrating relationships with men. You can only withdraw from the fray temporarily.)

Were your parents more concentrated on themselves than on you?

(This can leave you feeling like an outsider with people who are closest to you. With men this sense of being peripheral is painfully reenacted.)

Did you ever feel that if you were better, things at home would be too?

(A child often feels responsible for parents' failures. This sense follows you into your love life. It makes you come back for more, as if failure were up to you to correct.)

Did you always want to change your father?

(A father who holds out the hope that he will change and never does is opening an emotional trap for his daughter. She will try and try again even in the face of failure. With every lover you are trying to succeed where you failed with Father.)

Did you admire and love your father, even with his problems?

(The fact that you loved your father is in great measure why this pattern has a hold over you. If you could have hated him, you might have been able to dismiss him, write him off. Having seen his potential, you couldn't give up on him, as you cannot give up on other obsessed men.)

Did you feel your father was strong, but . . . ?

(A child may find it difficult to see a father as a troubled man. "He's really good, except for one particular problem." Compartmentalizing his problem, making it not part of him, leaves you unable to have a realistic view of men, to have an integrated picture of who they are, to see a man as a package deal.)

Did you ever try to keep your father from the thing that took him away from you?

(The little girl who has tried and failed becomes the grown woman who cannot tolerate anything that takes a man from her.)

UNLEARNING THE PATTERN

If you have answered most of the foregoing questions affirmatively, the chances are excellent that your pattern is one of trying to entice highly motivated men away from their obsessive ambitions that make them unavailable. If you think this sounds like you, begin to review your past critically and break your unfulfilling pattern. Unlearning will involve new thoughts, feelings, and actions. The first step in this process is to memorize your need. It is your need that keeps you pitted against a man's obsession, whether it is work, alcohol, politics, sports, religion, a cause, power, or money. Your need is to win a man from this all-consuming interest he puts above all else, including you. You must repeat over and over again to yourself the nature of your need. Keep it uppermost in your mind.

My need is to win a man away from his obsession that keeps him unavailable to me.

Make many copies. Put one in your appointment book. When you have to go to it to cross off another date missed because of his meetings, his deals, his business trip, look at it. Pin one to a formal dress you own, the one you might wear when an important man takes you out. Paste your reminder on the clock, the one you constantly check when he says he's leaving the office at eight and hasn't arrived yet by eleven.

Spending some time talking to a friend about your need can be invaluable. Tell him or her that your need is to make a man get close to you by getting him to drop his obsession. Explain what you mean by this and what you think made you develop this need. Convince your friend. Unless you can convince someone else, you're not convinced yourself. Work on yourself until you are thoroughly sold on your need.

Now that you have some insight, use it! Where else has this need appeared? Reflect on the men in your life. Whom have you tried to convert? Which of them have you tried to get hold of when they seemed to be slipping away? What man has been occupied or preoccupied with something, leaving you second, "out in the cold," "high and dry"? Review the men in your life. How has your need come into play? Is it the common denominator in your relationships? Can you evaluate your need to win men over?

Your Relationship Analysis

List all the men who have played a part in your life. Alongside each name write down anything about your experience that might have to do with your need to win men away, to get them to stop rejecting you in favor of something else in their lives.

This takes time and a great deal of thought because your need is not readily visible. Here is how Vanessa would analyze her relationships, for instance:

Mark, a second cousin

During the summer their families rented beach cottages next to
each other at the shore. Vanessa had a crush on him, even
though he was starting studies at the seminary in the fall. Only
by the end of the summer did she finally get him to have sex with
her. Vanessa was devastated when he stopped speaking to her
and left the shore earlier than planned. To this day at family
gatherings he avoids her.

Grandpa Cal

He ran like hot and cold water. He could be Vanessa's best
friend, yet if he were playing his daily poker game, he would
usher her out of the room and warn her that under no circumstances could he be disturbed. Totally absorbed with his cronies,
he had no time for Vanessa. As soon as he closed the door, Vanessa felt devastated and would cry angrily.

Mitch, the captain of the varsity football team and Vanessa's steady boyfriend in high school

Football season drove her crazy. She resented sitting home Saturday nights and begged Mitch to break his training curfew once
in a while. He never did. It was always beyond her how he could
give up everything for football. When he missed her sorority's
annual picnic because of an ordinary scrimmage, she had had
enough. She couldn't take the fact that she came second.

Daniel

As a nineteen-year-old sophomore, Vanessa was in love with and
planning to marry him. He was a director she had met during
summer stock two years earlier. Though she knew his life was the
theater, Vanessa was sure once they were married, he would find
more time for her. The spring before their June wedding, Dan
got an offer to tour Europe. He told her the wedding would have
to be postponed until the fall. Dejected, Vanessa dropped out of
school and moved to New York.

Ryan, an advance man for a national candidate

As a volunteer in a political campaign Vanessa met him before
the primary. She worked hard and enjoyed it, particularly because she spent most of the time in Ryan's company. They
worked day and night together. Immediately after the primary
was over Ryan moved on to the next state. Vanessa was shocked

that after all the time they had spent together, she heard absolutely nothing from him.

All of Vanessa's relationships center on a struggle to win a man from his ambition or obsession.

How about your own list? Gain an understanding of your past and confront your need's effect on your present.

Men You Should Be Alert To

Who should you watch out for?

- Workaholics
- Men who have "a drinking problem"
- Politicians on the move
- Fanatics of any persuasion
- Compulsive gamblers
- Driven men
- Overachievers
- Executives married to their companies
- Men who talk exclusively or excessively about their own thing
- Guys who cannot change their plans to suit you because something else comes first
- Men who meet with you only after ten P.M. because they just can't get there sooner
- Men who don't keep in touch regularly
- Men who make you feel second to that other thing in their lives and make themselves scarce because they "can't help it"
- Power seekers
- Money lovers

These sorts of men are unavailable, not because of someone else in their lives but because of *something* else. As you review the list, the common denominator begins to emerge.

These are men who are only partly available. Something dominates their lives other than you or any woman. These are men who correspond to your need. Put yourself on notice. Every casual pickup in a bar, every date, every man attractive to you or attracted by you must be checked. Interrogate yourself. "Am I starting a relationship with a man, or am I simply falling back into my frustrating pattern?" Spot your need and break out of your pattern.

4

Melissa

Melissa and Kevin have been living together in Kevin's garden apartment for the past three years. Thirty, short, petite, and good-looking, Melissa is an assistant personnel director for a department store. She is pursuing a graduate degree in marketing. She dresses well, but most of the time she appears washed out and fatigued, done in by her daily routine, which actually isn't terribly overwhelming. Melissa always looks as though she could use some color in her cheeks, a little makeup perhaps, something to bring out the sparkle you sense is there but hardly ever materializes. She is regarded by her friends as gentle, attentive, and thoughtful, a person who remembers anniversaries and birthdays and observes all the social amenities. She seems independent. She's a competent professional and has lived on her own since college. However, she has a helpless and hapless quality about her, almost as if life were batting her around. Things seem to happen to her. She never seems to be in charge of her life.

Any little thing seems to throw her off balance. Last year after the seasonal Christmas rush at the store, she couldn't even manage to stay for the office party, she was so distraught. It took her several weeks before she felt herself again.

If things get hectic or something unplanned pops up at work, she can feel overwhelmed. Occasionally at lunchtime she's so tense that she goes and sits in the cathedral near the store just to unwind. Even nominal daily pressures get to her. Currently, Melissa is stumbling through the last in a series of four long-term live-in relationships. It is probably not the last one. Once more Melissa has found herself with a guy who doesn't completely satisfy her. Something is missing, again. What it is that's missing eludes her. Sometimes Melissa thinks she knows. Lately sex has been only good, not great. But whose fault is it—Kevin's or hers? Typically she's not sure. Whenever she thinks of sex, she compares Kevin with George, her last lover. She is perplexed. Kevin is good-looking, has a job, cares about her. So many things sound right, yet Kevin is just not it. Or is he? George, that creep, might have been capable of being mean, but sex was great. Why didn't it work out between them?

This has been a rough year for Melissa. Her thirtieth birthday was a devastating experience. She couldn't believe she had reached thirty and was unmarried. Having no children bothers her; she wants a family. Time seems to be slipping by quickly. In spite of this pressure Melissa finds that she can't commit herself to marrying. Once more she feels that though Kevin is a really nice person, he's not the man she's looking for as a husband because she always has a sense that he's not totally with her. He just can't seem to accept her for what she is. Take her guitar playing and singing: everyone loves it, yet it irritates him. It also annoys her that she has to keep the lid on part of her personality when she's with him. It sometimes makes her feel awkward, especially in front of her friends. She doesn't see her friends too often because he doesn't go in for the kind of socializing she would like to do. She was really embarrassed by him when at her friend's lawn party he sat indoors, watching a baseball game.

Melissa wishes she could communicate better. She sometimes wants desperately to tell him how she feels—about sex, say—but a fear of stirring things up stops her from doing this. Her friends are no real help. Whenever she starts talking, more often than not they come up with advice she doesn't appreciate. How could people be so pushy, so sure of themselves, so smug? She doesn't intrude on anyone, and she expects the same in return.

Often she thinks of breaking up. But could she? Would she find anyone else? Whatever else he is, Kevin is nice. Why, then, can't she have that special feeling? He just doesn't do it for her. Where is that sharing she always dreamed of? What is it that stands between them?

Kevin has said he would like marriage, but he's not aggressive about it. Still, not being able to make up her mind is driving her crazy. With George it was different. Or was it? He said he wasn't interested in marriage. But would she have really said yes if he had asked? No, George wasn't the right man for her, either. Yet he still has a hold over her, and even though he lives with someone else, he calls from time to time—which would be fine, except that he still gets to her romantically.

She can smile now, thinking of her first serious affair with Edward and realizing how wrong they were for each other. It's hard to believe she spent three years of her life with him. Three years—is it possible? Still, she has a warm spot for Eddie, too, and they exchange birthday cards every year.

Sometimes what bothers Melissa most about her relationship is a feeling that she doesn't belong. Kevin seems to run the show; his opinions prevail. Though that's frequently a comfort, it can be excessive. Melissa lacks a voice in their relationship. And at times she feels she can't really be herself because Kevin can become so devastatingly critical and picayune on occasion.

Even vacations are complicated. Having contributed her share of the rent for their cabin in the woods, she now has mixed feelings about their vacationing together and whether she'd really enjoy it. Renting a ski lodge in the mountains last winter was fun, but the idea of splitting the rent this year isn't. As much as she realizes it is fair, it bothers her. Kevin makes much more money than she, and after three years it seems sort of ridiculous that they still do everything Dutch. Not that she wants to become dependent on him. That thought makes her wince. Yet, after all, they are a couple.

Melissa never did feel any passion for Kevin, even at the beginning of their relationship, but she had felt that he was good for her and that she should give it a try. Most of the time she could put aside her doubts, since it didn't seem to bother Kevin that she didn't want to marry. Even when he brought up his interest in starting a family, he never made demands on her. Their conversations about marriage were less and less frequent these days; their vacation plans seemed halfhearted. It was as if a kind of boredom had set in. They both lived in the same apartment, but they seemed less and less interested in each other. Even though nothing was seriously wrong—they didn't yell or scream—it just seemed as though there were no real purpose in staying together. Melissa felt there had to be something more to a relationship, and she felt certain Kevin also sensed they were going nowhere.

When the tenants of the apartment complex where they lived began holding co-op meetings, Melissa and Kevin started to talk about the possibility of buying. Melissa told Kevin she wasn't ready to make that kind of decision. Several days later Kevin angrily announced that he was buying the co-op and that it was time for them to split. Although upset, she could understand Kevin's feelings. After all, she hadn't been giving him what he really wanted. They decided it would be simplest to wait two months until the end of their lease in order to give Melissa time to find a new place.

Melissa had no bad feelings about Kevin. It just hadn't worked out. He was still her good friend no matter what.

This was one thing she felt very good about. Like George and Eddie, Kevin would remain an important part of her life and a friend.

DISCERNING THE PATTERN

Melissa wants marriage and a family. This is her wish: real togetherness with one and only one man. What she is not aware of is that this wish is colored by a need to keep her life on an even keel, to maintain a psychological equilibrium and keep her feelings under control. She needs to be attached to a man while remaining emotionally detached.

Conscious only of the wish, Melissa expects that each new relationship will flourish into a meaningful and intense love affair with someone whom she will want to marry and who will want to marry her, yet she responds to a man who is distant, reserved, rigid. For the third time in a row she is moving toward a relationship where she can move in with a man, assume all the trappings of a couple, and toy with the idea of getting married. Meanwhile the relationship moves nowhere emotionally, but Kevin is the distant, withholding sort who can tolerate a relationship on this basis.

Living with Kevin, she experiences a feeling of quiet desperation. On a daily basis things go well enough, but there is always that nagging feeling that they lack a real sparkle, that this is not the man she could spend the rest of her life with. For three years she experiences this attachment that doesn't ever advance or grow. Nothing changes. It doesn't get better, it doesn't get worse. It just is. It's just a matter of time until Melissa will give up. Melissa hangs in, waiting for something to happen. Disappointment awaits. Kevin, after a very long while when no commitment is forthcoming on Melissa's part, loses his patience and decides to end the relationship. Melissa is left feeling frustrated that she could

MELISSA'S CYCLE

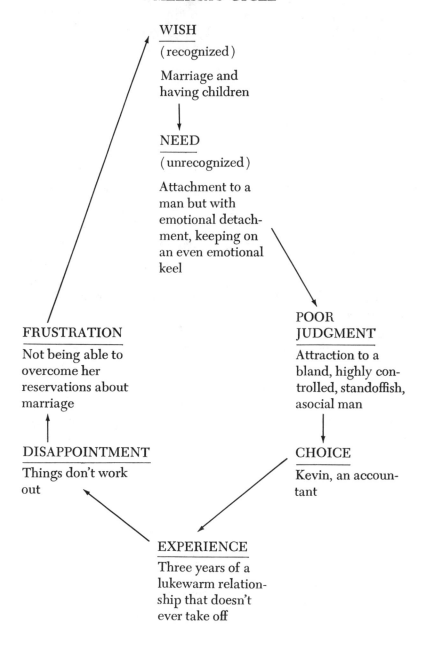

WISH
(recognized)

Marriage and
having children

NEED
(unrecognized)

Attachment to a
man but with
emotional detach-
ment, keeping on
an even emotional
keel

FRUSTRATION

Not being able to
overcome her
reservations about
marriage

DISAPPOINTMENT

Things don't work
out

POOR
JUDGMENT

Attraction to a
bland, highly con-
trolled, standoffish,
asocial man

CHOICE

Kevin, an accoun-
tant

EXPERIENCE

Three years of a
lukewarm relation-
ship that doesn't
ever take off

never overcome her reservations, her ambivalence, about marrying Kevin. Her wish to be married and have children remains unsatisfied. Her wish unfulfilled, her need unrecognized, she begins once more to think about finding someone else and trying again.

Where does the need for an essentially static relationship come from? Why does Melissa seem to be so noncommittal while she longs for commitment and marriage and a family? Melissa grew up in a family where everybody, although caring, remained aloof and only ritually involved with one another. Though she felt close to them, she couldn't say she really knew them. No one seemed to say anything personal, requiring Melissa to deduce what they were really feeling. There were no arguments, no fighting, even with her two sisters. Melissa's hardworking father, a grain dealer, never talked about himself but was absorbed in his own thoughts. He took his responsibilities seriously. The possibility of a drought, a flood, or anything that threatened the crops weighed heavily on him. Although constantly preoccupied, he could be counted on in a crisis. The neighbors really respected him, something her father was always modest about. Either busy working or worrying about his work, he would often sit silently at the evening meal. When and if he did speak, he invariably told fascinating (though often repeated) stories about his war experiences.

Her mother was also reserved. She attended to her husband's needs at the end of his long day and busied herself with cleaning, cooking, and caring for her children. Melissa could not remember her mother ever losing her temper. Mother had never been sad, never joyous. No one ever embraced. Always there were the same dutiful pecks on the cheek.

Her studious oldest sister struck her as intense and also remote. It seemed as if no one in her family ever said what was on his or her mind. Was there ever an explosion of any sort? Even when her parents disapproved of her behavior, they never expressed it harshly. They just held the reins a bit tighter—for example, the time she moved away from home. Though they never articulated their feelings to her that they weren't happy about Melissa's out-of-town job, they made sure that the following year she was home and locally employed. They didn't have to speak; their silent disapproval had its desired effect. In their own quiet way they were always in control.

Though Melissa realized her parents were reserved and kept things to themselves, she only became aware at the age of sixteen just how little they revealed themselves. She needed a costume for a school dance that year and scoured the attic for clothes. Stuffed in a box with old linens were several letters from a woman named Janice to her father. Melissa was astounded to read that this was her father's first wife and the mother of her oldest sister. She couldn't quite believe what she had discovered. Despite her astonishment and intense curiosity, she never once questioned her parents for fear of hurting them. The only one she could bear to tell was her pastor.

Her family was like a constellation, each member positioned perfectly in the system, never getting closer, never getting farther apart as they silently and intently moved through life. They were charged with feelings but frozen into an inflexible system, afraid and incapable of getting close to one another. It was a family that looked like a family but lacked the intimacy that makes it one.

This system of relationships was all Melissa had ever known. It is this model that she brings to her affairs with men. Though desiring otherwise, she can only handle people at a distance. Sharing—complete and honest sharing—is something Melissa just can't do. She simply doesn't know how to go about it. What's more, somewhere in her heart she finds the thought of intimacy frightening. She has absorbed a family message that it is dangerous to let go. She is used to relationships where feelings are modulated. She is attracted to men she senses share this inhibition. With them she can perpetuate the form of relationship she knows and is most comfortable in.

As an adult she reenacts this early pattern, and this need to be attached while remaining emotionally detached becomes the central theme of her love life. Though this unsuccessful lovestyle does little to bring her personal fulfillment, it does keep her in well-known territory. Any intensity, anything but emotional detachment, throws her off balance and is avoided. Letting go, being out of control, is an unacceptable state of affairs—threatening. Uncharted areas and unpredictable reactions are things Melissa cannot face exploring. It is this intimacy and its unpredictable consequences Melissa senses she must avoid. Unwittingly she responds to men who send out signals that they will keep their distance, men who care for her but don't want her to open herself fully to the experiences possible in love. Melissa chooses men who are satisfied with having a semblance of a relationship. Interestingly she is on good terms with her former boyfriends. It's as if, even after the end of the relationship, the emotional tone of their contact remains the same as before.

Learning from the Present

Does her lovestyle resemble yours? Are you a woman who gets involved with men but never really lets herself go? Do you keep men at arm's length? Are any of the important elements of this relationship like yours?

If you think your need is to be attached while being emotionally detached, where does this need originate?

If you have doubts as to whether your pattern is similar to Melissa's, ask yourself the following questions:

Are you serially monogamous, involved on a long-term basis with one man at a time?

(Is this your trademark: finding one partner and settling into a relationship you can keep on hold emotionally? In this way you limit the number of men who enter your life and the way you maintain your equilibrium.)

Do you move in together but never really feel as if it's your home?

("As if" characterizes the quality of your love life. You and your man are together "as if" you were true partners, but there is always a distance between you. You can never really feel relaxed or comfortable with him.)

Do you go Dutch and share expenses equally?

(The difficulty in merging your financial resources is symbolic of the difficulty you have in merging emotionally with a man.)

Do you have difficulty speaking about really personal things, things that are truly private, with your boyfriend?

(Sharing intimacies makes you highly uncomfortable. To be entirely known is to be entirely vulnerable. You can't risk it.)

Do you invariably have mixed feelings about the men in your life?

(Ambivalence is the key feature of this style. You can never make up your mind about your feelings. Swinging back and forth between emotions prevents any one feeling from taking over.)

Is your boyfriend a good person yet you sometimes wish things were more exciting?

(Excitement does not come from detachment. Excitement comes from letting go, losing control, something your need doesn't permit.)

Do you like being with friends but never really want or accept their advice? Is their advice annoying? Are you uncomfortable when they get too personal?

(Sensing your dilemmas about men in your life, friends respond to you "as if" you could use help. You feel intruded upon, as if they've stepped over your personal boundaries. You feel more comfortable left alone.)

Do you feel overwhelmed by life? Do you tire or get ill easily?

(You feel strained because life takes hold of you and not you it.)

Is sex adequate but never great? You can't tell your boyfriend what makes you feel good?

(This is another area of your life where you hold back. If he really knew what turned you on, you might lose control.)

Do you pride yourself on having no ill feelings about your former boyfriends?

(This is mistaken pride. Such sentiments suggest the emotional tone of your relationships doesn't change before, during, or even after an affair.)

Do your relationships just peter out or die of exhaustion?

(You let things happen to you. Even if you sense your relationship is going nowhere, you let it go on and on and on till it just fades away.)

Is your guy sometimes picayune, irritable, mean?

(A woman with your need holds powerful emotion such as anger in check. Often you pick men who express the feelings you can't.)

Do you end long-term affairs feeling no hatred? Do you

feel instead that "it just didn't work" or "it's better for both of us"?

(Your need leaves you an emotional coward. No matter what, you can't take a stand.)

Do you generally not scream or yell? Are knock-down-and-drag-out fights not your style?

(To you emotions are dangerous. If you let loose, you can't tell what might happen. Maybe you'd have to confront just how angry you really are.)

Does your partner inhibit you? Does your special thing (singing, joking, dancing) not go over well with him?

(Your style forces you into affairs where you sense you can't be yourself. You find someone who puts a lid on you.)

Learning from the Past

Do you feel you don't really know your parents as people?

(You don't. They didn't let you. What you understand about them is based on your inference, not their declaration. In your love life you are unknowable in the same way. The men you choose aren't the kind to break through to the real you.)

Are your parents quiet or reserved?

(These refinements are probably the manifestations of their own attempts to keep feelings under wraps. The civility you bring to your love life [for example, the way you graciously end an affair] is a carry-over from this model.)

You never really remember doing something wild, something outlandishly funny with your parents?

(Letting it all hang out was never your family's style. It is the same with the men in your life. You wish for gay abandon but don't practice it. In fact, you find men who criticize anything you do that approximates it.)

As a child, did you have equal feelings about your mother and father? You didn't prefer or dislike one more than the other?

(Such equality can't exist for a child. If it does, it's a manufactured, forced feeling. You allowed yourself to love but tried to control the range and intensity of your other feelings.)

Do you feel your parents cared equally for you and your siblings?

(Parents feel different things for different children, and invariably children feel more—or less—favored by them. Not to acknowledge any distinctions is an effort to deny or suppress feelings, to work at maintaining an emotional equilibrium within a family.)

Did your parents never seem to talk to you about important things?

(Tackling issues means a kind of face-to-face confrontation, something your parents steadfastly avoided with you. Something you cannot achieve with the men in your adult life.)

Were you always a good child, never feeling the urge to rebel?

(The family message was that the eruption of feelings, especially negative ones, such as anger, was forbidden. You still act with men as if you believed intense emotions are powerful, threatening forces.)

Could you never tell your parents anything truly personal?

(Parents can nonverbally communicate that they are fragile
and easily upset, that at all costs you must maintain the
status quo. It is a special form of control. "Don't tell us anything or do anything that might hurt us." As a child you
didn't.)

Are you unaware of the details of what's going on in any
member of your family's life? Is there little or no gossip?

(Here is the "as if" quality again. On the surface yours appears to be a loving family, yet in fact you are strangers to
one another. Loners. Afraid to ask. No one dares to know
too much.)

Have you ever found out about a skeleton in a family
closet? Are there secrets that no one has ever mentioned?

(In your family information is kept from people. It's better
not to know—that's the attitude. This is estrangement at
work. Each person knows more than they ever say. With
men you hide more than you reveal.)

Do you still do pretty much what your parents expect of
you, even though they aren't openly demanding?

(Quiet, passive control is the predominant style of your
family. It is yours in relation to men with whom you're involved.)

UNLEARNING THE PATTERN

If you find yourself answering yes to many of the foregoing questions, it is probable that your relationships can
best be described as attachments with emotional detachment. Is each a reenactment of the kind of reserved, controlled expressions of emotion you learned as a child? Are
you unwittingly attracted to men who slip comfortably into
this need?

The first step in breaking out of your routine is unlearning. Begin by making clear for yourself that your need gets you involved with men with whom you can have long relationships without great emotional investment or commitment, men who tolerate your ambivalence, your indecision, even your lack of enthusiasm for them. It's not that you don't care about the man in your life; on the contrary, your relationships are serious matters. It's just that you never feel *this is it*. As nice as he is, he's just not the person you see yourself spending the rest of your life with. Something indefinable is missing. Learn your need:

My need is to be attached to a man while remaining emotionally detached.

Understand that this need is the premise of every relationship you've had. Tape-record it. Play it back. Do you sound convincing? Keep recording your declaration of your need and listen until the sound of your own voice rings true. Let a friend listen. Does she feel you sound sincere? Does it sound to her as if you accept the true nature of your need? Keep repeating it and listening until you're truly convinced.

Write your need down. Copy it on several three-by-five index cards. Print it out on each card in bold black letters.

Use these reminders to disrupt your pattern. Let them jolt you into recognizing that you're acting out your need. Put one in your key case. When you come home after work, ask yourself if it really feels like you're home. Put one in your diaphragm case. When you're about to have sex that's good but not great, think about how you hold back. Put one in the pocket of your bathrobe. When you feel done in by your ambivalence and want a hot bath, where you can just stop thinking, read it.

When you go to pay your half of the rent, have one in your checkbook. Stop and consider that you can't even let go enough to make a financial commitment to a man. Paste one inside each of your old address books. When you fish them out to send greetings to an old beau, ask yourself why your need keeps you on this emotional even keel with every man in your life.

What should you be doing with these reminders if you're living with a man? With your pattern there are probably many areas of your life that are private. Perhaps there's a book only you would read, a drawer of your bureau he'd never go to. Put these reminders in all your private spaces. When you retreat to them (and from him), think about your need, how you put limits on your emotional contact with the man in your life.

Explore your history. What was your father like? Your mother? How did they get along with each other? Was reserve within the family the unwritten by-law of your house? Talk it out. Piece it together. Reconstruct the early experiences that have contributed to your unsuccessful pattern.

Work. Keep on working until you are convinced about your need and see yourself and it clearly.

Did you feel uncomfortable in the past when anyone tried to get too close or tried to break your emotional barriers? Do you run from or resent men who try to move into your innermost emotional territory?

Your Relationship Analysis

Go over all the men in your life. How has your need come to play in these relationships? List beside each anything that might have to do with your need to maintain emotional distance.

Melissa's relationships reveal a lot about this:

Grandfather Ethan
Since he retired five years ago to Naples, on the west coast of Florida, Melissa had seen him only once, at her sister's wedding. Though she hasn't paid him a visit, she always calls him around

the time of his birthday or any important holiday. Melissa keeps telling her mother that she wishes she could see "Big Dad" more often (she used to call him that when her father was away during the war). However, she never can get around to seeing him.

Cousin Clifford

After service in Vietnam, Cliff stayed on the West Coast to attend college and never returned to his parents, whose house adjoined Melissa's family's place. Melissa and he corresponded occasionally. When Melissa's friend returned from college in Southern California, she casually mentioned seeing Cliff and commented how well he got along in a wheelchair. Melissa was astounded that no one, not even Cliff himself, had ever mentioned this tragedy.

Raymond

All through high school Ray was the only boy she really had much to do with. Though she herself didn't consider him her boyfriend, everyone else thought of them as a couple. Things never got too serious between them. They never went beyond petting. Even when they went their separate ways after high school, she always had good feelings about him. About a year after he left to study design at the Fashion Institute, she heard gossip that he was gay.

Stuart

On the first day of her first year at community college she met Stuart, a fellow freshman. They dated steadily for two years. In the second year, when he had his own place, Melissa often spent the weekend. She was always comfortable with him. Even though they shared the same bed, he was never pushy about sex until she was ready. When school ended, so did they. They wrote to each other, and Melissa was pleased to hear that he had found a nice girl friend. At a class reunion Melissa got a chance to meet her and Stuart. They got along quite well. Stuart still writes but doesn't say much about his girl friend, so Melissa isn't sure if they're still together.

Mr. Brooks, regional director of the store where she works

Melissa always had an excellent working relationship with Mr. Brooks. They got along well and had the same sense of humor. After a while he began to delegate more responsibility to her and took Melissa under his wing. Mr. Brooks frequently talked to her at length, asking questions about herself and getting into some fairly personal discussions about her boyfriends. This made Melissa very uneasy. She didn't know how to get across to Mr. Brooks that she didn't care to get so personal. Finally, one day he went too far and asked her how she felt knowing that an old boyfriend, Ray, was probably gay. This was too much. She told her boss in no uncertain terms that while she liked him and liked working for him, it was just none of his business. Since the incident they definitely spend less time together, but Melissa feels it's better this way.

Now that you've read Melissa's relationship analysis, you can begin to see the theme that appears and reappears. Sometimes explicitly, sometimes subtly, her relationships are attachments with a very limited emotional range. Melissa never gets too close. In this way she never loses control or becomes overwhelmed. To grandfather, an important person in her childhood, she was always solicitous but avoided direct contact. With cousin Cliff her emotional distancing prevents her from knowing the most crucial event of his life, his paralysis.

For three years she could carry on a lukewarm relationship with Ray. Here her need to keep uninvolved enabled her to close herself off from an inkling of his true feelings about his sexual identity. Either in or out of a relationship, she maintains the same even-keel feelings about Stuart. Mr. Brooks is okay as long as he doesn't go beyond her emotional barriers and intrude on her personal feelings.

Now that you have an idea, conduct your own relationship analysis. Include any man who has been significant in your life. Relatives, friends, lovers, colleagues, peers, clergymen.

How does your need reverberate through your relationships? How does your pattern unfold?

The power of your need begins to emerge as you carry out this exercise. You begin to judge the power of your need as you recognize how it inevitably pervades your relationships.

Once you have conducted this self-analysis, you can have an idea of how it colored your past. Now you must confront how your need dominates your present, how it makes your current lovestyle unworkable.

Is your man reserved, shy, elusive, withholding? Is he controlled and withdrawn? Does he have any of these many different qualities that could give off the message "I can and will stand back emotionally; I'm a man who fits your need." This must be uppermost in your mind, and you must be alert to it at all times. You must always be aware that you are drawn inexorably, like a magnet, to such a man who will fit this need. And such men will remain the only males that attract you unless you learn to overpower this force by consciously controlling the need rather than allowing yourself to be controlled by it. Once you have the slightest sense or evidence that a man is in your life because of your need, stop. You must end things before they begin.

Men You Should Be Alert To

Whom should you be on the lookout for? Whom should you steer clear of? Men who

Are shy, withdrawn
Have few friends
Don't talk much about themselves
Brood
Seem like they have a potential to open up and never do
Don't talk about their feelings
Are not generous
Share expenses
Make you feel that "mine is mine, yours is yours"
Are rigid, strict, fastidious, tense
Make sex a routine
Don't excite you—especially sexually
Can wait forever for you to make up your mind
Even fleetingly strike you as gay

As you review these signs, a common element emerges. All are potential candidates for relationships where strong emotions and a range and depth of feeling are unlikely, if not impossible. The very reason such personalities appeal to you, the very reason you must be alert is that subliminally, these are individuals with characteristics who perfectly fit your need to be attached and at the same time detached.

Therefore, you must remain alert to your need and catch yourself as you respond. In each instance you must ask yourself if you are starting a true relationship or only beginning to reenact your old pattern.

Only when you can detect your need before it begins to govern your selection are you going to have truly gratifying experiences with men.

5

Jenny

"Jenny, Jenny, you're not listening to me; you haven't heard a word I've said."

Jenny's mother was absolutely right. For three days she hadn't listened to anybody, not since she saw the announcement of Richard's engagement in the paper. "And to think that a year ago he wanted to marry me. Peggy probably just caught him on the rebound. I'm sure Richard's not in love with her, not the way he loved me." Jenny went to the full-length mirror in the hall to reassure herself.

She remembered how he had acted; he just couldn't do enough for her. Flowers, gifts. It bordered on the ridiculous. Whatever she wanted was fine; the best restaurants, the best shows. "How could an insurance broker afford all this?" Jenny wondered, not that she really cared. It wasn't her fault that she never pretended to have any real feelings for him. As far as Jenny was concerned, their relationship was completely one-sided: He did all the calling, the chasing. She'd never said she loved him, but Richard was oblivious; her total lack of responsiveness never stopped him from professing his love.

Sex had been as one-sided as everything else. It had amused her to see how excited Richard got when she let him get close and how quickly he came. She wished she could enjoy it as much as he did.

Now reading the engagement announcement, Jennifer thought maybe she had judged him too harshly. "I'm sure things could have gotten better," she mused. "He didn't really seem to know what to do. I know I like men who take charge, but Richard could have become a good lover. It was stupid to have told him he needed more experience. He didn't say anything, but I'm sure he was hurt."

Jennifer felt mounting irritation, a knot that was getting tighter and tighter. Without even realizing it, she clenched her teeth together and muttered under her breath, "I shouldn't have turned him down when he wanted to marry me. If only I had another chance, I'd do things differently."

That was it. Deciding it was not too late to set things straight with Richard, she called his office. "After all, he's not married yet, is he?" At first, surprised to hear from her, Richard sounded a bit irritated. Friendlier by the end of the conversation, he thanked her for her good wishes on his engagement.

In spite of his reserve she sensed excitement in Richard's voice. She'd just have to keep trying.

The next day Jenny planned to be in the neighborhood of Rich's office and just casually drop by. Startled to see her, he was uneasy in her presence. Jenny was ready. Pulling out a form, she tossed it on his desk. "You're the only one in this whole office who's capable of straightening out this cancellation mix-up."

Reluctantly Richard solved her "problem" in a few minutes and got up to walk Jenny to the door. Close to him, she touched his arm and said, "I know you're engaged, but I don't believe for a minute that you've stopped loving me."

His reply came quickly as he removed her hand. "Jenny, I had a lot of feeling for you once, but it's over for me. I'm sorry. I'd rather you didn't come again. Someone else in the office can handle your business."

For the next two days her phone calls didn't get beyond Rich's secretary. She stopped by the office the next week, but his secretary foiled her again, claiming that Richard was in conference.

She was furious. That night she couldn't fall asleep. She came up with the idea of waiting outside his office building in the morning. Like clockwork he would arrive to work at 8:45 A.M. (She knew about his punctuality, since he used to get so irritated at her own lateness.)

If he ignored her, she could always threaten to make a scene, since he hated to fight in public. It would work; he would listen to her. Jenny knew how to get her way. She remembered in college when she had broken her engagement to Kent. Even though she made it clear that she wanted nothing to do with him, he kept following her. It was absurd. Kent went the whole route of the lovestruck boy, even showing up at her dorm window drunk and calling to her. If it had been a night in May instead of January, she would have cooled him off with a bucket of water. "And to think that at one time I was so wild about him that I made him break up with his high school sweetheart for me."

The next morning Jenny carried out her plan and managed to corner Richard in a coffee shop. They spoke for a few minutes until he left her for his office. She wasn't exactly sure where things stood, since he hadn't said a word about his fiancée. He couldn't have meant it when he said he would ignore her calls in the future, her letters, her visits. She was upset and yet relieved that she had a date that night with Edward.

Edward wasn't her type, but he was a good listener. He seemed to understand her problems with Richard and didn't mind that Jenny cut the evening short. Jennifer had to get to bed early. Richard was on her mind, and in bed alone she could concentrate on what her next move would have to be. If she didn't make exactly the right moves, Richard might be a lost cause.

DISCERNING THE PATTERN

Jenny's wish is to have a man around. To have his company while she makes up her mind about him. She wants time and freedom to resolve whether she really wants him. What she isn't aware of is that this wish is colored by an unrecognized need. Jenny's need is to be pursued by or to pursue men but to always maintain a distance in either instance. She is always just out of his reach, or he just out of hers.

She is attracted to men for all the wrong reasons. Why? Because psychologically her need overpowers her wish. This drives her to men who can be held dangling, men who are ardent, who chase. This is why Richard was her choice. In entertaining her, declaring his immediate love, he sent a signal that he would tolerate a one-sided relationship. While initially she had had Richard at her beck and call, eventually her relationship had deteriorated into a series of scenes complete with tantrums, demands, and pleas. Her disappointment at being ignored mounted. She became preoccupied, even obsessed, with plans to get him back, to undo her mistake. Finally she began to realize that Richard wanted nothing to do with her and that he would truly ignore her. This led to frustration since she had no possibility of renewing her relationship with him on any terms, no chance of having the attention she required.

Where is Jenny? Her wish to have someone around goes unfulfilled. Her unconscious need to be either rejecter or pursuer goes unrecognized. Jenny's pattern has come full circle, ready to begin the unrelenting cycle again.

Why does this need to be either the pursued or the pursuer dominate Jenny's relationships with men? Where does it originate?

Jenny comes from an old New England family and spent her childhood living in the country; only when she was in

JENNY'S CYCLE

WISH
_____
(recognized)

Companionship

NEED
_____
(unrecognized)

Being pursued and
rejecting, pursuing
and being rejected

POOR
FRUSTRATION   JUDGMENT
_____   _____
No chance for re-   Attraction to a
lationship to be   man who falls im-
renewed on any   mediately in love
terms; no com-   with her from the
panionship   outset and who
                                   relentlessly pur-
                                   sues her

DISAPPOINTMENT   CHOICE
_____   _____
Recognition that   Richard, an in-
he wants nothing   surance broker
to do with her

EXPERIENCE
_____
Eventually the
man's avoidance of
her and becoming
interested in some-
one else; her beg-
ging, pleading,
plotting to get him
back

high school did they move to town. Her mother, a high-strung, nervous woman always seemed overshadowed by her father.

"My parents were a mismatch. Mother is nice, but rather plain if you compare her with Father. He's so charming and cultured. If the two of them ever went anywhere together, it was my father who would attract attention, whom people liked to talk to. My mother has always been shy and uncomfortable in the limelight."

Jenny herself found being around her father gay and exciting. "Dad traveled a lot for work. I was always disappointed when he left. The house would get so dreary with just my mother around. Sometimes on an evening when he was expected, I'd hardly be able to concentrate on my schoolwork. Every time I thought I heard his car, I'd jump up and shoot over to the window. I don't remember this, but my mother said when I was very little, I would fall asleep waiting, and Dad would wake me up, even if it was midnight."

On his return he would often come with gifts for his "girls," and Jenny would perform the latest songs or dances she had learned in school. He would hold her, squeeze her, play with her. But he was a busy man, so the excitement of having him home was often followed by a letdown when he'd put in long days at the office and long hours working at home.

"He never had time to do things other fathers could do. I think, too, that in some ways he was never that interested in those things. He wasn't the kind of father who'd toss a ball with you. I know he loved me very much, but he only had so much time and couldn't be bothered."

Though everything in their family life revolved around father, Jenny's mother never complained about being neglected. She accepted everything he did, even closed her eyes to the existence of his mistress in Boston.

"I don't know how my mother took it. Maybe deep down even I knew that something was going on in Boston. I always wanted to go with him on a trip, but I never asked. Instead I'd spend time in my room daydreaming about how wonderful it would be. How we'd walk down the city streets together; how he'd even take me to a restaurant. I could get pretty carried away." Even when he was home, Jenny spent more time making up how she and her father would do things together than actually doing them.

What does this mean for Jenny in her adult life?

Jenny grew up in a home where she was forced to tolerate an unhappy relationship between her parents. A successful, selfish, self-confident father dominated the scene while her mother lingered in the background. Jenny had confused, ambivalent feelings about her father and felt sorry for her mother, who seemed at his mercy. When her father was away in Boston, she longed for him, idealized him, and often wished she had the power to bring him back home. His return confused her further. While she was eager for his return, she never entirely forgave him. His all-out enthusiasm for her was, secretly in her heart, met with reserve and disappointment. She never let her feelings go, since he would inevitably end up leaving or withdrawing from her and her mother soon after his tumultuous return.

Jenny's life became a kind of emotional seesaw. Father's leaving was a periodic rejection. A painful rejection that left her longing to be with him, to follow him as she would often dream of doing. And then the tables would turn: Her father would be back with a great rush of excitement and try to win back his "girls," only to withdraw again, using work as an excuse after this concentration of attention. At these moments Jenny was filled with a deep feeling of resentment toward him. She harbored anger toward this man who held out promises but disappointingly never delivered.

When Jenny becomes involved with men, she is reactivating this early pattern of relating. She is acting out her need. In a very fundamental sense this is the only way Jenny knows how to relate to men. Although Jenny's lovestyle never brings her a fulfilling relationship, it keeps her in safe territory. She is immersed in a predictable pattern of relating. As painful as her relationships may be, they are familiar.

Learning from the Present

You've read about Jenny. What is your reaction? Do any of the significant elements of this relationship sound like yours?

After you've broken up with a man, do you realize you've lost a good thing?

(Regrets play a big part in the love life of the pursuer/pursued. "Should have," "could have," and "what would have been" are the tag phrases of this style.)

Do you find yourself involved with men you don't think much of? The more he tries to win you, the less you think of him?

(The paradox "If he cares for me, he can't be that good" is burned deep into the heart of every pursuer/pursued.)

Do you find yourself involved with men who like you much more than you like them?

(The more he's turned on, the more you're turned off. His emotional ardor is the quickest route to your emotional withdrawal.)

Do you keep a man on a hook, even when you know you're not really that interested?

(A man who is kept dangling is a sure sign of this pattern. The pursuer/pursued is engaged in an emotional power struggle. Sometimes she gets the upper hand.)

Do you enjoy being admired and pursued and never take those who do admire you very seriously?

(Excitement and attention are the feelings you like to indulge in, but they never seem to bring real satisfaction.)

Does it annoy you when a man you've initially rejected turns around and rejects you?

(How quickly one forgets. You have a short-term memory for what you contributed to these rejections. Your hurt is related to your injured pride rather than to the emotional pain of rejection. All you can feel is abandoned.)

Do you find yourself thinking desirously about a man after you don't have him anymore?

(Only when you are at a safe distance can you let your feelings go. For you, the imagined and fantasized aspects of the relationship are best.)

Do men become more attractive to you when they start dating someone else?

(Although you're indifferent when a man is around, you feel lost, unsure of your worth, once he's out of your life. Another woman's interest increases your self-doubt.)

Have you dreamed that your man would break up with the other woman and come back to you?

(Hope springs eternal. The pursuer/pursued often replays scenarios so that they have a happy ending. Despite facts that may contradict this, she feels that the man who's left still really loves her. There's no such thing as a man who is gone for good, even if the only way he's around is in her wishful thinking.)

Have you ended up "stealing" a man from another woman and then regretting that you even bothered?

(A pursuer/pursued's juices start to flow if there is a man who ignores her, especially if it's because his attentions are turned toward another woman. Once the challenge is there, you stop at nothing. Since it's the chase that excites you, winning means little.)

Do men always seem more appealing at a distance? Once you know them intimately, is there always something missing?

(A pursuer/pursued has enormous difficulty accepting a man for what he is. At a distance a man can be idealized, glorified.)

Do you go after a man against all odds, even if he indicates he's not interested?

(You keep a relationship going even when a man has called it quits; clean breaks are not part of this style.)

Do you think sex would be better than it used to be if he came back?

(Your self-doubts about sex run high. You wonder why a man who likes you doesn't excite you and wish you had a chance to try again.)

Do you feel you could have a man back if not for circumstances or because of another woman?

(You have a hard time thinking about the negative feelings a man might have about you. You need to tell yourself that circumstances, rather than his hurt, anger, frustration, and so on, are responsible for keeping you apart.)

Have you exchanged harsh words with, or leveled bitter accusations at, a man who's left you—or wished you could?

(Angry feelings may be part of this style. They are there all the time but only surface when they can be blamed on the man.)

Learning from the Past

This next set of questions can help you identify and isolate some past experiences that may have created your powerful need:

> When you needed your father, were you unable to have him?

> (A child who needs a father and doesn't have him is a child who may feel abandoned, rejected. These are the feelings that are pervasive in the pursuer/pursued and that interfere with intimacy in adult life.)

> When your father tried to be nice to you, did you hold back? Did something seem to be missing?

> (Emotional memories leave deep impressions. While your father may have been able to ignore or forget or try to make up to you for his unavailability, you couldn't forget the pain, you couldn't trust him fully. This pulling back from men who are demonstrative is central to your pattern.)

> When you think of your parents, is your father the dominant figure?

> (This preeminence of your father in your early life is responsible in some ways for the fact that in adult life you often find yourself preoccupied with a man. Men are everything.)

> Were your parents very different, a mismatch? Was your father much more interesting than your mother?

> (With this imbalance of feeling about your parents, a father can become overvalued. The message may be that mothers, women, are not as worthwhile. This self-doubt is easily stimulated in the pursuer/pursued.)

> Do you have mixed feelings about your father—you

missed him when he wasn't around and resented him when he was?

(In these feelings lie the core confusion about adult men. The lover who leaves stimulates these feelings of longing; the one who is near rekindles the pain and is rejected.)

Was your father involved with another woman, or did you suspect as much?

(Whether in fact it was another woman or not, there was a sense that his interest was not fully with the females [wife, daughter] in his family. Such suspicions may give rise to fantasies about Father when he is out of sight. In adult life this translates into a preoccupation with a man's experiences away from you.)

Did your father try to make up to you for having hurt you?

(Every man who is nice to you is, on some level, a man trying to make up to you. Since your father hurt you repeatedly, it's no wonder you don't take these men seriously.)

Did your father never really understand how you were feeling inside? Was he never really available for you?

(You keep this emotional distance from men in adult life.)

Did your father force his own mood on you? Did he insist that you be happy in his presence?

(As a child you suffered from your father's lack of empathy, from the discomfort of being urged to feel the way he wanted you to feel. When a lover comes on strong, you feel that, like Father, he is emotionally out of sync with you.)

Did your mother tolerate a lot of abuse from your father? Did she accept being second fiddle, even being ignored?

(Observing this treatment makes a girl feel she doesn't deserve to be treated well. It leaves her with a poor self-image.)

Was your mother meek, submissive?

(Mother's message was that men are to be submitted to. When you pursue a man, you're acting this out. In a way you're laying yourself at a man's feet.)

Was it exciting being with your father? Did you enjoy his attentions, but much of the time he wasn't that involved with you?

(Fathers who run hot and cold are the starting point for your relationships. In your love life, feelings run to extremes. Every man is either turned on or turned off in regard to you. You are either excited or indifferent. As there was not any middle of the road when it came to your interactions with your father, there's none with the men in your love life.)

Did you sometimes find yourself really admiring your father, whereas other times you felt disappointed in him?

(As a child it is often difficult to cope with contradictory feelings about your father, to accept that one person can be both good and bad at the same time. These irreconcilable feelings are the split you feel toward men as an adult. Men are either admirable or disappointing, good or bad, idols or bastards.)

When your father did spend time with you, were you his "girl"? Did he tickle you, hold you, put you on his lap?

(This excitement, this all-out attention, is something that you try to reestablish with lovers. It becomes a built-in expectation of how men should respond to you and how you should feel about them.)

Was your father very involved in his own activities—business, sports, hobbies?

(At the center of your style is a self-absorbed father. You never had practice getting close to a man.)

By now you should begin to get a good sense of whether your lovestyle is that of the pursuer or the pursued, rejecter or rejected. Critically review your past in an effort to understand your own special personal history that is reflected in this lovestyle and that established this need.

If this resembles or is even close to your lovestyle, what follows will help you to change.

UNLEARNING THE PATTERN

In order to change or break the pursuer/pursued, rejecter/rejected pattern you must unlearn your habitual ways of responding to men and learn new ones instead. Unlearning involves moving in new directions.

To move in new directions, begin by thinking through your pattern. Consider the kind of trap your need gets you into, a cycle of ups and downs. The men who are near and nice never seem to satisfy. Only when they are unavailable do they seem to fit the ideal you are seeking. When a man gives you the attention and admiration you seek, it actually does him in. If he wants you, how good can he be? If he doesn't want you, he can't be anything but great. Your image of what a man could be spurs you on, while what a man actually is turns you off.

You are angry and hurt, but you still long for a man.

Once you clearly understand the nature of your need, you can work on keeping it at the forefront of your thinking. Whether you are working, taking a bath, or out on a date, continuously be aware of this need.

The notion of pursuer/pursued must become your personal obsession. Literally keep your need in view—write it down:

My need is to be pursued by a man I've rejected or to be rejected by a man I pursue.

Make copies. Use them to remind you. Tie them into the pattern of your lovestyle. Try putting one under your pillow. Think about it as you lie in bed dreaming up ways to get him back. Put one on your mirror. The next time you give yourself the once-over to see how you compare with the new woman in your boyfriend's life, read it.

Where do you keep the scissors? Put a reminder there. Look at it the next time you clip a social announcement or a newspaper article about a man you passed up.

Keep one with the vase you use to put the flowers in that your admirers send you. Think about how your need makes you react to such gestures.

Put one on the phone. Review it as you talk with the man who's called to invite you to the best show in town.

Keep one with your phone book. The next time you try to track down the number of a man you used to date (at his home, club, office), be reminded of your need and the real reason for your search. Let thought begin to replace action.

Work on yourself until your understanding of your need is firmly planted in your mind and heart. Once you're saturated, sure you have a grip on it, it is time to make the next move: relationship analysis.

Your Relationship Analysis

Now use your insight into your need to reflect on the men you have pursued. Who has pursued you? Who has been involved with you in both ways? Think about all the men in your life—your friends, lovers, idols, relatives. How has your need been reflected in your feelings toward them? Is this need to be pursuer/pursued the motivation behind your involvement with different men? Is it the common denominator in your relationships. How can you find out if pursuit and rejection are the twin themes running through your relationship to men. How do you confirm it?

List all the males who've been in your life. Alongside each name write anything about the relationship that might have to do with pursuit and rejection. This is not easy: Don't forget that this need is often hidden.

Here is Jenny's relationship analysis:

Cousin Elliot, a younger cousin of Jenny's who always wanted to play with her
Jenny just couldn't stand him. They played together only when her mother forced it. Then she teased him mercilessly. They often fought. At one point things got so bad that their parents decided they shouldn't play together. The separation didn't last long, since Jenny insisted that she play with Elliot again because she missed him. Once they were back together again, nothing had changed.

Eric, an older brother
Jenny idolized him. She always wanted to be with him and his friends. As far as he was concerned, she was a pest. Despite her anger toward him she used to come home from school and bake brownies for him to eat when he got home later.

Seth, a senior when Jenny was a sophomore
Jenny was dying to date him. Although he would often catch her eye and smile, he never came over and asked her name. Her friend, who knew Jenny's feelings, would push her in Seth's direction whenever he was near. Jenny joined the school paper, of which he was the editor, just to be around him. But he acted as if she didn't exist. Seth had a girl friend, but Jenny just couldn't see what he saw in her.

Warren, a classmate
Jenny felt as if she had known Warren forever. They had started grade school together. In high school she thought he was a creep and never even considered dating him, even though he was always asking her out. After all their dateless years he still invited her to their senior prom, but she refused. ("I didn't want to be seen with him.") She got no other invitation and spent the night at a slumber party. "We all sat around and talked about what we were missing."

Phillip, a creative writing instructor
Phillip wanted to get into Jenny's pants from the first class, lavishing praise on her about her literary gifts. She wasn't the least bit interested in him. She thought he was overly romantic and silly. He once sent her a poem that embarrassed her to no end. He'd call and she'd say she was out or even just refused to speak to him. He finally took the hint. Next semester she ran into him on campus. He was with another woman and didn't even acknowledge her with a greeting. Jenny felt annoyed by his treatment. When she saw him in the cafeteria several weeks later, she said sharply, "I'm sure that girl isn't as good as me. You really missed out, didn't you?"

Look over these descriptions. It becomes clear that pursuit and rejection are very central to Jenny's relationships. There is always that feeling of imbalance so typical of the pursuer/pursued's need.

Her cousin Elliot wanted her attention, but Jenny made him miserable. Yet when she couldn't have him under her thumb, she missed him. When he was available again, she was back to her old tricks.

Eric, her brother, was idolized like her father, and equally out of reach. His overt rejection angered Jenny but that didn't stop her from trying to win his attention.

High school senior Seth was attractive to Jenny precisely because he was uninterested. By contrast, Warren, another classmate, was unappealing because he was too nice. It's as if each boy represented one side of Jenny's need. Seth was the pursued, Warren the pursuer.

Phillip, her creative writing instructor, was typical of Jenny's entire pattern. His admiration was scorned, and he was regarded as foolish and ridiculous. As soon as he ignored Jenny, he stimulated her interest in him.

Now it's your turn to make your own relationship analysis. Don't forget any man who may have been important to you: lover, boss, colleague, peer, friend, enemy, doctor, teacher, cleric. Once you have reviewed your past, you must attempt to come to grips with how it affects the present, how it controls your love life.

Men You Should Be Alert To

In order to loosen the hold your unconscious need has on you, you must become hypersensitive to anything about a man you like, a man who turns you on, a man you find yourself involved with, for anything that even remotely connects to your need. Is the relationship unbalanced? Does one person care more than the other? Can one person be portrayed as in pursuit? Is there rejection in even the subtlest forms? These are the men a woman with your need must watch out for. These are the men who signal the beginning of an unbalanced relationship. Men who

> Claim love at first sight
> Sweep you off your feet, call you constantly, shower you with gifts
> Wine and dine you, write you love letters, want you to meet the family right away
> Talk about marriage soon after meeting you
> Put you on a pedestal
> Carry a torch for an old love
> Are romantics—write poems to you, bring you one red rose, celebrate your one-week anniversary, fall all over you
> Do all this while you have little or no feeling for them

These are the pursuers. But beware. Your list doesn't stop here. You must be alert to *your* tendency to run after men who don't have the same feelings for you. Men who

> Are confirmed bachelors (especially those over forty years old)

Are too busy to see you
You don't know well but who seem terrific
Come to a party with another woman
Seem to meet with success after you stopped dating
them
Tell you they don't want to see you anymore, are elusive
Don't return your phone calls, ignore you
Give you their office phone number, not their home
number
Were old boyfriends of yours but are now dating some-
one else
Are seriously involved with someone else
Travel a lot, live out of town
Have been dropped by you in the past
Have unlisted telephone numbers

Confronted with these lists, you can see that behind each
type of man is the specter of the pursued or the pursuer.

Be alert. You must catch yourself *in the act* of starting to
respond. Every casual meeting in a bar, every date, every
man who seems attractive or is attracted to you must be
checked against this list. Once you become aware that a man
is even slightly associated with your need, this relationship
must end (even before it has begun). Only when your need
is under control can you really be free to choose a man with
the potential for a mature experience.

Linda

On her eleventh birthday Linda figured out that she had only 2,555 days left until she would be eighteen and could get away from home. Daily she would advance the countdown, marking a red X through each square on a small calendar in her desk drawer. At age thirty-two the old calendars are neatly piled in her drawer and are an irritating reminder that she never made it, she never got away.

Linda can't fathom why she is still at home. It's not that there is a shortage of eligible men. With her thick, honey-blond hair and a figure that was perfect since her teens, Linda was always meeting more men than she knew what to do with. In fact, people are always shocked to hear she's over thirty. Friends say she still looks like she did as a teenager. And then there is always Mark lurking in the background, a guy who would marry her if she really insisted on it. In fact, Mark and marriage have been on her mind lately, and the subject had just come up between them once more. "After five years I have the right to know where we stand," she told him directly. Mark's answer was disappointing, even confusing. What had he meant when he said, "I'll marry you if that's what you want"? This was hardly the enthusiastic proposal of the Prince Charming she had envisioned, the man who would sweep her off her feet and ride with her into

the sunset. Mark's lukewarm concession to marry just confirmed her feelings about him. He and their relationship
would never amount to anything.

Not that many things about Mark didn't appeal to her. He
was the only one with whom she could have sex. After all
their years together she felt sure he wouldn't think she was
easy. Yet she had to admit she wasn't altogether comfortable
with sex. There was always the small, nagging feeling that it
wasn't proper. And she still didn't like it when Mark pulled
the covers off so that he could see her naked body. No matter how many times it happened, she was aware of her discomfort when he looked at her directly. Once he had wanted
to make love standing in front of the mirror. It only happened once. She preferred the lights out, lovemaking at
night in the dark, in private. In the end she usually did enjoy
sex but was glad they didn't live together. She liked being
able to be on her own when it suited her.

What Linda admires about Mark is the way he bucks con-
vention, the fact that everything, including work, is second-
ary to his music. He really isn't motivated by money, and
that's rare, but at the same time she can't stand it when she
has to pick up the check for dinner so often. Not that she
doesn't have the money. After eight years of teaching, she
earns a good salary, most of which she can put in the bank
because she lives at home. It's just the idea that usually he
isn't able to pay and doesn't mind it that bothers her.

Mark is really quite a contrast to her father, who takes his
responsibilities as a provider so seriously. Ever since she can
remember, he has had two jobs. Even now that all four children work and contribute to expenses, he still keeps at it,
selling carpeting to businesses during the week and women's
shoes on the weekends. Maybe this is the reason her parents
disapprove of Mark. His attitudes about life are so foreign to
them. Much as she hates to admit it, she can understand
their feelings. But then Jonathan, the electronics engineer of
whom they do approve, is so predictable and so straight that

it's sickening. Short, dark, pudgy, he looks so awkward in his three-piece suit. He just doesn't fit her image of a desirable guy. If he only stopped calling, because he really has no chance.

"Whenever I think of marrying someone like Jonathan, I feel like I'm going to suffocate. I just can't bear the thought of a totally predictable, boring life," she tells her sister Lauren. "A life like our parents', a life that just happens to you, is the last thing I want." She confides her feelings to Lauren because she has always been able to depend on her to understand. They have always been each other's best friends. In fact they have never really had any other friends outside.

Although their two other sisters are younger, there is a real sense of togetherness between the four sisters. They don't seem to need any outside friends. Lauren, like Linda, is also afraid that marriage would tie her down. The idea of having to answer to anyone, being controlled, makes them both shudder.

Even Millie, their younger sister, who lives with her boy-friend, Jim, feels the same way. But Jim is so fly-by-night, they wouldn't be surprised if Millie returned home someday. Sometimes they hardly feel that she is gone at all. Every week, dirty laundry in hand, she arrives for Friday night dinner. They can see how upset Dad is about Millie. When it's time for her to go, he glues himself to the TV and barely nods good-bye. Everyone really misses her. It just isn't the same without her.

It was strange how she first moved out and then came back to announce her departure. While they miss Millie, both Linda and Lauren are happy to have more space at home. Lauren finally has her own room, and Linda loves the extra closet she's inherited. One less person to share clothes with. Raiding closets had gotten out of hand—even mother was in on it. For a time, Linda considered putting a lock on her door.

Despite Millie's move, all three are again traveling together for three weeks this summer, this time to Greece and Israel. Next year Jeanie, their seventeen-year-old sister, will be joining them for sure. Of all the reasons for not moving out, this was the most important. They simply couldn't pay for their own apartment and travel as well.

Still, Linda has mixed feelings about living at home. It's convenient, cheap, and no one really hassles her, but as Lauren recently pointed out, "You know, it's getting embarrassing to bring men home. I lied and told this new guy at work that Millie and I live together. He's picking me up at her place next week. I just hope I can pull it off without a problem."

Linda suddenly remembered the family's annual Mother's Day outing the following Sunday. They would all pile into the station wagon and go have lunch with Grandmother. They'd done it every year since they moved away from her. Even before the first hello Linda knew she would hear Grandmother ask, "What's new with the girls?" The table conversation would consist of a monologue from her about their unmarried state and their advancing age. Linda sometimes felt like strangling her grandmother. True, she was hardly a teenager, but she felt herself to be a long way from being ineligible. Sometimes she wondered if the only real reason she wanted to marry was to shut everyone up.

After these outings Linda could understand why Lauren had declared, "I want to marry an orphan." This family business was just too much.

DISCERNING THE PATTERN

Although she enjoys the freedom of being single, Linda knows she should be looking for a committed relationship. Although she's not sure she wants children ("Not that I can see myself without them"), she knows she doesn't want to spend the rest of her life alone. This halfhearted interest in settling down is her wish. As she approaches thirty-five, this wish is becoming increasingly important to fulfill. What she is not aware of is the influence of her need to remain secure within the family fold, to stay in the only emotional environment in which she feels safe and at ease.

Not aware of her need, Linda attaches herself to men who have no potential, men with whom she cannot develop the kind of commitment she wishes to have. Instead she responds to men who offer no lure, no pull strong enough to dislodge her from the family unit. On the contrary, these men have something that is a decided drawback. For Linda, these are men who are unpredictable, unreliable, poor providers. Men whose marginal life-styles suggest anything but a committed partner and secure future. Not the type of man whom a girl like Linda leaves home for.

Mark, an unemployed musician, becomes her choice. Her need drives her to a relationship that can never have the kind of stability that leads to living together, marriage, or any sense of seriousness that might require her to leave the nest.

Mark, living on unemployment, working only to eat, never on time, frequently high, offers a relationship that leads nowhere. For five years Linda hangs onto Mark. Her experience with him is filled with minor ups and downs that are part of their "unconventional" relationship, a relationship that is punctuated by periods where both of them see other people, only to return to each other. Disappointment mounts as time passes and the relationship never takes hold. Linda, compelled to test it, pushes Mark to clarify where they stand. Mark's lukewarm concession to marry "if that's what you want," is the halfhearted response she gets. Though neither shocked nor surprised by his answer—she has had no cause to expect anything else—her frustration with the situation mounts. What she had dreamed of was a declaration of

LINDA'S CYCLE

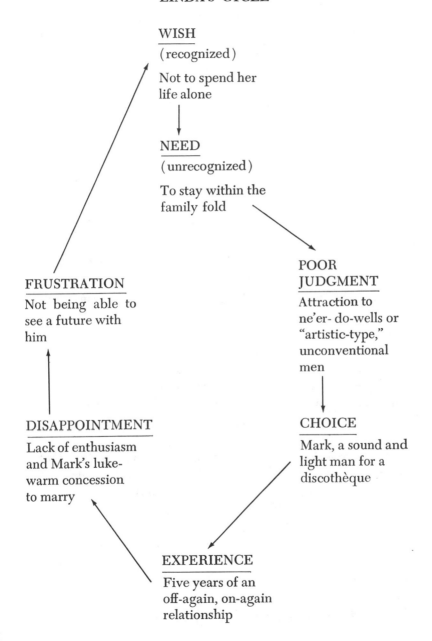

WISH
(recognized)

Not to spend her
life alone

NEED
(unrecognized)

To stay within the
family fold

FRUSTRATION
Not being able to
see a future with
him

**POOR
JUDGMENT**
Attraction to
ne'er- do-wells or
"artistic-type,"
unconventional
men

DISAPPOINTMENT
Lack of enthusiasm
and Mark's luke-
warm concession
to marry

CHOICE
Mark, a sound and
light man for a
discothèque

EXPERIENCE
Five years of an
off-again, on-again
relationship

undying love and passion, not a reluctant concession. Her feelings for Mark haven't changed, but she has to save face, so she breaks up with him, only to reestablish their loose routine later. As has happened in the past, pushed by her need, he gradually drifts back into her life. Linda is back to square one. Her wish for a stable relationship is as out of reach as ever. Once more she is at the mercy of her unconscious need. She will not involve herself in a relationship that would take her away from her family. That is the governing factor.

What is the difficulty? Why is Linda's need to remain tied to her family so powerful? Why does it keep her more attached to home than to a man? Why does she become involved with men who offer so little incentive to leave? For that matter, why is the prospect of involvement never alluring?

Linda spent her life in a large, tight-knit family. The members of her immediate family were intensely involved with one another. The closeness extended beyond her parents and sisters to the entire side of her father's family. However, they were never close to her mother's family. Everybody knew everybody else's business. Everyone was devoted to and worked hard for one another.

Mother worked hard raising four girls on a tight budget in tight quarters. For many years the six of them occupied five rooms of a two-family house, with Grandmother Dora and Uncle Jack taking the upper floor. Mother's devotion paled by comparison with Father's efforts. While his two jobs left him little family time, the girls and Mother knew he was doing it for them. He never missed time at either job, just as he never missed his morning phone call to his mother at his first coffee break. No matter what his other failings, no one could criticize his efforts at being a provider.

Life centered on the house. At any given moment someone could be found upstairs, downstairs, or in the tiny backyard. The girls always came home directly from school and rarely played in the street. Mother didn't permit roller skates or bicycles, since she was afraid of accidents. From time to time they wondered why Mother felt the neighborhood streets should be off limits for them. Maybe it had to do with the strangers she was always warning them about after a neighborhood girl was said to have been molested on the way to school, though years later it was found that she had exaggerated the story.

While Mother never had anything against friends, other kids didn't come to play at the house, either. Things were so cramped, there just wasn't room for anyone else. Also, Linda and her sisters were embarrassed for friends to see the way they lived. They regretted not having special friends, but the four girls were best friends anyway. As children, they never really noticed that no one besides family visited. It was something they thought little about. Only when they grew older did they become aware how different they were from their neighbors. They realized Grandmother and their parents also had no outside friends. In fact Mother and Father, as far as Linda could remember, simply had no outside interests, no hobbies, no clubs, nothing at all. Dad provided for them, Mother took care of them, and Grandma Dora had a comment to make about everything.

The way they lived, privacy was a real problem. Getting the bathroom for yourself was no easy task, and anyway the door didn't lock. Linda often ended up dressing in a closet or sometimes under her blankets. If Father wasn't around, Uncle Jack, who hardly ever worked, was always walking in on them with little warning. While they had little personal privacy in their home, outside it was something else. In fact the unwritten rule was that talking to anyone about private family matters was a kind of betrayal.

How do these early experiences relate to Linda's present way of thinking about and behaving with men? How does her past influence her present?

Linda is part of a family that can't and doesn't want to let go of its members. This way of relating is deeply ingrained in her. It carries over several generations. Father, first and foremost, is a son to Grandma Dora. His brothers and sisters also hover around Grandmother in the same way, and Uncle Jack even lives with her. In his own home, ironically, the same phenomenon occurs with Linda's father. Even though absent a lot of the time, he becomes the dominant figure around whom all relationships revolve. He is the family's hardworking provider, the center of their universe. Everyone's role is defined by their position in the family. Mother is wife and caretaker, never involved in the outside world with friends or community. The girls are first and foremost daughters. They are unwittingly encouraged to maintain childlike behaviors. Linda's very youthful appearance and her self-image as "still young" are qualities suggestive of a girl reluctant to assume the role of woman. This reluctance is there because these daughters never have permission to assert their independence and to be separate, to be on their own physically and emotionally. On the contrary, there is a kind of intense dependence and interdependence. Family comfort and familiarity create a cozy security that make all four sisters reluctant to leave. This desire to stay at home, within the fold, was always strengthened by the sense that the outside world was potentially hostile, dangerous, and suspect and that alone Linda would be sure to fail. To stay within the family is, therefore, a prudent thing to do. Relationships with men can only be maintained if they don't interfere with the ties to the family. Men are sought out who can be dated, even over a long period of time, but who never provide a pull strong enough to dislodge Linda.

All of the sisters, but particularly Linda—who is expected as the eldest to make the first marriage—are therefore unconsciously attracted to men who will not draw them away from the niche within which they so snugly fit. Mark qualifies. Because of his precarious, unstable life-style he will never really amount to a serious candidate for marriage. He doesn't have what it takes to sweep Linda off her feet and wrench her from her family's hold. Linda coerces him into a lukewarm proposal—more a concession, actually—just to convince herself that he's not suitable. In some way Mark's unconventional ways help reinforce Linda's youthful, childlike view of herself. A serious relationship might mean that she would have to relinquish the feeling.

Jonathan, the engineer, is the man in Linda's life who has the potential to be a provider, unlike Mark. He is considered by Linda to be a bore. This sense of an ordinary, predictable future with a man like Jonathan is something Linda wants no part of. Thus Jonathan, like Mark, never succeeds in becoming a strong enough attraction to wrench her away from her family. Ironically, both Mark's instability and Jonathan's stability offer Linda the same dead end. Men, no matter which way you slice it, are not good enough to leave what Linda already has.

Learning from the Present

Is Linda's lovestyle reminiscent of yours? Are you a woman who looks for the nonexistent Prince Charming? A woman who finds men who will never make her break away from her family?

Do you still live at home even though you could afford not to?

(When you are able to leave and don't—beware. It's emotional, not financial, dependence that's the problem.)

If you've moved out, do you still refer to your parents' place as home? Is your room as you left it?

(Don't let the fact of having your own apartment fool you. While you are physically separate, you're still very much part of the fold.)

Do you drop by at your parents' house for dinner, to do the laundry, to pick up the winter clothes you've stored there?

(Each act says loud and clear that you're still the child, that you can't do it on your own.)

Do you have other siblings who are also single and who also live at home?

(Remember, all members of the fold are subject to its pull.)

Do you wishfully envision a Prince Charming coming to sweep you off your feet?

(What you are saying is that you need some incredibly powerful magical pull to sweep you out the front door of the family abode. This unrealistic expectation allows you to stay at home, waiting.)

When you think about men in your life, has there always been some major drawback? Something significant about their values, character, life-style that disqualifies them from being part of your future?

(Disqualifying men as serious candidates is an important feature of your pattern: You never find someone worthy enough to leave home for.)

Are you never able to find a man who appeals to all sides of you?

(Your style draws you to men who are either too unconventional [and you're too stable to risk your future with one of them] or too conventional [you want something more than a boring future]. The net effect is that you have no reason to budge.)

Is your family involved in your social life? Would you bar-hop, date, or travel with your sister, for example?

(When you leave home, you take a little bit of it with you. Traveling with a close family member is a sure way to discourage invasion. You send a message to men: "We've got one another, and that's enough.")

Do you tell yourself that you could leave home at any time but that this way is just easier, cheaper, more convenient, more comfortable, gives you a chance to travel and spend more money on clothes, and so on?

(These are the excuses, the rationalizations, you develop to keep you from taking a chance.)

Do you like sex but never really feel it's the right thing to do? Are you prudish at heart?

(Sex symbolizes breaking away. It's no wonder you can't own up to liking it.)

Are you uncomfortable being naked in front of a man? Do you prefer making love in the dark, under the covers?

(Men are outsiders, not members of the family fold. You're a little leery, embarrassed, afraid of them.)

Do your family members have keys to your apartment?

(With your style, moving out can simply mean an extension of the family hold, this time to include your apartment.)

Do your parents always talk marriage? Is every date judged on his eligibility?

(This is a case of all talk and no action. Since their mere comments don't affect your behavior, your irritation at them helps you to ignore the issue.)

Does the idea of getting married fail to turn you on, to excite you?

(Your pattern leaves you feeling that you're supposed to get married, that you should have children, but without any urge to do so.)

Despite all the drawbacks, is your personal motto "Be it ever so humble, there's no place like home"?

(The sense you have is that while you're not living in paradise, it would be worse "out there.")

Is your heart never really in any of your relationships? Deep down do you know that you're just going through the motions?

(Dating men gets you off the hook. It makes you appear independent.)

Do you break off with a man for a while, often drifting back into the relationship without any major changes?

(This is pseudo-movement. It makes you feel as if something is happening, when in fact you're going nowhere.)

Do you think that children are important but that it's a big and permanent step?

(This is self-deception. Children are not the problem. Growing up is the frightening prospect for you.)

Have there been times when your dates picked you up someplace other than home?

(There are times with men that even you are embarrassed by your tight connection to home.)

Do you feel that you "have time," that you're not that old?

(Feeling young is part of your self-delusion. It permits you to feel and stay the child.)

Learning from the Past

Do you consider your family close, tightly knit, clannish?

(These words mean trouble for you. What may lie behind these labels is a sense of the emotional grasp your family has over its members.)

Did you grow up feeling it's "us" (the family) and "them" (the outside world)?

(As you were growing up, your family may have made the world at large seem like a dangerous place. No wonder you don't want to strike out on your own.)

Did you not have many friends in the neighborhood? Did your parents? Was no one invited home, for example?

(You've learned that you can't trust people, that others are intruders.)

Did your mother feel that you weren't safe on the streets? Did she discourage bicycle riding and skating and instead encourage sticking close to home?

(The message is twofold: It's a tough world, and you can't be safe on your own. Striking fear into you was a way of keeping you in control.)

Did you feel that you lacked privacy? Was everything shared—clothes, bathroom, bedroom?

(A lack of privacy between people may give the sense that there is no separateness tolerated. Feeling this, you can't commit yourself to a man, for it would mean asserting yourself as a separate human being.)

Did your family live close to your grandparents, aunts, uncles? Did you share a house?

(You learned as you grew up that no one ever gets away.)

Were you close to one side of the family and not to the other?

(The other family half was the competition and therefore to be ignored. Consolidating the ranks and eliminating the men who compete for you is your variation on this theme.)

Have you always thought of your father and mother as first and foremost a son and daughter to their parents, especially when they are in their presence?

(In your adult behavior you carry on this family tradition.)

Was your father devoted to his family role as provider (not necessarily successful)?

(His degree of devotion doesn't permit you to believe that anyone else's could come close. You don't trust that a man would have your father's capacity to take care of you.)

Do you have single aunts or uncles? When someone divorces, do they head back home?

(You learned that moving away doesn't happen—or only temporarily—that children are expected to remain satellites orbiting around parents.)

Even though you may be friendly, are you really a very private person?

(Sometimes the only escape from an intrusive family is to

go deeper into yourself. Having so precious little private territory, it's difficult to share it with a man.)

Has anyone in your family ever eloped, run off, married a foreigner while abroad?

(Such actions may indicate just how tight the grasp of your family is. The only way out is in the dead of night.)

UNLEARNING THE PATTERN

Your need is to remain within the family fold. This is where you feel most comfortable, relaxed, secure. This is your territory, your safe and comfortable place.

Within the family context you have meaning and importance. Your very being is defined by this affiliation. In fact the warning is that outside of this you may not really know who you are at all. Your family doesn't release you; you have neither permission nor support to go it alone. In some way the family message transmitted to you since your earliest days is that any outside relationship will not bring real satisfaction and, even more ominous, that you can't make it if and when you leave the protective nest. So you are drawn to men who unconsciously signal that they will not tamper with your situation, who will leave you where you are and will neither challenge you nor push you to break away. These are the men to whom you respond, men with whom you cannot envision a future. You involve yourself either with men who don't take life seriously and would not make acceptable mates or else the responsible types who conjure up visions of a life of unending dullness. Neither offers an incentive to leave home. Strikingly the men in your life don't demand that you make major changes. You keep dating them but nothing happens or develops. You remain tucked away within the family.

Breaking the hold of this need and dislodging yourself from your family clutches depends on keeping these ideas about your need active, vivid, and conscious. Unlearning this pattern must go hand in hand with the recognition that this is your self-defeating pattern.

Write down your need on an index card:

My need is to stay within the family fold.

Rewrite this need on a dozen more cards. Don't just scribble it across the paper, give yourself some time. Each time you complete a card, try reading it out loud. You may feel awkward at first, but listening to yourself can be another useful way of imprinting your need on your mind.

Once completed, each card can be used as an effective visual reminder. Put one in your wallet. When you're with a man but have to pay the check, think about how you have come to be involved with unreliable men, men who aren't candidates for serious commitments.

Keep a reminder of your need at work. Consider your situation: Despite your proven ability to support yourself, you are making no move toward real independence.

Place one in your savings book. When you deposit your paycheck, think about how you use fears about money and security to keep you close to home.

Write your need next to the number of your travel agent, the one you use for the trips where the last stop is always home. Put a reminder in your suitcase, the one you should be packing to leave home instead of on a guided tour.

Since being part of a tightly knit unit is central to your pattern, try to use these reminders to break out of this. Give one to each sibling. Let your sister put it on her closet door— the one where she has the clothes you like to borrow. When you ask your brother if he's doing anything Friday night, let him remind you how your need makes the family the social center of your life.

Put one on the door of your room. Let it remind you of how your need makes it difficult to keep yourself "off limits" to your family.

Your family will inevitably react to all this. Perhaps they will be angry, offended, or dismiss this as just another one of your quirks. Watch out. These reactions are part of the emotional pull your family exerts on you. Don't take down and don't hide these reminders; don't move back into the fold.

If you are in your own place, put a reminder on the inside of your front door. Every time you open it to head to your parents' home for dinner or to drop off dirty laundry, think first.

Put one on the outside too. When you're coming in, having just stopped by to say hi to your sister or to pick up something from your old room, think. You may be in your own place physically, but your need keeps you tied to home. Work on disrupting your pattern. Work on dislodging yourself.

Your Relationship Analysis

Recognition of your need to remain securely within the family fold may now come to bear on a review of your past relationships with men. Linda's analysis is provided here. In her review of relatives, friends, and lovers, the theme of her need emerges in a variety of ways. Evaluating her past experiences with men is a starting point for your own analysis.

Uncle Jack, a bachelor, who lives upstairs with grandmother
He was always around, filling in for father, who worked non-stop. Jack baby-sat, ran errands, and generally helped to cope with Linda and her sisters. Even when Linda was a teenager, he would tuck her into bed, talk to her, and rub his hands up and down her thighs and back. Linda remembered mixed feelings about this; it felt good, but she was uneasy. They are still very close. If she's upset, Linda goes upstairs to Uncle Jack's and Grandmother's rooms. Just being there makes her feel better.

Cary, Linda's boyfriend through two years of high school
Cary was a secret from her parents for several reasons, primarily because her parents thought she shouldn't go steady. Secondly Cary wasn't from the same religious background. Linda was also embarrassed to have him meet her family and see the way they lived. The only time they saw each other outside of school was when they could meet at another friend's house.

Stuart, Linda's boyfriend for two years following high school
He was nice, someone to date, but nothing really exciting. From the very outset it was a low-key relationship, even though he was the first man with whom she had sex. Their relationship was so casual that Lauren would come along on dates. It wasn't at all unusual for the three of them to go to a movie on a Friday night or spend a Saturday night at a favorite jazz spot. By the finish of the second year Lauren ended up dating and sleeping with him. Linda was glad that Stu and Lauren hit it off so well. Years later they got a kick out of comparing notes on him.

Kyle, a bartender
Linda always went to the same bar and grill during her lunch hour. Kyle worked there, and every lunch hour she'd flirt with him hoping he'd ask her out. He was strikingly handsome, and Linda had heard stories that he was a gigolo. More than once he had even teased her by saying she didn't have enough money to keep him. Despite the sense that Kyle was looking to be "kept," Linda started dating him. She told herself that she understood Kyle's intentions and that dating him was just for fun. The relationship ended when Kyle quit his job to travel in Europe with an older woman.

How is Linda's need to stay tied to her family reflected in her relationships? With Uncle Jack the key element is that he provides Linda from childhood to adulthood with everything she needs. He's everything from surrogate father to confidant to a pseudo-sexual partner. Note that Jack keeps himself tightly within the family, too. He's a bachelor, lives with his mother, and shares a house with Linda's family. The message is that there is no reason to look further, that everything can be gratified within the family.

Linda's need emerges differently once the men are outsiders. First there is Cary, a boyfriend who is kept on the periphery. Their relationship is limited, thus he poses no threat, stirs up no disloyalty. He can't—the relationship is a "secret." Cary never comes to her home. He's a 9 A.M. to 3 P.M. boyfriend.

Trust Linda's need to drive her to find a boy like Cary who tolerates being peripheral for two years as they "go together." Also note how Linda manages to find seemingly legitimate reasons for keeping Cary away. She's not permitted to go steady; he's a different religion; she's embarrassed by her home and its furnishings.

Stuart is a boyfriend who's barely a boyfriend. The relationship is long-term but casual, almost incidental, unimportant. He's nice but not exciting. Dates are a threesome. Stu gradually becomes Lauren's boyfriend. Even in their romantic life the two sisters are intimately tied together.

Kyle is exciting but unstable, yet Linda responds because she knows there is no future with him. And no future with a man assures her future in the family.

Utilizing Linda's model, you should be able to pursue your own exercise in relationship analysis. How would you analyze the men in your past? Where and when has your need revealed itself in your past?

Men You Should Be Alert To

Once you've analyzed your relationships, the next step is to see the way in which your need operates in your current adult involvements. This next phase involves putting yourself on notice. Beware of men

Whom you regard as having very different values
Who are easygoing guys who don't take life seriously
Who place no demands on you
Who don't excite you, don't turn you on

Who are unacceptable to your family
Who let you get away with murder
Whom you could have sex with but don't feel like
waking up with
Whom you don't really respect but like their company
Who are nonconformists
About whom you can say, "We're just friends"
To whom you drift back after a breakup
Who just seem to be around
Who don't mind that you live at home
Who would shock your family
Who, from the outset, have some major drawback

These feelings, thoughts, and ideas should serve as a
warning system. You'll have to give up these men who fit
your need. It's a challenge, but you can do it.

Vivian

How could she have wasted three years of her life staying married to this man? Vivian wondered.

"Your Honor, this man doesn't deserve to see his child. One weekend with his father and my grandson comes back to my daughter's house upset for a week. Every visit it's another woman. Furthermore, his father works half the night and leaves him with a stranger."

Vivian knew her mother was right, but the way she put everything so strongly made her cringe. From the corner of her eye she could see Ted frowning at his ex-mother-in-law. As much as she couldn't stand Ted, she had to admit he wasn't that bad. And Keith was his son, after all.

Vivian hated this hearing about custody interference. The only hope was that a court ruling would get Ted out of her hair and let her live her life without his constant badgering.

Everyone had warned her about Ted. "Any kid who drops out of school to join the Marines has to have problems," her mother had commented. Only her father seemed to accept him. Once Dad knew that Vivian was serious, he even talked about going into business together with Ted. That was her father's goal. "Working for yourself is the only answer, don't make my mistake. Get out on your own when you're young enough. Before the kids and the bills and the ulcers come along," he advised Ted.

Mother hated these conversations. She resented anything that got Vivian and Ted closer. Making her disapproval clear to everyone, including Ted, she always brought up Vivian's old boyfriends. According to her mother, everyone but Ted seemed to be a doctor or a lawyer. "And what's your latest professional interest," she would snidely ask Ted. "I hear bartending is a very promising career these days," she'd remark.

Her mother's nastiness didn't blunt her determination. Mother was wrong about him. It was true he wasn't the professional she always pushed for, but Mother just didn't see the qualities in Ted that Vivian saw. He would often talk to her about the plans he had. He had had several different jobs after the Marines, and that experience had helped him develop ideas about his future. Vivian wanted a good husband and she knew that with her support Ted would be one. If her mother would only relax, she'd have the good life her mother was pushing for. It just took time. You just don't wake up married to a success story, you work on it together. In fact, Vivian was happy her father talked to Ted the way he did. She really felt it was possible for them to do something together. She liked the idea of Ted's assistance being able to make it easier for her father. That would make her mother happy.

When Vivian set the wedding date, her mother exploded and threatened not to come. They battled for weeks. Only when Vivian countered by threatening to elope did her mother give in. "It'll be a small wedding. I'm not wasting my money on him."

Vivian started secretarial work after their June wedding. Ted tended bar and signed up for a training program as an X-ray technician. When Vivian missed her first period in July, the bottom fell out of their plans. School was out. In March

Keith was born. Ted couldn't give up his job until Vivian could get back to work the next fall.

Fall came, but by then it was clear that Vivian's salary by itself couldn't carry them along. They'd have to find another way. Vivian started to read the business page. At breakfast she'd read the advertisements aloud. Ted listened but sometimes he left the table, furious. It was her father who spotted the advertisement for an ice cream franchise nearby. He had been investigating it for a while and thought that together they could do well. Vivian pushed for it. There was three thousand dollars in wedding gifts. Mother had five thousand she'd saved over the years of unspent Christmas Club accounts. Between Vivian and her father they finally got Mother to use it as a down payment. "I'm doing this against my better judgment. It's money down the drain," she snapped as Ted signed the promissory note for all five thousand.

Six months after the store opened, the town started construction of a new highway. At year's end what had been the busy intersection where the ice cream store sat was only an alternate route. They were out of business in eighteen months.

Mother was livid. "Who doesn't investigate these things before they throw their money into it?" she ranted every morning on the phone to her daughter. Vivian couldn't stand to look at Ted. He was back to tending bar again. They argued. Every day he left a little earlier and came home later.

Vivian couldn't stand Ted touching her. They hadn't had much sex anyway since Keith was born. She couldn't trust him not to get her pregnant again. Anyway, the few times she was willing, he couldn't get an erection. Her mother was right. Ted was a waste of time.

Several months after the business failure, her father's ulcers got bad. Vivian went to help at home. A few days away from Ted and she knew she wasn't going back. "Don't worry," her mother had said, "you don't even have to go to the apartment. Give me the key. I'll pack up your things and bring them home. Look, be glad you can get out easily while you're young. There are still plenty of good fish in the sea. You'll go back to your music. Get a better job. Meet people more your caliber. I'll watch Keith. You'll see, things will get better."

The judge's gavel startled Vivian out of her daydreams. She looked at Ted and she was angry. She hated everything about him. Ted's mother walked over to her, touched her on the arm.

"Vivian," she said, "for Keith's sake, let him see his father."

"Get away from me," Vivian snapped. "I don't want anything to do with you or your son." She shot off out of the courtroom and raced to the restaurant where Jeff, her new beau, was waiting. When he didn't show up, Vivian worried. Jeff was a wild driver. It was something she had brought up many times. But it never seemed to help. Anyway he was probably okay. Being on time was just not his best quality.

In a few minutes Vivian found herself doing a slow burn. She tried to stop her mounting anger and to think about how much she cared for Jeff; he could be so much fun to be with. Even though he had no college degree, he was interested in learning, in new ideas. She knew he admired her. When he found her flute in her closet, he was impressed with her musical interest. It was Jeff who encouraged her to play and pushed her to audition for the local orchestra. When she made it, he was prouder than she. "If only he pushed himself the way he pushed me," she mused. "He's definitely got what it takes."

Vivian had liked Jeff the first time they met. He was a close neighbor, but they only met when he asked to use her

phone in a minor emergency. He was embarrassed to tell her
that his phone was turned off for overdue payments. He was
so cute, almost little-boy shy as he stood in the doorway.

Now sitting at the bar a whistle interrupted her thoughts.
Looking up, she saw Jeff right in front of her. He smiled and
waved sheepishly, pointing at his watch. "I've been standing
here waiting for you for five minutes," he teased. Disarmed,
Vivian hugged him and muttered, "Damn it," half playfully,
half angrily. "Surprised it's only five minutes and not my
usual half hour? See, your lectures really help. Another few
and I might even be early." He gave her a playful kiss behind the ear. "Just tell me we don't have to stop by your
parents' to pick up Keith. Let's just go home and screw."

Vivian didn't let him say another word. "Why, mother will
bust a gut if I don't show up. As it was she was annoyed that
I didn't go home directly." Vivian hesitated for a moment.
"Hell. Let's go home."

As they drove along, Vivian smiled to herself. "Jeff's driving is not that wild. I'm really too critical sometimes." For
Vivian Jeff was a relief from someone like Ted. He came
from a fine family: His father and brother were both doctors.
His mother was a real lady, soft-spoken and elegant. Dinner
at their house was a pleasure. Jeff enjoyed his family but was
a little self-conscious. He was the late bloomer, but finally
at twenty-eight he was coming into his own. He wasn't wild
about his job. However, with Exxon he had a future. It was
Vivian who suggested he apply for the company scholarship
program. With his brains, she had said, they would most
certainly subsidize his education.

In the car Vivian wondered out loud when they would
hear about his scholarship application. Jeff didn't say a
word. He rubbed his head as if it ached. Vivian immediately
sensed something was off. Whenever Jeff was uncomfortable,
he got this way. "What's wrong, honey?" Vivian asked, trying to control the urge to raise her voice and demand an
answer. Nothing. "Jeff," she snapped, "what's going on?"

"Damn it, Vivian. There's not going to be an answer because I never sent in the application. I just couldn't see myself staying a small fish in a huge corporation. You know I was never really happy there."

Vivian wanted to scream. "I can't believe it," she sobbed. She didn't know if she was angry or just plain miserable. This morning had brought back too many memories. She wanted something better. She needed time to think, to be by herself. She was tired of taking crap from every man in her life. "Jeff," she said sobbing, but this time without any ambivalence in her voice, "take me to my mother's."

DISCERNING THE PATTERN

Vivian's wish is to settle down and marry a man who can provide her with the good life. Not necessarily easy street, but someone who can give her the comfort of some luxury. This desire is something Vivian recognizes about herself.

What she is unaware of is her unconscious need. The need is to remake a man, to take an unsuccessful man and turn him into a success. Her need is to transform a losing proposition into a thriving venture.

Unable to recognize this need, Vivian's poor judgment goes into operation. Unwittingly she is drawn to men whom she unconsciously believes can be transformed, changed for the better, men she subliminally senses have untapped potential that she will succeed in releasing. The need overpowers her wish. She doesn't find a man who will fulfill the wish for a better life. Rather the strength of her unconscious need drives her to choose men who can be worked on and improved. Ted is chosen because his dropping out of high school, joining the Marines, his poor reputation, his numerous jobs, his "plans," were the signals to which Vivian responded. Jeff, the late bloomer, is the black sheep of a decent family. Unconsciously he fit her need as well. Both men are functioning below their capacities, a situation ideal for Vivian's need.

Her experience with Jeff is strikingly similar to what she had with Ted. Vivian pushes. The man tries but invariably fails to meet the goal. Vivian pushes harder. The inevitable disappointment follows. The man doesn't make it, and his promise goes unrealized. Despite her urging and her support, he doesn't change, and frustration mounts.

Why does she always get stuck with losers? Although initially rejected, her mother's criticism eventually rings true. Why does she waste her time with such men? These are not men with whom she is going to find the good life. This growing discontent makes Vivian realize she is a long way from satisfying her wish. Neither Ted nor Jeff will be a man who will provide her with the comfortable life she wishes to have. Her relationships are terminated because she cannot satisfy her wish.

Ungratified as well is her unconscious need. Vivian does not succeed in remaking her man; she does not transform him. Both wish and need go unsatisfied. Vivian finds herself angry and disgusted with men. Unaware of her unconscious need to remake a man and still seeking to have her wish for a good life come true, she will begin once again to carry out her unsuccessful lovestyle, the pattern that keeps her from a truly meaningful relationship.

In Vivian's house her mother ran the show. Father was a likable guy but a pushover. A man with an artistic flair, his youthful dream of pursuing a career in art never materialized. He married at twenty and wound up taking an occasional art course at night. He ended up assistant art director

VIVIAN'S CYCLE

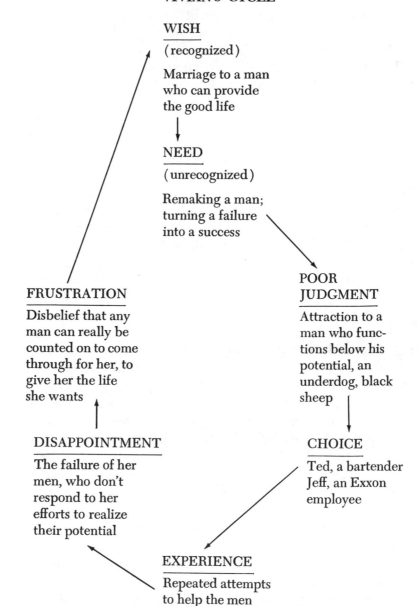

WISH

(recognized)

Marriage to a man
who can provide
the good life

NEED

(unrecognized)

Remaking a man;
turning a failure
into a success

POOR
JUDGMENT

Attraction to a
man who func-
tions below his
potential, an
underdog, black
sheep

FRUSTRATION

Disbelief that any
man can really be
counted on to come
through for her, to
give her the life
she wants

DISAPPOINTMENT

The failure of her
men, who don't
respond to her
efforts to realize
their potential

CHOICE

Ted, a bartender
Jeff, an Exxon
employee

EXPERIENCE

Repeated attempts
to help the men
succeed

of a trade magazine. "It drove Mother crazy that he never became the director. I thought it was ridiculous too, but this was typical of my dad—always taking a backseat."

Even when she was young, Vivian felt her father was a defeated man. "I like Dad," she recalled, "but there's something sad about him. It's as if somewhere along in life he had given up, given in. He never complained out loud, he just seemed to swallow everything. I guess at this point in his life he's resigned."

This defeat Vivian sensed about her father has taken its toll. She recalled what happened at thirteen. "Father acted strangely, locked himself in his room, barely ate, didn't wash or shave. After a week of this my sister Pam and I came home to find him gone. In the evening I overheard Mother on the phone. 'Harry's had a nervous breakdown. The doctor says shock treatments will snap him out of it.'"

Vivian remembered feeling terribly sorry for Father and being angry at Mother for putting him in a mental hospital. As far as she was concerned, this breakdown was her mother's doing—it was those fights. "Even through the closed doors you could hear my mother yelling, 'Why don't you do this? Why don't you try harder? Look at other men your age!' It's hard to believe, but even after all this he'd still defend her. Once Mother was nasty to a neighbor. Dad tried to smooth things over. 'My wife's very high-strung,' he said. 'She's got an artist's temperament. She's really a wonderful woman. Please accept my apologies.'"

"Wonderful woman" was never the term Vivian used to describe her mother. "She really didn't treat Dad right. He needed a push, but her way was not right for getting the best out of a man."

Pushing was not limited to her father. "Just because Mother didn't make it as a singer and ended up a music teacher, I was supposed to be the musician. The trouble was that according to my mother's scheme of things, I was also going to be the doctor's wife. I suppose that's why I never took music that seriously."

This constant interference made for a volatile relationship between mother and daughter. Sometimes they could be the best of friends, but at other moments they'd fight ruthlessly. Particularly as a teenager, Vivian could scream viciously at her mother's intrusiveness: "Do you want to drive me into a nervous breakdown like you did Daddy? I hate your guts. I hate being your daughter. The last thing I'd want to be on earth is anything like you."

As she matured, Vivian felt pulled in different directions. On the one hand she sensed she should do something with her life. On the other she had an almost embarrassingly out-of-fashion feeling that marrying and having the right husband would give her what she wanted.

Vivian grew up in a home where the central theme was Father's obvious lack of success and Mother's pushing and continual disappointment in him. What was less clear was Mother's unhappiness and frustration with herself. A talented, intelligent woman, she never lived up to her potential, never met her own expectations.

Vivian felt contradicting feelings toward her father. She did understand Mother's angry disappointment. But at the same time she was sympathetic toward her father, feeling that with a better wife he'd have turned out a better man. Vivian felt that by seeing how poorly her mother treated her father, she knew the right way to act toward him. She could be the kind of woman to bring out the best in him.

The irony of her parents' relationship is that her father's lack of success makes him the most prominent and focused-on member of the family. Her mother has created a situation in which the family's happiness, or lack of it, rides on the back of this one man's success. And this is what Vivian brings to her relationships. She finds a passive and pliable man like Ted or Jeff whom she can remake. Each relationship is not simply the repetition of her parents' style but an attempt to succeed where her mother has failed. Vivian tries to turn a man around, as if to prove that Father were a good person after all. With the right woman—Vivian, not Mother—a man can do it.

Vivian sets herself up for an impossible task. For what she fails to realize is that the passivity of a man like her father is deeply embedded in his character; it is part of his nature and cannot be altered by outside pressure. With Ted it was first school, then the drive for his own business. Later Jeff is pushed to be more responsible, drive carefully, be punctual, win a scholarship, look for job promotion. Having failed in her attempts to transform these passive men into aggressive hustlers, she is angry at herself but blames them. She is enraged, despite the fact that although they went along with her, they never promised anything. It was Vivian who read the want ads, thought up the money-making ventures, filled out the scholarship forms.

Vivian's anger has another dimension. As it becomes increasingly apparent that these men are no different than when she began, her mother's criticism begins to ring true. Vivian's frustration with her men inevitably forces her to agree with her mother, to eat humble pie. She grudgingly submits to her mother's "I told you so." Disgusted with losers, her mother becomes her only ally. The alliance creates a mother-and-daughter team bent on "getting the men" who have failed them. Unable to understand her rage at herself and her mother, she vents all her hostility on the men. Vivian and her mother's angry attempt to deny Ted visitation rights is an example of the teamwork.

Breaking up is a confirmation of her failure—failure on four counts. Vivian has no success in changing a man. She is not able to do a better job than her mother, that is, succeed with a man where Mother failed. She can't prove that her father is not a failure. And Mother was right after all. All men are disappointments. A terrible consequence of this failure is that Vivian ends up back under her mother's control. This situation leaves Vivian enraged. Unable to understand her rage, she vents all her disappointment and hostility on the man. Overflowing with anger, she wants to get back at the man, wants nothing to do with him or anyone connected with him. She wants to deny Ted custody, make him miserable. She can't even bear to be physically near Ted's mother. Likewise, Jeff is abandoned in a tearful, frustrated rage.

This is the nature of Vivian's pattern. She is a woman with dashed hopes. Under the spell of this cycle and with the irritation of her controlling mother in the background, she will no doubt after a time begin again to turn toward a man with the unconscious need to transform him.

Learning from the Present

Is Vivian's pattern anything like yours? Do you end up in a lopsided relationship with a passive man whom you are forever prodding? Do you start out expecting that he only needs the right support to fulfill his promise? Do things end up very different from your expectations? To help you see if this pattern in part resembles yours, review the following:

> Are the men you choose those with potential, promise, men who may not be doing well but who seem to have the capability to do better?
>
> (It is not what he is but what you think he will become that turns you on.)
>
> Do you find yourself criticizing, correcting, finding fault?
>
> (Beware—a woman with your need isn't just asking for a bit

of self-improvement. You want major remodeling from a man.)

When you criticize a man, does he generally take it from you? Does he even come back for more? Does he often agree with you?

(This reaction is seductive. It keeps you trying. The question is that although he seems to want it, can he take it, can he change?)

Are you full of suggestions on how a man can improve himself: dress better, go on to school, get a better job, go into business?

(Your intentions are always admirable, your suggestions beyond reproach. What this obscures is your total lack of acceptance of the man for what he is.)

When you think about your future success, do you think primarily in terms of the success of your man, for example, his salary, his title, his prestige?

(You doubt your own self-worth. The pathway to your feeling good about yourself is basking in reflected glory.)

Do you give men a number of chances to make it? Do you take them back or help them get a fresh start?

(If at first you don't succeed, you'll try, try again. Each time your frustration mounts.)

Are the men in your life often not as educated or as hardworking as you? Do you pull more weight when it comes to responsibility (for example, he moves into your apartment or you pay the bills)?

(These inequities let you feel you have the right to push a man, to remake him. You're allowed to take over and you do.)

Is yours the stick-and-carrot approach? ("I love you but you have to do better")?

(What you're really saying is that for you love is conditional: It depends on his success.)

Do you go for a guy whom your mother is critical of?

(If Mother thinks no, the juice starts to flow. You're all set to prove her wrong.)

Do you go with a man against your mother's wishes and often end up agreeing with her?

(This is the trap of your pattern. You inevitably end up humiliating yourself, having to admit you were wrong.)

When you break off with a man, do you get support from your mother? She'll pack, help you retrieve your things from his place, get your old room ready for you, pay the lawyer's fee?

(Your mother is central in your pattern. She does not want you to succeed where she has failed. She'll gladly make things easier to get you back under her control and prove she's right.)

Does your mother always know what's cooking in your relationship? Is she especially alert to bad news, always ready with "I told you so"?

(Because you're both in competition to see who's the better woman, your mother is ready to declare victory when she senses your defeat.)

Did your mother always want you to marry a professional, someone who was a ready-made success?

(Your mother would like to live through you vicariously. What she couldn't have, you will.)

Have your boyfriends ever admitted that they were

frightened of you, that you gave them headaches, stomachaches, pushed them to drink or to drugs or to staying out late? Were they afraid to come to your door?

(Your need drives you to drive men. You pick fragile men who want to be changed but can't take the pressure.)

Does breaking up leave you in the pits, enraged and depressed at the same time?

(These are the emotions that charge through you as you recognize your failure to remake a man and face having to go back to Mother.)

When you end a relationship, are you extremely angry at your man? Does your anger extend to anyone or anything connected with him?

(This suggests the extent of your rage at your own impotence. Anyone or anything related to your man is a reminder of your defeat.)

Do you find that you team up with your mother, gang up together on a guy?

(In your moment of defeat you identify and join with her.)

Do you feel you take a lot of "crap" from men?

(You fail to comprehend your share in a relationship, how you helped to engineer your failures. The only thing you see is how disappointing men can be.)

Learning from the Past

Could you describe your father as henpecked, whereas your mother wore the pants?

(This is the basic model for all your relationships. Men are targets for women to aim at.)

Are some of the words you might use to describe your father *schlemiel, nebbish, Milquetoast?*

(You learned from your father's model that men have no control over their lives, leaving the way for women to take over.)

Did you think your mother pushed too hard? Were you angry at her for it? Did you want your mother to get off your back?

(Even as a child you felt and struggled with your mother's control. It's a battle that carries on into your adult life.)

Were you surprised that despite the way your mother dumped on your father, he still liked, admired, or praised her?

(Admiration in spite of abuse—this is the kind of relationship you seek. A man who thinks you're better than he, grants permission to be remade.)

Did you think that given different circumstances your father could have done better?

(As a child it was too hard to see your father's contribution to his own problems, to confront his limitations. So you developed a fantasy that it's not his fault.)

Was your father someone who never made it, never lived up to his potential, never realized his talents?

(Your father was the first man of unrealized potential you tried to love.)

Do you want to be very different from your mother but sometimes are scared by how much you're like her?

(You identify with your mother and fight this at the same time. This is why with men you often behave as she does and hate yourself for it.)

Have you tried to rebel, to break away from your mother, only to find that she wins?

(The theme of your childhood is the theme of your adulthood. Only as a woman you try to use men to help you break her hold.)

Did you get confusing messages—on one hand to pursue your own talent or career and on the other to find a well-to-do man?

(One root of your pattern lies in your mother's personal frustration and anger with herself. This resulted in a set of mixed directives to you, her daughter.)

Do you think of your mother as a frustrated woman?

(You may not, but her domineering quality is born of her frustration. She couldn't control her own life, so she tries to work on others.)

Are you surprised that despite their fights and bickering your parents stayed together?

(Your parents were locked tightly together in their struggles. Your reluctance to give up on a man despite numerous attempts to do so suggests that you are reenacting the one and only model of a relationship you know.)

UNLEARNING THE PATTERN

Your need is to remake a man, to transform him—to take a man who is functioning below his potential and have him realize his promise. Your own sense of satisfaction and accomplishment is rooted in how far your man can go. You need someone who will initially admire you, strive for you, perhaps regard you as his mentor. A weak man who is passive, receptive, and looking for your encouragement is the key element in your pattern. Such men stimulate you into action on their behalf. You think up new business ventures, pursue want ads, investigate some form of college training, encourage ambition. Think about this need and all its ramifications. It has long been part of your unconscious agenda with men. Loosening its grip depends very much on keeping these thoughts about yourself conscious and uppermost in your mind. Unlearning these deeply ingrained drives to make your man a success has to be preceded by an honest acknowledgment that this is, in some way, your lovestyle.

Helpful techniques for keeping your need in mind depend on using devices that reinforce your memory, that interrupt your pattern. Write down your need on a sheet of paper:

My need is to remake a man.

Make a lot of copies. Each has to be placed in a strategic spot in your home where you will come into contact with this reinforcement device. Keep one next to your degree—the one you have and he does not. Put one on the dashboard of your car—remind yourself that you drive the better model (or he doesn't even own one). Keep one at work. Think about how you seem to keep a job and he can't, or won't. In each instance, make yourself consider how your need inevitably drives you to a man who's not on a par with you.

Put one with all the college catalogs, government brochures, power of positive thinking books you have amassed in your effort to help better your man. Think about how your need compels you to push him.

Put one wherever your guy stuffs his speeding tickets, unpaid bills, pawn shop stubs, uncompleted assignments. Think about how your need makes you hope a man will reform for you.

Keep a box of notes of apologies from your guy. Write your need boldly on top. Whenever you add one to the pile reflect on how your need makes you try again and again and again.

Put one with your divorce papers. Consider how your need leaves you bitter at having failed in your efforts to remake a man.

Your Relationship Analysis

The self-awareness that can begin to emerge as you move your need into focus can be further strengthened by relationship analysis. Insight about your need to remake a man should be applied to a review of past relationships. This technique involves examining all significant male relationships you have had. It may include friends, relatives, lovers, men you admire. Assess whether and how your need has come into play in these experiences. This evaluation needs time and can be difficult. Your need may not be easily discernible. Nonetheless careful analysis will bring out the repetitive theme of your need in your relationships. The analysis of Vivian's relationships is offered as a guide to your own exploration.

Steven, a classmate in fourth grade
He had a crush on Vivian. Vivian was teacher's pet, and he was just getting by. She teased him, pushed him around. Despite everything he always wanted to play with her. When she was dodgeball captain, she'd feel sorry for him and pick him. If he missed the ball, she would get angry and threaten that she'd never pick him again. Once she let him copy test answers but got angry when he copied too much. She reported Steven to the teacher. He was so embarrassed, he didn't come to school for the rest of the week.

Dennis, a tough kid in high school
When Vivian got to ninth grade, she went from a neighborhood school to a district high school with a diverse student body. She got into a very different crowd. Her first year was spent with a group of tough kids from "the other side of the tracks." Dennis

was one of the gang. Whereas Vivian was basically a good student, Dennis spent most of his time cutting classes. She liked knowing that she was better than any of his old girl friends, and Dennis rubbed it into them, too. She knew she was the only girl he didn't sleep with. She made it clear to him he was not going to get the things he got from other girls. Vivian knew he respected her for her stand. Her parents, however, were so upset that they actually thought of taking her out of school. After a summer during which she was shipped off to camp, Vivian lost interest in Dennis and his group and moved back into her own circle of friends.

Roger, a young soldier who was confined to a veteran's hospital

Vivian met him while she was serving as a volunteer during her senior year of high school. She liked him immediately and started to encourage him to think about planning his future. Every week she'd come with brochures, and catalogs, and ideas about professions he could enter despite his injury. Vivian grew very attached to him and began to talk more and more about him at home. When her mother sensed that Vivian was in love with Roger and wasn't put off by his disability, she spoke to him directly but without Vivian's knowledge. Roger's manner changed abruptly. Although Vivian raged at her mother's interference, things were clearly beyond repair. Roger asked her to stop coming to see him.

Lester, a dancer

Vivian met him when she was playing with the civic orchestra. Lester was quite talented on stage but had been making even greater headway as a budding manager of other dancers. He was not overtly homosexual but was delicate and sensitive looking. Vivian became close with him and knew that he was tormented and struggling with his sexual identity. Feeling he had a lot to offer, she sensed that if he could have sex with a woman, he would feel more sure of himself. Although it was a difficult decision, she worked it out that he would stay at her apartment for a time. The arrangement was supposed to be platonic, but Vivian crept into bed with him after the lights were out. She couldn't get him to respond to her, and Lester finally insisted, "Enough, Vivian!" Furious, she blurted out, "You fag!" Realizing her cruelty, she begged for forgiveness. Lester left without saying a word. He never spoke to her again.

Abdul, Vivian's brother-in-law

Abdul had been a student with her sister in college. He came from a well-to-do Egyptian family but wanted to immigrate to the United States. Pam married him before they graduated so that he wouldn't have difficulties about being allowed to remain in the country. Once they were married, Pam complained that he treated her as if they lived in the Mideast. This was one time when Vivian was in full agreement with her mother; she encouraged Pam "not to take that crap from him." Their mother confided to Vivian that she was sure Abdul married Pam just to get his papers. When Pam complained that Abdul's parents weren't helping him financially as they had expected, Vivian eventually repeated her mother's comment. Later Pam agreed she had made a mistake. After six months the marriage was annulled.

How does the need to remake a man emerge in Vivian's relationships? With Steven, her young classmate, the key element is Vivian's attempt to encourage him, to give him a chance, followed by her putting him down.

With Dennis the central issue is Vivian's control over someone inferior. She enjoys feeling superior and having control over whether or not they have sex.

In Roger's case his physical handicap stirs up her need to make a man realize a potential in spite of his limitations. Mother's disapproval is another hint that her need is at work.

Lester is another impossible mission. This time Vivian's focus is an attempt to change a man's sexual identity. Her rage at this failure, her annoyance at a man who doesn't meet the goals she sets, is an indication of her need in action. Her anger is a hint of what her reaction later in life will be to failure with men.

Abdul is another example of her family's pattern of helping a guy in need with the hope that the investment will yield a return. Disappointment in him is swiftly followed by punishment. He is thrown out of the family; the relationship is nullified. Since Abdul isn't Vivian's own man, she can easily identify with her mother's critical view. Again the women team up to get rid of the man.

Vivian's relationship analysis demonstrates how her need comes to the fore in a variety of ways. How about yours? Which men would you include? Spending time and thought on your own relationship analysis is important, since it is a tool for demonstrating to yourself the pervasiveness of your need. It gives you a way of seeing how your personal variation of this need resurfaces and reemerges throughout a lifetime, beginning in your early childhood.

Men You Should Be Alert To

Having achieved this understanding of your past, the next step is to understand how your need currently affects your adult relationships.

Remember that your need drives you into relationships where you try to remold a man into what you think he should be. You are then likely to be attracted to men who admire you, look up to you, and give you a feeling that you know better. The men who fit your need are those who submit to your judgment, plans, and decisions but are not likely to stick with them or follow through. If you are interested in a gratifying relationship with a man, then you must be alert to the men who match your old pattern. These relationships will lead to failure for you. Be alert to men who

> You sense have unrealized potential
> Have made many job changes
> Are waiting for "the right opportunity"
> Submit easily to your influence
> Seem inferior to you
> Are impressed with you and claim little for themselves
> Are drawn to your friends and your life-style and see you as a way of bettering themselves
> Are black sheep, dark horses, long shots

Are guys suffering tough breaks, victims of circumstance
Have shortcomings, defects, or handicaps you feel they
can overcome if they just try hard enough
Are waiting to be discovered or rescued
Won't qualify in your mother's eyes
You find yourself giving a second chance to
Promise to reform for you
You feel sorry for

Keep in mind that it is not a man who is the problem.
Rather, it's how he fits into your need that causes the difficulty.

Reflections and Reactions

At this point in your exploration of unsuccessful lovestyles a number of things may be happening.

You may have found a story that is strikingly similar to your own, so much so that you hardly feel as if you need to read on. But you do go on because you sense that each exploration can only add to your growing awareness of the power of the unacknowledged need in influencing your life.

On the other hand, a less dramatic event may have taken place. You may have found only a part of yourself in one of these six illustrations of other women's situations. And you will move on to see if the next six women and their patterns will help expand your understanding.

Perhaps nothing strikes you as familiar yet, but you are ready to continue this course of self-exploration and read on. All of these reactions are perfectly fine. However, there is a far greater likelihood that your response may not be so placid.

Exploration and recognition of your own pattern may be accompanied by a variety of feelings:

144

Anger ("Are you trying to tell me that's why I am not happy with the men in my life, that it's me and not them?")

Shame ("Could that be me? I would not like to think so.")

Guilt ("Could I really be like that? Is that really what I do to men?")

Fear ("If I am doing this, I'm in trouble. It scares me to think I have so little control over myself, over my life. What will my future relationships be like?")

Despair ("I'm caught. How can I ever change? What will become of me?")

These responses are an expected part of the difficult, often trying process of self-discovery. Your need is unconscious in large measure for the very reason that it is *unacceptable*, that acknowledging it means facing complex and difficult issues.

If you are flooded by feelings of anger, shame, guilt, or even despair, don't be hard on yourself. Try to accept your emotions as a normal part of the complicated process of change and growth. Understand that while you may feel otherwise, you are not alone.

No matter what your emotional reaction, the important consideration is that in spite of these feelings and their intensity you go on in the pursuit of self-awareness. As long as you are open and willing to go on, there is room for growth.

These emotional reactions do not exhaust the range of responses you may have, however. You may be feeling something else entirely at this juncture. It is possible that the sense you have is that there is nothing in this book so far that pertains to you nor probably anything in the pages that follow. Your reaction may be one of the following:

I am unique. I can't be categorized. I'm different, and no one else is anything like me. I won't find me in this book.

I think this idea of a pattern is ridiculous. An unrecognized *need*? You've got to be kidding. I don't believe in an "unconscious" anything.

Look, all this has nothing to do with me. There just aren't any decent men around. That's the only problem.

I am perfectly happy and adjusted to being alone. I don't need anyone to tell me otherwise.

This is a new era. Genuine careers are finally possible for more than a few women. Relationships aren't important the way they once were.

Who needs men anyway? I don't have to depend on anyone but myself for happiness. It's ridiculous for women to be so concerned about men.

If you feel compelled in any of these ways to reject the information and possible motivations posited here, be careful. Remember, it is not unusual when someone is faced with new ways of looking at herself that the process creates turmoil, even anxiety. For some a flat rejection of thoughts that challenge one's self-image is the only possible alternative. If you sense yourself mounting this kind of denial, perhaps that is what's happening. Rather than facing the turmoil, you may be struggling to keep things under control. Try to think about this possibility. Are you rejecting the ideas about relationships, needs, patterns, and lovestyles because it is too difficult to do otherwise?

Try to reevaluate your feelings. Keep in mind that the reasoning you develop to support your rejection may sound logical, thoughtful, modern, correct. Who could, or would want to, for example, argue with the idea that "you are unique"? However, if these thoughts act as deterrents to your self-exploration, to your willingness to examine your behavior, thoughts, and feelings, if they permit you to stop this important process, then they are ultimately only excuses and obstacles to change.

9

Vicki

Dear Mom and Dad,

The personnel office at the hospital must have my diploma in order to approve my permanent appointment as staff physical therapist. Please have it photocopied for me and send it right away, special delivery. It's very important. If they don't have it by the end of my first six months (a week from Thursday), it's grounds for automatic dismissal.

Things are fine here. Boulder is so different from Boston. I know you think that my staying here after my two-week vacation was a rash decision, but really it's so peaceful and beautiful here. If you saw this place, you'd understand. I really want some quiet. Things were just too frantic in "the big city."

Gotta go. Have to be at work in a few mins.

Will write again in a couple of days.

Love,

Vicki

While Victoria tried to convince her parents how right Colorado was for her, she actually had mixed feelings about her decision to stay. At least one thing was better for sure: Her parents were easier to take at a distance. For one thing she didn't have to hear her mother's daily health reports or her father's insistent commands to do this, do that. Or his constant put-downs of her mother. And maybe now, with Rod out of the picture, local life would also settle down again here in Colorado.

Rod was the very first guy Vicki had met in Boulder. Even though she had only skied once before in her life, she managed to join his intermediate ski class. He had the looks she loved: slim, dark, wiry. She didn't know the color of his eyes because he wore sunglasses all the time, but even through the glasses, when he looked at her, she was turned on.

She hoped he would notice her, because the competition was tough. There were some really great-looking women in her class. Frankly she was amazed when halfway through the course he just said, "Meet me at my cottage at eight. It's the one with the blue Porsche in front. We'll have dinner in town."

From that moment on, Vicki was so excited that she didn't remember a thing he taught. She just looked at him and kept thinking in disbelief, "How come me?"

When eight o'clock came, she knocked at his door. Surprisingly he was in a robe, not yet ready. "We'll eat at ten," he announced, offered her a drink, sat down next to her on the couch, and didn't make a move to finish dressing. "Let's fuck," he said, matter-of-factly. "That way we can relax through dinner."

Vicki was taken aback but terribly excited all the same. By the time she reached the bedroom, she knew he had nothing on under his robe. In a minute they were both lying naked on a huge flokati rug in front of the fireplace. It was wild. They didn't speak at all, but Rod made it clear what he wanted from her. Part of her wanted to protest when he pushed her facedown on the rug, another part of her was excited beyond belief.

Vicki remembered every minute of that first night and unfortunately everything that followed as well. They never made it to dinner. The next day on the slopes it was as if he didn't even know her. Two days later, when he came to her room unannounced at midnight, she was furious. He was higher than a kite. She was amazed by the first words out of his mouth: "Who was that son of a bitch you skied with today? You'd better keep your ass away from him." Vicki answered that he was being ridiculous. "Don't give me grief" was his response to Vicki's anger. "Let's screw." In spite of her anger, Vicki was turned on. When he grabbed her wrist, she didn't protest. This time they never even made it to the bedroom. Vicki didn't even feel the cold of the floor until much later, in the early morning hours, when she awoke and found herself alone.

Now, as she reread her letter, she couldn't believe she had tolerated this crazy relationship for half a year. They didn't go anywhere or do anything together. He hardly ever made a date to see her but just showed up, having not called for a week. Only sex seemed to keep things going. Vicki couldn't remember being as enraptured with anyone as she was with Rod. Christopher, back in Boston, had come close to this, physically, but Chris's temper had been impossible. More than once he had knocked her down or pushed her around. Once he had slammed her into the corner of his dresser, and she was so angry and so ashamed of the large black-and-blue mark on her arm that she told no one and wore long-sleeved shirts for weeks. When her friend at work asked her about it, she could only explain that she had fallen off a stepladder at home. She thought she had sworn off guys like Chris and Rod. Yet somehow these dark, silent, athletic types always did her in.

She could hardly believe such good-looking men could be attracted to her, the least popular girl at East End High School. But then these relationships never amounted to anything. Invariably she never had anything important in com-

mon with any of her men. She couldn't remember ever
having had a decent conversation with either Rod or Chris.
What conversation could you expect from a ski instructor or
a manager of a fast-food stand? Mostly they ended up arguing about their relationship. Actually there was never anything with either man that even resembled a relationship.
She couldn't remember a dinner out. Rod never arrived until
late. If Chris and she ate together, it was Chinese take-out
food or pizza delivered to her apartment. *What's wrong with
me?* Vicki wondered. *Why do I always end up with the
SOBs of this world? It's so crazy. All I want is a little peace,
to curl up in bed with a big box of chocolate-covered raisins
and a bunch of Agatha Christie novels, and I'd be happy.
Instead I'm bouncing from one bastard to another. Why
can't things just settle down?*

She found herself crying. *Why me? Why me? Why am I
even staying here? What's here for me? The job is decent,
but big deal, it's nothing so fantastic to make me hang
around if I'm miserable. But at least here in Boulder people
are friendlier than in Boston.* When she thought of friendli-
ness, her neighbor Arthur came immediately to mind. She
couldn't stand thinking about him and didn't understand
why, but the thought of Arthur made her cry even more
now. He was unbearably kind. Whenever he didn't see her
leave for work, he would call to see if she was okay. One
time, having noticed she had a cold coming on, he came
over, piled down with groceries, and fixed her some hot soup
while she took a bath. Too bad. Despite everything he did
for her, Arthur didn't turn her on.

From the first day she met him when he had helped her
move in, she had known it. Vicki made it clear to him that she
wasn't interested. But nothing she said or did seemed to faze
him. He was always there. Arthur held no attraction for her,
and Vicki would ask herself why not. He was nice, had a
good job, was presentably good looking. But still there was
something unbearably clean-cut about him. The few times

they casually had sex, he was such a gentleman, so kind. It
depressed her. A wave of sadness came over her even now as
she thought about it. She hated this feeling. It was a terribly
lonely kind of sadness. Even as a very little girl on the
swings alone in her backyard she'd have this feeling. Left
out, alone, not belonging. A deep, tight lump throbbed in
her chest. She remembered her fantasy on the swing that she
wasn't her parents' child. A kidnap at birth had torn her
from her real parents, the ones who truly cared for her,
about her. Now, so many years later, it still made her sob.

Suddenly the phone startled her. Vicki let it ring a few
times while she grabbed a tissue and blew her nose. Before
she could finish her hello, the voice at the other end coolly
announced, "I'll be there in an hour," and hung up. It was
Rod. "Damn," she cursed as she slammed down the receiver.
Vicki didn't budge from the seat for a full ten minutes. But
then the sadness she was feeling started to lift.

Now she needed a cool shower. The water pouring over
her head made her feel better. She took the handshower and
ran it up and down her body. It felt good. Sadness was replaced by a sense of anticipation. So what if Rod was a
bastard. He was fantastic, wild. He could make her forget.

DISCERNING THE PATTERN

Vicki's *wish* is to be left alone, not to be hassled by any man,
not to have relationships, since they all turn out to be unbearable. What Vicki is unaware of is that her wish is influenced by an unconscious *need*. Her need is to be a victim, to
be abused, and at the mercy of a man. To be involved with
an uncaring man to whom she can't say no. A man who
mistreats her at will. A man she is afraid of, a man who takes
over, who's the master of her emotional life.

Not aware of this and thinking only of her wish, Vicki
believes that if she tries hard enough, she'll find a haven

from involvement, a peaceful niche where she can remove herself from men and not be bothered. She stays in Colorado, yet despite all her resolve, she cannot resist being attracted to men who are cool, aloof, physical—men whose interest is clearly limited to rough sex. She is drawn to men with whom she has little in common, men who are unpredictable, undependable, even volatile.

Vicki's need draws her to these men. Her need to be a victim overpowers her wish to find peace. With this need in ascendancy, judgment is impaired, and her choice of men leaves her with Rod in Boulder and Chris in Boston. They become the men in her life because with them she can carry on a relationship of abused and abuser, victim and victimizer. She becomes his emotional doormat. She has no say, no rights; she is available on demand.

Vicki's experience with Rod is agonizing: pain and humiliation punctuated by moments of sexual excitement. Her disappointment is that her involvement with him never really resembles a relationship at all. Instead it is a string of unpredictable encounters. Her frustration mounts as Rod confirms her view that men are bastards and a source of trouble rather than a source of satisfaction. She feels further than ever from her conscious wish for a peaceful relationship. Vicki becomes increasingly convinced that she has to swear off men, give up on them if she wants to have a life free of turmoil. She resolves that she's through with them. The problem is that Vicki's need to be at the mercy of a man is still the force that drives her into any relationship. So her resolve is pitched into uncertainty by Rod's next phone call. Her need will no doubt bring Rod or someone like him into her life once more.

Why does Vicki's need to be abused dominate her relationships with men? Why does she get into situations where

VICKI'S CYCLE

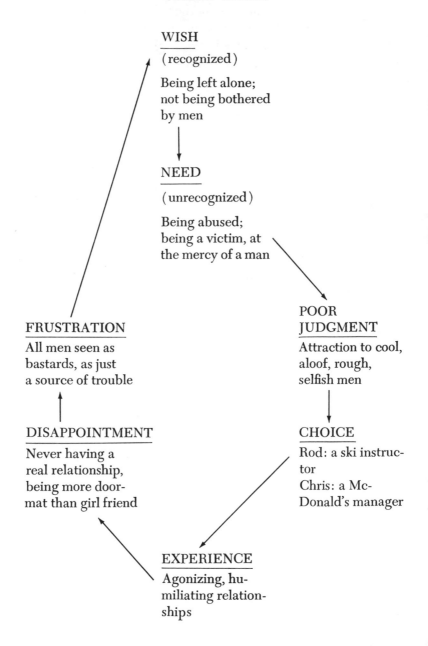

WISH

(recognized)

Being left alone;
not being bothered
by men

NEED

(unrecognized)

Being abused;
being a victim, at
the mercy of a man

POOR
JUDGMENT

Attraction to cool,
aloof, rough,
selfish men

FRUSTRATION

All men seen as
bastards, as just
a source of trouble

DISAPPOINTMENT

Never having a
real relationship,
being more door-
mat than girl friend

CHOICE

Rod: a ski instruc-
tor
Chris: a Mc-
Donald's manager

EXPERIENCE

Agonizing, hu-
miliating relation-
ships

she becomes the victim? Where did this particularly self-destructive need come from?

Throughout her childhood Vicki couldn't remember a day when her mother wasn't in bed for one reason or another, when the room was dark and the shades closed. She had had migraines. Bouts of arthritis would come on rainy, cloudy days. And then, every month, for reasons Vicki couldn't quite understand, her mother would lock herself into the bedroom, curl up, and emit painful groans from time to time. Only years later, when her mother had a hysterectomy, did she hear about the tipped uterus and difficulty in conceiving.

Vicki's first brother was born when she was three. Despite her mother's reputed anatomical difficulties, over the next three years two more brothers arrived on the scene. Often Vicki wondered how the family managed. Dad, after a stint at everything from salesman to Laundromat operator, finally got a civil service job when Vicki was ten. But still, finances were always tight. And then there was her mother, who hardly did anything in the house. By the time Vicki was eight, she was making beds and fixing dinners. Dad did the shopping. The laundry awaited his days off.

Vicki's father had little time for her. He only seemed to talk when things went awry, and then it was more shouting than talking. If Vicki couldn't keep her brothers quiet during dinner, Father would explode. When he'd bang his fist on the table, Vicki felt a tight lump in her throat and a knot in her stomach. At those moments Vicki felt miserable and terribly alone. All she craved was a little attention, someone to talk to her rather than order her around, shout at her, and then ignore her.

Vicki always remembered being lonely; she felt her loneliness grow more acute during her adolescence. She felt isolated, abandoned. She never had a really close girl friend. Only at her aunt's Thanksgiving dinners did Vicki have any contact with her relatives. The rest of the year, except for one cousin who lived nearby, they ignored her. No one called her or invited her anywhere. She spent most of her time by herself. She'd close the door to her room, lie in bed, and do little but daydream.

At twelve, when her breasts began to develop, Vicki became terribly self-conscious. While her undershirts embarrassed her, she couldn't bring herself to say the word *bra* to her mother, let alone ask her to buy one. Baggy shirts, hunched shoulders, and books held against her chest were Vicki's attempts to hide her changing body. Menstruation was another source of embarrassment. It was the school nurse, not her mother, who gave Vicki her first lessons about being "unwell."

Looking back at Vicki's past, it becomes increasingly clear that she grew up in a home in the shadow of an unhappy, frustrated relationship between her parents. Vicki lived with miserable and unsatisfied parents who dragged the family along, managing to get by without giving the time or making the effort to understand or even acknowledge their children's needs or to give their children the love and attention they desperately craved. Vicki's feelings and thoughts were of little interest to her parents. She was unimportant to them. Thus, she felt herself an outsider, neglected, abandoned, left out. Useful and used (often to take over her mother's responsibilities), rather than loved.

How does this relate to Vicki's adult relationships? How does this influence her experiences with men? How is her need related to this early experience?

The lack of attention and caring Vicki endured left her with deep-seated feelings of worthlessness. These feelings were reinforced by the model of a mother who seemed to have little self-respect and a father whose harsh and tyrannical behavior conveyed the message that women were not entitled to feel valued or valuable. The result is that Vicki's self-esteem is nil. Though on the outside she appears otherwise, her childhood left Vicki a deeply sad and bitter person. The emotional isolation and abandonment of her childhood is a pain that lies locked inside her. On her own now, an adult well past the years when these feelings began, the wounds of her childhood have not left her. She is emotionally scarred. Though Vicki's parents did not physically abuse her, she did suffer a kind of emotional abuse. Without being able to identify it as such, she not only saw her parents victimize each other but was a victim herself. Where does this leave her?

Being a victim is the sort of treatment Vicki continues to anticipate and expect from any close relationship. She tolerates poor treatment and even cruelty because she knows no other alternative for a relationship. Even unfounded jealous rages from Rod are acceptable to her. In some way Vicki takes jealousy as a sign that she is important to a man. Even if Rod is irrational and hostile, in some fashion she means something to him.

Vicki expects and accepts abuse from a man because she has been made to feel so worthless and insignificant. Abuse is what Vicki senses she deserves. After all, if her parents thought so little of her, why should anyone else feel any different?

Never taken seriously as a separate, real person by her family, a person with feelings to be respected, she cannot see herself that way in her dealings with men. Vicki doesn't feel entitled to think of herself as a sovereign individual with rights, needs, demands, so she cannot ask it from men.

There is another important reason Vicki stays involved with an abusive man such as Rod. These men enable Vicki to keep her painful emotions, her true sadness, bitterness, and anger locked away under control. A relationship with an abusive man keeps all of Vicki's thoughts and feelings focused on the abuse, the cruel treatment, the aggressive and explosive sex. Abuse becomes a strange form of protection. A tumultuous, unpredictable relationship gives her no time to reflect, recall, feel the ghosts of the past. Vicki's real self, her real hurt, her real anger are suppressed. The bastards of her life keep Vicki from having to acknowledge her unhappiness. As long as they are around, Vicki must focus on their aggression rather than on her own emotions. By contrast Arthur, her thoughtful neighbor, brings out her innermost feelings of sadness.

Vicki's rejection of Arthur, the one man who is kind and caring in her life, is directly tied to this. Arthur's kindness evokes Vicki's true sadness and longing. His tenderness makes her realize the love and kindness she missed. His reaching out to her is the painful reminder that no one, neither her mother nor her father, ever reached out to her before. The fact that Arthur cares about her as a person, just because she is herself, opens up her emotional floodgate. It is painful to the point where it is intolerable. It is also frightening, since the floodgate may release the angry bitterness Vicki harbors within her. Abuse and cruelty by a man like Rod are relief by comparison.

Learning from the Present

Is Vicki in some way like you? Do you run into one bastard after another? Are the men in your life cruel, mean, uncaring? Do you think your need might be that of the victim? Do you need to be part of an abusive relationship? Do you wish for a little calm and quiet in your life yet find men who make your life anything but that?

Reflect on your own pattern. Ask yourself the following questions to help identify whether your lovestyle is that of the victim. The way you respond to these questions will help you identify if your pattern is similar to Vicki's.

Do you know from the first moment you meet a guy that "It won't be good; he means trouble," but you go ahead anyway?

(Although you do see the signals, your need makes you disregard them.)

Is sex for you a form of aggression, rough, violent? You don't look for rough sex, it's just what ends up happening in bed.

(For a woman with your need, sex and mistreatment go hand in hand; you don't expect better from men.)

Do you have fights that end (sometimes against your will) in sex?

(Even if the sex is great, if you have no say, your feelings are ignored, or you are simply overpowered or outmaneuvered, you are being abused.)

Do you pick men who are below you educationally, intellectually, financially, or socially?

(A woman with your need doesn't feel worthy, and this is reflected in your choice of men.)

Are you attracted to exploiters?

(Being used by men is another form of abuse.)

Is a relationship always on "his terms"?

(Know that "his terms" may really mean that there is no respect for your feelings.)

Is your man unpredictable, volatile? Does he get angry easily, at little things?

(When you find yourself unsure as to whether he'll be adoring or assaulting, calm or agitated, apologetic or accusatory, you are being victimized by a man's mood.)

Are the men you date extremely jealous?

(With your need the kind of attention you get is negative.
While he doesn't declare his love for you, he berates you if
he suspects that another man wants you.)

Did a man ever hit you or come close to it? Do you feel
a potential for violence?

(There is no clearer sign of your need at work than if you
remain with a man who has even come close to hurting you.
Physical and emotional mistreatment are inseparable.)

Do you tell yourself that enough is enough and swear
off a man—till the next time he calls?

(You have a tremendous capacity to forget just how bad
things were.)

Are you surprised at yourself for getting involved with
"that kind of guy"?

(This disbelief is what allows for your involvement. Never
really feeling it's happening to you, you don't try to stop it,
you don't take responsibility.)

Do you get turned off by "nice" guys?

(You reject these men because deep down you don't feel de-
serving of them. In a way you're rejecting yourself as unfit.)

Is being with a guy who's sweet depressing to you?
Does it sometimes even make you cry when a guy is too
nice?

(The calm and quiet that a kind man brings into your life
allow the deep-seated hurts you carry to emerge. The pain
is too much.)

Do you know your man's Achilles' heel and go for it,

criticize his bad habits, bring up his failures, mock his sexual performance?

(Angry but afraid to directly express it, you take sideswipes at your man.)

Do you have difficulty asking for things, making your needs known, especially with men?

(With men you feel as if you have no rights, that you're not entitled to have them. This feeds into your role as victim.)

Are your macho types very touchy about their masculinity? Do their egos need constant inflation?

(You invariably choose men who probably could never be content or secure no matter what your efforts. This keeps you busy. Working on keeping your man happy gives you little time to be in touch with your own pain.)

Learning from the Past

Were your parents very absorbed with each other?

(In a home where a child goes unnoticed, she begins to believe there is nothing about her worth paying attention to.)

Was your mother selfish, preoccupied, or sickly?

(A child cut off emotionally by a mother feels isolated and unwanted. Relating to an abusive man may be your attempt to forget this.)

Did your mother never take on the job of being a mother? Did everyone else take on her responsibilities, especially you?

(Mother's refusal often means that an angry father saddles his daughter with early responsibilities. In this way a girl learns to expect being used by men.)

Did you feel you were the family scapegoat? Do you think of your family as being unfair to you?

(If you were positioned low on the pecking order as a child, you assume it is your correct position as an adult.)

Did you feel rejected and ignored? Did you feel useless, worthless?

(It is this essential feeling of worthlessness that lies at the root of your adult relationships.)

Could your father be demanding and get excessively angry? Could he be very frightening, autocratic?

(With a father like this there is no permission to be angry back. It is no wonder you can't be direct about your feelings with men.)

Do you remember yourself as being a sad and unhappy child? As a child you were lonely, had few friends?

(Your tumultuous relationships serve to divert you from these painful memories, the way biting your tongue can help you to ignore a larger pain.)

Was your adolescence the worst part of your life?

(Adolescence is not easy for anyone. For an isolated, lonely, insecure child it can be hell.)

Were you deeply embarrassed by your physical development, your breasts, menstruation? Did you hate the idea of becoming a woman?

(You learned that women were not valued, thus the signs of your own womanhood held out no hope of joy or relief, only fear and shame.)

Did your father act harshly or critically toward your mother?

(This is another aspect of your negative self-image. You were made to feel that there is always an open season on women.)

Did your parents pick on each other or on the children?

(Aggression was your family style.)

Do you sense your parents lack respect for each other, that they are frustrated, unhappy people?

(Where there is no respect between parents, there may be little self-respect in children.)

Were you treated harshly, picked on, criticized, made to feel like dirt, unimportant?

(Constant criticism may leave a child feeling she can do no right. That such failures deserve no love is the feeling you bring to your adult relationship.)

Do you feel bitter about your parents and their relationship to you?

(An inner core of bitterness lingers into adulthood. It surfaces in the cynical distrust and disgust you can sometimes feel toward men.)

Did your father beat you? Was he ever violent?

(In the history of abused women there is often a father who was himself an abuser of women.)

If you find yourself nodding in agreement with some of these questions, it is likely that your lovestyle draws you into abusive relationships. As an adult you continue to carry on the victimization of your childhood. Is this you? Do you unwittingly respond to men who fit your need? If this may be you and you are interested in escaping this vicious cycle, follow the next steps.

UNLEARNING THE PATTERN

Begin by unlearning your automatic reaction to abusers. Understand, memorize, convince yourself that your need to be a victim is the central theme of your relationship to a man, that you respond to physical aggression and intimidation, that being pushed around is the way you expect to be handled, and that you tolerate it. Acknowledge that raw sex is the hallmark of your lovemaking. Arguments and fights are not infrequent, often ending with sex. Your man comes and goes as he pleases, shows up when and where he wants. You are at his disposal. Men you are attracted to are invariably the jealous type. Somehow you stay with these guys, swearing off one or the other but never sticking to your resolution.

Being a victim in your relationship to men is your unconscious need. Overcoming it, breaking out, involves keeping the idea of this need and all that it means conscious. Bear in mind that it's not easy to keep your need out front. Your subconscious will try to suppress this unpleasant thought about yourself.

One way of preventing this from happening is continually to remind yourself of this unpleasant truth about yourself.

A useful exercise is to work with a friend. Attempt, with her, to discover the particular ways in which your need to be a victim has run through your love affairs. Try to find the pattern of your lovestyle. It is helpful to draw your own pattern analysis diagram, filling in the characteristics of men who have attracted you, your choice of men, your experience with them, and the disappointment and frustration you felt.

Keep this pattern analysis. Date it. Periodically review it, particularly if you begin a new relationship. Review this pattern again with your friend. Who is the new man in your life? Does he fulfill your wish or your need? Again use your friend, a more objective outsider, to help you analyze your relationship and find your pattern.

Review your diagram on a regular basis. Perhaps once a week is sufficient or perhaps every other day is best for you. The most important thing is to make a regular commitment to this kind of self-confrontation.

Try writing your need out on index cards:

My need is to be abused, at the mercy of a man.

Disrupt your pattern. Replace action with thought. Place a reminder on your phone. When he calls up at all hours to see if you're available, consider why you can't put limits on the kind of behavior you'll tolerate from a man.

Put one in your medicine cabinet. If you *ever* find yourself in need of first aid because of a man, you must confront the role a tolerance for physical abuse plays in your affairs.

Keep one inside your refrigerator. When you put in the soup your friend made or the groceries he brought inside, think about how kindness from men affects you.

Keep one on the front-door chain lock, the one you had installed so he couldn't get into your apartment, the one you may well unlatch to let him in. Understand your ambivalence, how you get embroiled in relationships with men you really want nothing to do with.

Put one with the travel brochures and the apartment and classified ads you keep. With your need you sometimes sense that running away is the only way out. Ask yourself how your need gets you into such desperate situations.

The more you can create opportunities for this self-confrontation, the greater will be the chances for controlling your emotional destiny.

If you begin to sense that you may have a need to be abused, begin another relationship analysis, this time of all the important men in your past. See if these past relationships were marked by cruelty and abuse.

Your Relationship Analysis

Review all the men in your life—relatives, friends, lovers. How has your need played a part in these experiences? Is it the common denominator, the recurrent theme, of your relations with men? List all the significant men in your life and write beside their names anything that might have to do with your need to be abused. Vicki's relationship analysis follows. Closely examine how her need has given her an attraction to a special group of men all through her life.

Cousin Robert, the only cousin with whom she had any real contact
When they were both nine, they were quite close, and Vicki confided in him. He proceeded to tell her brothers everything. They teased her relentlessly about her secrets. She never confronted Robert with what he had done to her. Although she stopped confiding in him, she still stayed friendly.

Uncle Jay, her father's youngest brother and only five years older than Vicki
He was the only reason she looked forward to the occasional family gatherings. He paid attention to her; she'd do anything for him. When she was fifteen, he began, whenever they were alone, to fondle her. She couldn't believe he was interested. She'd never even had a single boy look at her, let alone touch her. She knew it was wrong and she tried to resist at first. Jay threatened her. For several years he insisted that she let him carry on this way. Vicki always submitted. She never told anyone about it.

Bob, the older brother of Janice, a classmate of Vicki's
Vicki, who had never had a boyfriend throughout high school, dreamed about Bob. She tried to keep on Janice's good side so that she could hang around him. Janice took advantage of Vicki, from borrowing her best sweater (returning it torn) to getting Vicki to do her math homework for her. Bob used her as an errand girl too. One Friday when she came to call on them, the house was noisy and full of people. Janice's mother came to the door and told Vicki that her children were busy. Vicki cried all

night, realizing that after everything she hadn't even been invited
to their big party.

Paul, Vicki's drama teacher in her senior year
After graduation Paul asked Vicki to be a mother's helper during
his family's vacation on the Cape. She was very happy, since,
though she never told him directly, she admired him tremen-
dously. By the second week of summer she was doing more than
admiring him, she was in love. One rainy afternoon when his wife
had taken the kids to the movies, Paul, who was sitting next to
her, reading, began to kiss her on the neck. Vicki lost her vir-
ginity that afternoon. Throughout the summer they carried on an
affair. As Labor Day approached, Vicki started asking Paul how
they would meet in the winter. He always had the same answer,
"We'll see." By mid-September she hadn't heard from him. She
made a trip up to the high school. When she came into his class-
room, he was with a very pretty student who was getting after-
hours help. Without saying anything to him, she knew where
things stood.

Vicki's attachments have a theme that follows her into her
adult relationships with men. Her loneliness, isolation, and
lack of self-esteem drive her into relationships in which she
permits herself to be used. She allows herself to be victimized by men. She trades off a little attention for a lot of
abuse. Her eagerness for affection impairs her judgment. She
places her trust in someone like Cousin Robert, who doesn't
deserve it, and even once she's humiliated, she doesn't reject
him. She hangs on to whatever little he gives her. She's confused about her Uncle Jay and goes along with his actions.
She doesn't reject him because she never considers that she
has the right. And anyway, something is better than nothing.
It's obvious how she is used by Bob and Janice. The hurt of
such humiliation is swallowed. She never fights back, never
unleashes any anger she may be feeling.

Though Vicki may not sense it, Paul is the predecessor of
the Chrises and Rods of her life. The only thing she gets
from this man is sex, and it's on his terms. Thus what echoes
through Vicki's relations is abuse, being pushed around, ex-

ploitation, humiliation. Vicki feels she doesn't count, so that's the way she permits other people to treat her.

Now that you have explored Vicki's relations, try to do your own relationship analysis. Recall all the men who were significant: relatives, friends, lovers, colleagues, clergymen, doctors. Can you understand how your need to be abused drove you into your relationships?

This analysis will help you understand why your present relationships inevitably are dead ends and why the peace you seek remains elusive. Recognizing how this happened in your past must be followed by an awareness of how your need operates in the present.

Men You Should Be Alert To

In order to change your current relationships with men, you must be on guard, alert to those characteristics in a man that fit into your need to be abused, that would mean the start of another unsuccessful pattern. It means putting yourself on alert.

Become hypersensitive to any attitudes, actions, or behaviors that even vaguely suggest you're in for abuse. Is a man an emotional volcano, ready to erupt? Is he looking to use you as a doormat? Do you find some magnetic attraction that inexorably draws you to a man who will think little of you as a person and act accordingly? This style of relating will remain the only thing you know unless you consciously interrupt this need to be abused that unwittingly propels you toward these men.

What are the signals? What should you watch out for? Men who

Are the jealous type
Get greatly annoyed at little things
Insist on everything being their own way

Dominate
Tell you how to dress (even on the first date)
Have a hot temper
Don't think or act as if you have any rights
Are "macho"
Put you down, both publicly and privately
Make you feel like you're worth two cents
Threaten you
Seem as if they could be violent
Drop in unannounced (mostly for quick sex)
Advocate master/slave relationships
Are below you socially or intellectually
Want to end fights with sex
Get you furiously angry
Continue to be attractive to you, even though they're cruel to you
Never ask you what you want or what you think
Physically push you around

As you run through the list, the theme emerges. Men with these characteristics harbor the potential to fulfill your need to be abused. These men will never be the bearers of the acceptance and security you desire. Quite the contrary, the very reason these men appeal to you is that subtly, subliminally, unwittingly they send you signals that they will satisfy your need to be a victim.

Don't permit the vicious cycle to take hold. Be continuously alert. Catch yourself in the act of responding to your need. Every man has to be carefully evaluated. Are you starting a true relationship with a man or are you simply beginning to reenact a pattern of abuse? Are you on the road to intimacy and love or are you simply perpetuating your unsuccessful lovestyle?

Once you can detect your need and interrupt it, once you can break the pattern of victimization, you can be open to gratifying relationships with men.

10

Gladys

By five o'clock Friday the federal court building was nearly empty. Unlike the others Gladys was in no great rush to leave. As long as she was home by seven to feed her pets, she could finish typing. It had been a hectic day. Judge Reuben Kaplan was in a foul mood. If she hadn't fended off most of the visitors and screened the phone calls, it would have meant disaster. She knew the Judge's moods like the back of her hand. She knew what was best for him better than anyone else, including Mrs. Kaplan, and she knew he appreciated this understanding. While the Judge wasn't one to go around patting people on the back, Gladys understood that she was indispensable. In fact yesterday, in the midst of the trial, with all the reporters hovering around, he'd found a moment to praise her in front of the Chief Justice. Not that she needed to hear it. After all, it would be fifteen years at the end of January with the same boss. It would be a great occasion to celebrate, but February 2 would be her fortieth birthday, and it put a damper on the idea of a party. Being forty and still alone was a somewhat unsettling feeling for Gladys. While she didn't really look forward to her birthday, she knew it wouldn't be the disaster everyone predicted. After all, as she put it, "Between traveling, church, my pets,

work, and Mother, I hardly have a free minute. Really, when
I think about it, I'm not missing anything, am I?"

There were occasional Sunday afternoons in the spring
that found Gladys less content and less sure of herself. Her
thoughts sometimes wandered back to Jeremy. She had been
twenty then; he had been twenty-two and had just been
drafted. They became engaged before he left, even though it
had meant rushing their plans. Though they had known
each other since high school, they had both had it in mind
not to marry until they finished college. As much as she had
been in love with Jeremy, she had been troubled by not
being able to figure out how her parents really felt about
him. When asked, Mother would just comment, "As long as
you're sure, it's okay with me." Her father would end any
discussion about her fiancé with the same comment: "Princess, is he really good enough for you?"

Within a week after leaving home Jeremy's first letters
began to arrive. All he could write about was how much
he missed her. But after a few months Jeremy's letters didn't
come so often. He explained that he was busy and the mail
was slow, but Gladys couldn't help being annoyed, especially since he didn't really seem to pay much attention to
her feelings. Whereas she used to wait excitedly for the
postman to deliver his letters, she now felt disappointed by
the time she finished reading them. Jeremy wasn't the same.

When Jeremy returned home on leave a year later, she
really started to doubt whether he was the one for her. He
had changed. He was definitely not the same; he was much
more aggressive and so physical. He almost forced himself
on her sexually. Gladys couldn't believe he wanted to go
"all the way." His behavior, his cockiness, assured her that
he had had experiences in Korea she just didn't want to
know about. Not that she was jealous; on the contrary, she
was disgusted. The idea that he could have fooled around
with a foreign girl whom she hardly knew was sickening.
This is not what she imagined or expected from her future

husband. When Jeremy was discharged six months later, she was certain he was not the man she wanted to spend the rest of her life with. All his war honors and medals made little impression on her. He was everyone's hero but hers. When the break came, Gladys felt she had woken up. As she admitted to herself, "I really knew all along that it wouldn't work out, and finally I got jolted enough to do something."

Immersed in these thoughts, Gladys was startled to realize she had stopped typing in the middle of a page. Why Jeremy occupied her thoughts today was hard to explain. Maybe her upcoming birthday was getting to her more than she'd like to admit. Gladys was irritated with herself. After all, she could never have stayed with him. His actions made it clear that they were worlds apart. The war had made him different. It was really a shame that this had come between them. How hurt she was, how much she had loved him—the only person she had ever loved!

Maybe she had moved too quickly. Only recently at lunch her niece, Barbara, commented that she hadn't given Jeremy a chance. She wasn't the first person to say that. Her friends had often made similar remarks.

Gladys looked up at the clock and then at the unfinished page: It was full of stupid mistakes and needed retyping. She had no hope of completing it in this frame of mind. She'd come in early Monday, which was easy, since she rose by 5:00 A.M. anyway. Getting up, she put on some fresh lipstick and combed her hair. Instead of quickly grabbing her coat, she lingered for a long while in front of the mirror. She didn't like what she saw. How could people tell her she looked young? Even though the blond rinse covered her gray streaks, there seemed to be more lines than ever around her mouth. She got hold of herself. After all, she really looked well, despite Barbara's comments that she looked fuddy-duddy. Of course, she didn't get caught up in the latest fads. She wore what suited her and what was becoming for a judge's secretary. She thought it a waste of money to get rid of perfectly good clothes just because someone else told you what's nice. Mrs. Kaplan, the Judge's wife, was one of those women who was a slave to fashion. If the Judge were my husband, she thought, I'd never be that way. She often wondered what the Judge saw in his wife, who was just a social butterfly, good for parties but with nothing really substantial about her.

When Gladys reached home, she heard tiny paws scratching on the door. As she opened the door, her pets excitedly jumped all over her. This welcome never failed to delight her. She felt needed. Poor sweethearts, alone all day without her. Despite the animals, her place was immaculate. Her home gave her a great deal of pleasure, especially her collection of foreign dolls—all souvenirs from her cruises and trips abroad.

Gladys loved the sounds of scurrying and barking when she came home. After her last trip, when they were still in the kennel, the house had seemed like a tomb. She had hated the dead silence. After that experience she made sure that following any trip, she picked them up before coming home.

Though tired tonight, Gladys perked up knowing she had quite a bit to do this evening. It was her turn to have the girls for Saturday lunch. Her silver needed polishing. She'd use her good silver and china. She always did when the opportunity arose. After all, she had it, why not use it. She could thank Oscar for her having all this. Though she had always had a hope chest (Aunt Mimi had given her the one she had as a young girl), only when she met Oscar did she really collect things. Her silver and china were purchases she had made thinking of her life with him. Thank goodness she had never let him know how carried away she had been!

Their relationship had been intense. He was the dashing young man of her dreams, an adoring suitor. At their very first meeting he had sent a note to her table in the restaurant. The romance was like a dream from the start. Seeing each other a few days each week—every time his flight schedule brought him to Chicago—generated a lot of excitement. It felt so wonderful to be so totally loved. She felt like a princess. Gladys loved Oscar in his Lufthansa uniform and was always thrilled when they'd go to a restaurant just before a flight. He looked exactly the way she had thought he should—tall, blond, suave. Almost before she knew what was happening, she went to bed with him. It was the first time in her life, but she did it because she knew she'd marry him.

After half a year she was surprised that he hadn't proposed yet, even after he told her how much he loved her and couldn't stand being away from her. It all became clear with a late-night phone call from a woman. In a heavy accent she had told Gladys that Oscar was a married man. Gladys had been devastated. When Oscar arrived next, she wouldn't even open the door. He came back several times asking to explain, saying he loved her, but she would have none of it.

After this blow her only saving grace was her job. She threw herself into her work. Judge Kaplan was at least a decent man. She felt as if the Judge and Dad were the only men she could respect and trust. They would never hurt her as Oscar had.

Serving Saturday's baked tuna-and-macaroni casserole to the girls, Gladys was chatting about the Judge's brilliant speech. By dessert the topic had changed from work to men. Of the four, only Hilda was married. Hilda could always be counted on to push for marriage. Gladys responded that the only man she'd have gone for was JFK. Proving her point, she pulled out her JFK scrapbook, full of years and years of clippings. Before long other scrapbooks were out. She had never thrown anything away. Everything important to her was captured in these pages. All the important events were there—cheerleading, sports, Sunday school, Junior Achievement, National Honor Society. It was hard to believe that high school was so many years ago. She still felt close to those times, to her sisters and her brother, and to her parents.

Although her luncheon was lovely, Gladys ate very little. She had one of her frequent burning stomachaches and didn't have much of an appetite. She would have to ask the Judge to recommend a good physician; this had gone on much too long.

The girls were hardly out the door when the phone rang. It was her mother calling to find out about her luncheon. Gladys always gave her a minute-by-minute description. She knew her mother enjoyed hearing all the details, especially now that she couldn't get around so well herself. Since Father's death two years earlier, Gladys was really worried about her mother. Her grandmother had died within twenty-four hours of Grandfather's death, and Gladys was frightened about the effect on her mother of living alone. Gladys thought it would be right for Mother to move in with her, but as Mother wasn't that eager, she hadn't pushed it. Gladys was relieved: Mother had very definite ways. The dogs, for example, would have to go. While Mother was a good traveling companion, living with her would be far from easy. Still, the time seemed to be coming when Gladys would be doing just that.

Mother kept talking on the phone, but Gladys's thoughts were somewhere else—with her father. Although she loved both of them, it was Father who was special. "As far as Dad went, whatever I did was right. If I had wanted the moon, I could have had it. His pride in me was boundless. My hair, my freckles, the way I dressed, pleased him like nothing else." It was not simply her looks he enjoyed but her high spirits, her opinions, and especially the way she showed her love for him. She was his companion; he was her best friend. "Dad was the most wonderful man I ever met."

Gladys finally hung up, telling her mother she'd speak to her tomorrow so that they could arrange going to mass together. The priest would be disappointed that they wouldn't be there for box lunch, but her brother had invited them instead. She hoped Mrs. Grayson, Mother's dearest friend, wouldn't miss them too much. Mother's friends always counted on seeing her at the box lunch. She enjoyed their company, and they never failed to praise her for being such a wonderful daughter. Their daughters were married and spread out all over the country, so they were envious. Thank goodness the weekend was so full, otherwise the four walls could creep in on her by Sunday night if she didn't make a point of planning things to do.

When Monday came, Gladys was up by five. She was used to getting up early. It was almost predictable now that she couldn't sleep past five, even on weekends. When she arrived early Monday morning to finish her work, the chambers were eerie and still. Gladys sat down to type without her usual container of coffee, since Saturday night her stomach had been jumpy. She was happy to be back at work. If not for Sunday lunch at her brother's and the friend they had tried to pair her up with, she probably would have felt better. Gloria, her sister-in-law, still thought she would eventually come up with the right man. Gloria's efforts were sweet, but she really just wasn't interested. "I don't want to be hurt again," Gladys thought. This time Gloria's choice was a widower who had a car dealership in the neighborhood. He was a quiet, reserved, but friendly man who tried hard to make conversation, and although there was nothing really wrong with him, she just wasn't interested.

By five minutes to nine the typing was completed, the desk was straightened, and everything was in order. The Judge would be pleased. She was glad for the five minutes— time to comb her hair and put on a little lipstick and start the day.

DISCERNING THE PATTERN

Gladys's *wish* is to be a wife, to be in love, to have a husband and a happy home.

At this point in her life, however, the search to fulfill this wish is suspended. Gladys is resigned to her way of life and feels that it is too late for this wish to be fulfilled. What she has never understood is that this wish has always been influenced by an unconscious, unrecognized *need*. A need to find the perfect man, a man who thinks she is "most wonderful" and whom she can, in turn, admire. A man who holds out the promise of a mutually adoring relationship that will be forever. Her need is to adore and be adored.

Not recognizing this need, she becomes infatuated with men who are "crazy" about her. She responds to men who, like Oscar, sweep her off her feet or to her childhood sweetheart, who went marching off to war and allowed her to be caught up in a romantic dream. Thus by not recognizing the need, Gladys exercises poor judgment. As soon as a man gives the slightest indication of infatuation, he stimulates the feeling that he has the potential of being her ideal, her adoring lover. Gladys plunges into relationships because they satisfy her need, not her wish.

Caught up in her need, she ignores the total person and chooses Oscar, for example, the dashing European suitor in uniform. However, inevitably, with time, she sees other parts of the men or learns more about them. In Oscar's case it means finding out that he is a fraud, that he is married. Gladys typically moves from an overidealized relationship to a profound disappointment that this is not the man of her dreams. Shattered, she rejects the man. She feels a sense of frustration, since there is no possibility of staying in love with such a person. What she learns about Oscar prevents her from sustaining the mutually adoring relationship her need requires. Deeply hurt and pained by her pattern, Gladys suspends her search to satisfy her wish.

Gladys feels "burned." These experiences leave their scars. The chances that she will allow another man into her life, that she will pursue her wish, grow smaller as the years go by.

How did Gladys develop this pattern? Where did her need to be part of a mutual admiration society come from? What motivates her to become infatuated only when a man fits her fantasy of how "the perfect man" should be?

Having come from a large family, Gladys was always perplexed by her father's seemingly unlimited interest in her. As she recalls, "Ever since I can remember, no matter what scrap of paper or clay concoction I'd bring home from school, Daddy would rave about it. I could do no wrong. Despite a houseful of people, with my father I always felt like there was just the two of us in our own special world."

Gladys was her father's favorite, his pet, the person he singled out to be his special partner. While her mother never interfered, she managed somehow to convey her disapproval of her husband's behavior toward Gladys: "When Daddy surprised me with a microscope after I won the high school science fair, the first words out of Mother's mouth were, 'When it comes to Gladys, you spend money like a drunken sailor.' "

Gladys's mother felt abandoned by her husband in favor of her daughter. She failed to realize that her husband's neglect and lack of interest was very much related to the criticism she heaped on him and the children and her attempts to run the show. The net effect of Gladys's parents damaged relationship was that with their disappointment in each other, her father found a new and receptive focus for his affection in Gladys. And Gladys found herself Daddy's girl.

GLADYS'S CYCLE

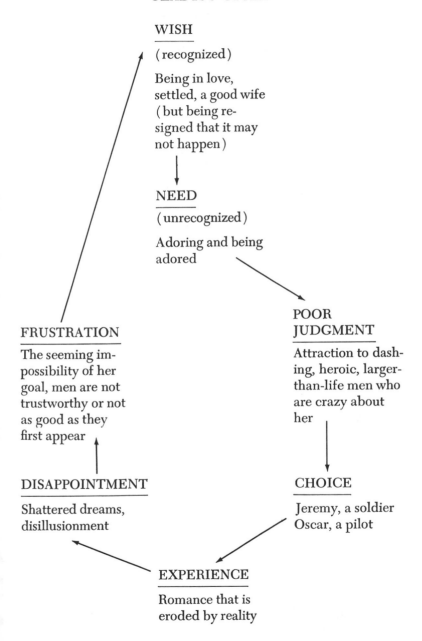

WISH
(recognized)

Being in love,
settled, a good wife
(but being re-
signed that it may
not happen)

NEED
(unrecognized)

Adoring and being
adored

POOR
JUDGMENT

Attraction to dash-
ing, heroic, larger-
than-life men who
are crazy about
her

FRUSTRATION

The seeming im-
possibility of her
goal, men are not
trustworthy or not
as good as they
first appear

DISAPPOINTMENT

Shattered dreams,
disillusionment

CHOICE

Jeremy, a soldier
Oscar, a pilot

EXPERIENCE

Romance that is
eroded by reality

"Sometimes I imagined I was Bonnie Blue with Rhett But-
ler for a father. On my birthday I almost expected my father
to lead a pony into the house for me."

Only as an adult, when she reread *Gone with the Wind*,
did Gladys get a sense of how her mother may have felt
about this "idyllic" relationship: "One paragraph really left
me thinking about my mother. 'Sometimes a dart of jealousy
went through Scarlett because Bonnie at the age of four
understood Rhett better than she had ever understood him
and could manage him better than she had ever managed
him.' "

Gladys felt that was true about herself. She knew and
understood her father better than anyone else did, better
even than her mother did. Feeling this way, she saw herself
as a pillar of support for her father. As she grew up, the
whole family came to depend on her as well. She could recall her father's need for her vividly, even as a little girl:
" 'My little burro,' he would say to me, 'carrying so many of
my burdens on your tiny shoulders.' It gave me the warmest
feeling when he called me that."

Though Gladys moved out of her home as an adult, she
maintained her "favored status." As Gladys recalls, "Father
didn't make a decision without consulting me. When the
phone would ring near midnight, I knew it was Dad needing
to speak with me."

As youngsters her brother and sisters had been jealous of
her special position, but this didn't last. Gladys was good to
all of them. They all knew when in need, call Gladys; she
never failed them.

When Gladys started to date in high school, she found the
boys too childish. It annoyed her that they all had only one
thing on their minds, and she wasn't that type of girl. Gladys
remembered thinking how awful it would be to get pregnant. It had happened to a girl who lived on her block. The
family had hushed it up, but still it was a scandal. What a
disappointment this girl was to her family, Gladys thought

at the time and vowed it would never happen to her. She couldn't do it to people who thought so much of her and she especially couldn't do it to her father.

How does all this affect her pattern? How does it come to bear on her adult relationships?

Gladys is looking for a man who will awaken in her the same idyllic feelings she had with her father. Father was a perfect man, a model, a standard against whom all men in her life are either consciously or unconsciously measured. Any signs of imperfection in a man are intolerable, since they burst the bubble and deviate from the ideal relationship that Gladys expects.

Her fiancé was an object of her affections only as long as she could be caught up in the romance of his military heroics. His return to her as an "imperfect" man, a man with sexual urges, shattered her fantasy. He became unacceptable when he showed his human frailties. Oscar met the same fate. Gladys could become infatuated with him because his romantic intensity and demeanor allowed her feelings of an ideal relationship to take hold. As long as a man serves to perpetuate a magical world of mutual adoration, he can be loved. Thus she never questions Oscar's origins, for anything realistic could undo her feelings for him, and only a midnight phone call disrupts her dream.

By contrast the widowed car dealer at her brother's home holds no interest for Gladys. His pleasant manner and friendly interest in her do not serve to trigger the excitement she expects from a man. She must be swept away or she feels nothing. An average, down-to-earth person cannot generate the unreal feelings she needs to experience. Disappointed, unable to find a perfect man who will treat her the way her father did, Gladys resigns herself to the notion that a man for her just doesn't exist.

Yet Gladys's urge to be reunited with Daddy is not laid to rest with this bitter truth. The need to be immersed in such feelings of mutual admiration drives her to find a man, in this case a boss, Judge Kaplan, who can in some way offer this. Here is a man she can admire, focus her attention on, and even secretly love. In return for this she pleases him, works hard for him, protects him, supports him. In this way Gladys satisfies some of her most basic needs. Yet this is only a tragic compromise solution, since the Judge can never really be hers. When the workday ends, she returns to an empty house filled only with further substitutes, her adoring pets.

Gladys is frozen in her relationship to the Judge. She knows only one part of him, and this allows her to perpetuate the fiction that he is ideal. This is a relationship that leads nowhere. A frozen frame out of a childhood film.

Learning from the Present

Is your need similar to that of Gladys? Do you unconsciously require adoration from a man and want to feel this in return? Clarify whether or not this is your need and how your past may contribute to its creation.

> Do you have an outstanding boss—maybe tough and demanding, but super? Were you ever secretly in love with your boss? Do you sometimes feel you'd make a better wife to your boss? Has no one ever worked for your boss as well as you do?
>
> (A man in authority drives your need into operation. You make him into the image of what you want him to be— perfect. Then you proceed to adore him and compete and excel for this object of your own creation.)
>
> Are you a conservative dresser, not usually getting caught up in the latest fashion?

(Your need makes you a woman who holds on to the past, who thinks what was is better than what is.)

Are you involved in church, synagogue, or philanthropic activities? Are these a big part of your social life?

(If doing good is your central social activity, what may be at its root is a need to be thought well of.)

Are your pets very important to you? Are you overly involved with them?

(Animals are important because they depend on you totally. For your efforts you are appreciated by them above all else. This is a feeling you need to have. It's an escape from having to work at real relationships.)

Do you plan your free time? Are you never without something to do? Would you be likelier to take a cruise or a guided tour than a vacation with no special destination?

(Planning ensures protection. Love, work, and even fun must be 100 percent perfect.)

Have you been disappointed by a man (jilted, betrayed, abandoned) and feel as if you're scarred forever?

(In your love life there is likely to have been at least one fallen idol, some shattering experience that excuses you from other attempts at loving.)

Has your romantic life been made up of a very few but very important relationships?

(Involved in the pursuit of perfection, you expect a man with such potential to come along only infrequently.)

At this stage of your life have you resigned yourself to not being able to find the right man? Are men not really what they seem, not good enough?

(If this is your feeling, question the standards you use to judge men. Aren't you making it impossible for anyone to ever measure up?)

Do you feel that your relationships broke up because it was his fault, because he wasn't what you thought he was?

(The difficulty is your failure to recognize that you expect too much, that fallibility disappoints you.)

Do you feel that the men you're introduced to are just not special enough?

(To make this judgment, you have to believe that you are the "most special" and deserve only the same.)

Are you a romantic at heart? Do you love to be swept off your feet, worshiped?

(You envision scenes that happen only on the silver screen. Men in the flesh are no match.)

Do you tend to be very caught up in your relationship and then become disillusioned with a man, sometimes bit by bit, occasionally all at once?

(You start with an illusion of what a man is. It's no wonder it takes little to disillusion you, to burst your bubble.)

Do you admire men from afar, but often once you get to know them, you're disappointed?

(This is another instance of your overidealization.)

Are you looking for a man like your father? Do you compare men to him?

(Watch out. If you knowingly make comparisons, you are guaranteed that with your need no man will ever look good enough.)

Learning from the Past

Even though you're no longer a girl, do you think Daddy is the most suitable name for your father?

(If you still like that name, you may still like the feelings that went with it.)

Did your father have a pet name for you as a child?

(A child who is overly favored and favorite may grow into a woman who cannot tolerate any other position.)

Did you dream or pretend you were a princess or a favorite character from a book? Did you feel special?

(The romanticizing you began as a child follows you into adulthood.)

Were you a real source of support to your family? Did they count on you?

(Being a good girl is your trademark.)

Did you feel that your mother or siblings envied your relationship to your father?

(This is the secret triumph of a little girl who is adored. She beats out all competitors.)

Did you enjoy winning honors, excelling, doing your best? Did you feel it was appreciated especially by Daddy?

(Perfect girl—perfect woman—looking for a perfect man.)

Were you your father's confidante?

(By singling you out he gave you the message you're Daddy's girl.)

Do you feel as if your father were the greatest guy you ever met?

(If you've met the "greatest man" already, what's the use of looking further?)

Were you kind of prudish? You thought sex was wrong?

(Chastity and purity are all part of being a perfect little girl.)

Do you think you'd have been a better wife for your father than your mother was, that you understand your father better than she did?

(Being able to have this sense confirms your feelings that you're central to his life, better than anyone else.)

Would you have done anything, sacrificed anything for your father?

(You'd do anything for him and he for you. In adult relationships you look for this mutual admiration.)

UNLEARNING THE PATTERN

Start unlearning your tendency to overidealize a man and to want that same level of adoration in return. Understand that your need is to be swept off your feet by the best (handsomest, most honest, purest, kindest, smartest . . .) man in the world. Be aware that you get turned on by anything that gives a man an image of being ideal or perfect and that you fall for this image, though not necessarily the man. Start to realize that you want a Lancelot in shining armor and you wish the role of Queen Guinevere for yourself. But once you are close and see the chinks in his armor, the magic is gone and his appeal is lost. Similarly the man who begins to think of you as anything but a princess is headed for rejection. This need makes you a pushover for uniforms, dashing foreigners, brilliant thinkers, for the Errol Flynns of life—if they could climb down off the screen.

Your expectations about your men are so unreasonably high that disillusionment is inevitable. The disappointment is a crushing blow, and the hurt feels everlasting.

Overcoming this need to adore and be adored involves being constantly aware of it, recognizing it as a force in your love life.

Recognition of your need is particularly difficult since it may jar your self-image. Conscious acceptance of a need long buried and long unacknowledged and the repetitive pattern in your love affairs may be an uncomfortable step. This natural resistance to accepting your need is a chief reason to make a real effort to reinforce it in your memory. There are many ways to help ensure that this self-knowledge will not slip away. Make yourself a set of reminders:

My need is to adore and be adored.

Where can you place them? For a woman with your pattern they must be tied in to your work. Question the role your devotion to your job and your boss play in your pattern.

Put one with your good china or silver. Try to understand why you find yourself using it for your girl friends when it was probably intended for a trousseau.

What about putting copies in your scrapbooks, clippings, photo albums? Stop and think why your need makes you idealize and hold on to the past.

Put one with the pet food. Consider why you have no problem being devoted to animals yet great difficulty in establishing realistic relationships with men.

There are other places you can find if you consider the particular features of your pattern. No matter what the location the effect must be to arrest your attention. Insight into your behavior creates change only if it becomes an active part of your life. Applying your insight to modify your behavior is the route toward personal growth.

Some people find visual cues an effective tool for memorizing. Others remember what they hear. Writing and reading in combination may be a good method for strengthening memory. Keeping in mind that each individual responds differently, choose from among the techniques suggested.

Whatever technique you adopt, bear in mind that awareness is the goal. Conscious awareness of your need is essential for interrupting your unsuccessful pattern. Thinking about your need is a deterrent to acting it out, and as you work on memorizing your need, you can heighten your sensitivity to its effect on your life by attempting a relationship analysis.

Your Relationship Analysis

The theme of adoration repeats itself in one form or another throughout all significant relationships, not only those of adult life. Gladys's relationship analysis follows as an example of how this need runs through her life. Once you see how it colors other relationships, you can begin to develop your own analysis.

Mr. Mack, Gladys's seventh-grade teacher

Unquestionably she was teacher's pet, at an age where all her peers took pride in being wild in school. When everyone else was disruptive, Gladys was quiet as a lamb. When no one had an answer, Gladys's hand shot up with the correct one. Homework was always neat and on time. Extra points for special projects were frequently earned. She was the only girl who still wore a pinafore, matching bow, and Mary Janes to school each day. The fact that the other children couldn't stand her hurt her feelings, but she could always count on hearing nice things from Mr. Mack.

Great-grandpa Obadiah

The picture of Great-grandfather is now in Gladys's living room. When her mother moved from a large house to a small apartment, she offered the portrait to Gladys, who had always loved it. Terribly interested in the details of his life (he was a captain in Custer's army), she spent hours taping her grandmother's glowing reminiscences about him. Grandfather often teased them, saying, "Obadiah was in charge of the stables. The only weapon he carried was a currycomb. If you want to hear the facts, listen to me, young lady." Gladys reassured herself that Grandma's recollections were the accurate ones.

"Joseph," a kind of boyfriend

Gladys was the first girl on her block to talk about her dates. Ironically her first boyfriend was imaginary. When she was alone Saturday nights, she pretended to be with "Joseph." She made him up by choosing the best qualities of famous people: He had the looks of her favorite movie star, the body of a famous athlete, and the brains of a scientist. She even had a picture of a man from a magazine in a frame. It was inscribed, "To the most beautiful girl, Gladys, your love, Joseph." Putting a picture of her fourteen-year-old cousin in her wallet, she showed it around to her jealous friends.

Father O'Reilly, a missionary in Africa

As a child in Sunday school, Gladys's class adopted Father O'Reilly's orphanage as their charity. From the first she was touched and impressed by his devotion. Even as an adult this remained her primary charity. She and Father O'Reilly correspond and still exchange Christmas cards without fail. She used to laugh thinking that she was probably the only person from Sunday school that still remembered his name.

John F. Kennedy

During the early 1960s Gladys was all absorbed in the President. She began a JFK scrapbook. As the election neared, she joined the campaign. Hearing that he would be in her state, she drove over three hundred miles just to catch a glimpse of him at an airport. His assassination was devastating to her. She never included anything about it in her scrapbook. "I always want to remember him as he was," she told a friend.

How does Gladys's need to sustain and maintain mutual adoration and idealization show itself? Being teacher's pet for Mr. Mack is an example of a relationship in which Gladys directs all of her energies into being perfect and in return is treated as special. Likewise the teacher himself is elevated, worshiped. Keep in mind that he is an older man, in a place of authority, whom Gladys knows only in one context and at a distance. This kind of situation reappears again and again in her life. Great-grandpa Obadiah is also glorified by Gladys. His heroic aura excites her, while she ignores or rejects any facts that make him simply human.

Joseph is the ultimate in perfection. As a fantasy he can be anything and everything she wants and needs. Her rejection of the real boys around her emphasizes the drive behind her need, a drive that makes realistic relationships almost impossible. Father O'Reilly's heroic devotion stirs Gladys, too. He is never known as a person outside of his good works, so he can be admired by her forever. Likewise, it is predictable that JFK would be her idol. Everyone's hero, he was for Gladys a modern-day Lancelot.

After evaluating Gladys's relationship analysis, begin your own. Which men have been significant in your life? Think about your behavior, attitudes, and feelings toward them. Does the theme of perfection, idealization, or adoration turn up? Is there a relative, colleague, or friend who has been tied to you because of your need?

Men You Should Be Alert To

The foregoing exercise helps you supply yourself with evidence about the nature of your need and the way in which it affects your personal life. This is your past. The next phase of change focuses on your adult relationships—today and in the future. This involves placing yourself on alert. The object is to make yourself acutely sensitive to anything about a man that may indicate that he fits your need to be idolized.

Your task is to become vigilant to qualities in a man that suggest you are out to reenact a pattern of relating. The point is to interrupt your urge to involve yourself with men on whom you can project all sorts of fantasies, whom you can glorify, or make larger than life. The inevitable consequence of this is disillusionment as the real world encroaches on your ideal one.

For you an added dimension of the need alert is to be on guard against men with whom you can have only limited relationships. Knowing a man only in some limited situation can permit you to keep the idealization of him going forever. When this happens, you run the real danger of fulfilling your need and not continuing the search for your wish. The boss whom you continue to idolize and who idolizes you is fulfilling your need. The fact that you know him only on a nine-to-five basis—he doesn't see you without makeup, you don't see him before he's brushed his teeth—helps keep reality in check and therefore helps to keep anything from spoiling your view of him. Understand that permitting these part relationships is a serious block to finding a "whole" man for yourself.

When you recognize that your need is at work, *stop*. Continuing with these men will inevitably mean a reenactment of your unsuccessful pattern. Be alert to men who

> Seem to have no faults
> Are in uniform
> Are dashing, romantic
> Have seemingly pristine characters
> Are older and are authority figures, such as clergymen
> Are totally unselfish, devoted
> Seem to be as wonderful as Dad
> Are perfect
> Are too good to be true
> Sweep you off your feet
> Idolize you

Say they've never met a woman as pure (kind, lovely,
and so on) as you
Seem to deserve your admiration, although you know
them in only one context or on a limited basis
Make you fall in love with them at first sight

The recurring warning you must heed is to keep alert. Any
sense that your need is being stimulated must signal a warning. Once you can begin to interrupt this cycle, you have a
very good chance of finding a man with whom you will have
a mature relationship.

11

Dianne

"Ladies and gentlemen, the captain has removed the No Smoking sign. However, we advise you to keep your seat belts buckled while you are seated. Have a good flight."

Dianne had been waiting for this moment since the plane took off. Although she didn't feel ill, she was nauseated beyond belief, and even before the captain signed off, she had climbed over Gail, who was already sleeping in the seat next to her, and raced to the lavatory.

Back in her seat, with her stomach beginning to calm down, Dianne thought of her week in Guadeloupe. The plane's steady course made her realize that the flight had little to do with her wooziness. It was the week at Club Med she was sick about. Her tan was the only thing she'd have to show for the trip, a tan and an eight-hundred-dollar credit card bill at month's end. She could have guessed it would be a bust. Club Med was just one big singles bar with a little bit of a French accent. But the men were typical.

Everybody was just out to get laid. Dianne was annoyed at herself for going along with it. She tried to get things straight with the first guy she met. Dianne even told him point-blank, "I'll talk to you, but I'm not going to sleep with you." She had meant it when she said it. Of all places, Di-

193

anne knew, if you were easy here, you'd never even see the guy again. But by the time dinner was over, Dianne realized that this man had no potential. "What the hell," she had thought. "Nothing can come from this. What difference does it make if we do end up in bed." This was her first night at the Club.

Her second date was a type Dianne had seen in action before. He was a stockbroker out to make the most of his vacation. He cruised the beach, jotting down as many telephone numbers as he could in a week. The squirrel collecting nuts for the long winter. His time limit was five or six hours per person. He and Dianne spent an afternoon together. He offered to look over Dianne's stock portfolio "back in the city." She gave him her number. He was cute, and she liked the fact that he wasn't pushy about sex. She wouldn't mind hearing from him again sometime.

The third day she and Gail were sitting at the bar when an incredibly good-looking, deeply tanned man moved up and stood between them. He put an arm around each of them and started talking as if they were long-lost friends. Dianne couldn't figure out which of them he was making a play for.

When he left for a minute, Gail immediately announced to Dianne, "Hands off." Dianne was furious with Gail for being so sure of herself but didn't even have time to answer. She left the two of them at the bar and went to her beach mat to do her nails and finish the last chapter of a novel. Dianne was reading so intently that she jumped when someone sat down next to her. It was him. Gail was still at the bar, talking to another guy. Dianne was really excited. He really seemed to like her. The next few days were great. They spent most of the time together. She slept in his hut, which was just as well, since Gail was still annoyed.

He had a tiny portable stereo and some great tapes, so for a couple of evenings they stayed pretty much to themselves. He was wonderful in bed. Having her back scratched, cuddling, and holding were better than sex as far as she was concerned, and he was a "holder." She told him that she liked him and was so glad he wasn't one of the European guys but someone who lived near her in the city. Dianne was really excited, because he had so much potential. Things were getting to be so good that she hated to leave bed in the morning for her tennis lesson. In fact, on the third day they were together she left the lesson after five minutes. Dianne nearly died when she went back to the hut and found Gail in bed with him. She couldn't believe it. What a jerk she had been to think this guy cared, that he was any different. As for Gail—forget it.

This slap in the face threw Dianne into a frenzy. The wave of nausea came over her again as she thought of how she had carried on in her last three days in Guadeloupe. She couldn't remember the last guy's name she'd been with, but unfortunately she could remember the night on the beach. She hated oral sex, and he loved it. She went along with it but had never intended to let it go that far. She got sick as a dog thinking about how she had just let herself be used. Gail was right. "They all want it. If you don't give, they don't ask you out, and the moment you do give, they don't marry you." Dianne couldn't really stay angry with Gail. It wasn't Gail's fault that guys ran when anything looked the least bit serious. The littlest bit of potential and they all take off.

There would be a lot (too much) to talk about with her shrink on Wednesday. Her shrink. Dianne wondered if it was even worth going to him. He was a nice guy, but after six months she wasn't feeling very different. Dianne could only afford it because her parents picked up the bill. As it was, on her teacher's salary she could hardly pay the rent for her two-bedroom apartment in the city—and that was split three ways. But her mother had heard at her beauty parlor that a psychiatrist had helped someone's daughter "land a husband." So at her mother's insistence her parents offered to pay.

As lunch was served, Gail woke and made some comment about having traveled a thousand miles to find the same bastards sitting on the beach as they'd found sitting on barstools. "Why don't they insist on truth in advertising? 'Seven lays and six nights' should be the Club's motto," quipped Gail. "And to think I lived on grapefruit for three weeks for this trip," she moaned.

Dianne always laughed at Gail's wisecracks. Unfortunately, Gail's jokes were not only funny but painfully true. Both of them refused the Salisbury steaks the stewardess offered.

"Why waste calories on this garbage?" Gail announced. They talked instead.

They came to the same conclusions they had reached before. The men they met didn't want to get married. Forget children. Guys were more interested in their sports cars, their stereo systems, or their new jobs.

Talking reminded Dianne of Fred. He prided himself in being laid back. He never got serious about anyone. Dianne knew it was true, since she had dated him a couple of times last year. Dianne still knew his schedule by heart. Work until three; squash on Monday; Tuesday through Friday, the singles bars; Saturday, a "real" date; Sunday, his regular softball game.

As Gail would say, "Cross him off the list, there's 'no potential.'"

Even though Dianne sensed it before they went out, he had been nice, so she didn't refuse him. They had a pleasant enough evening. But when he fell asleep right after sex and mumbled for her not to leave but "come cheer for me at tomorrow's softball game," she felt as if it was something he must have mumbled to a million women. She had been back in her apartment by 6:00 A.M. Watching the late show that night and binging on her favorite chocolates, Dianne sighed deeply and wondered if there were any men who cared. Sometimes it was easier to sit home alone with a big bag of

Reese's Peanut Butter Cups than face the prospect of another one-night stand.

As the plane began its descent, Dianne thought about her parents, who were probably there waiting at the airport. Her mother would be expecting her to parade off the plane on a man's arm as if the 747 were Noah's Ark and God had assigned her a special partner in Guadeloupe.

Her prediction was accurate: Mother was at the gate, craning her neck to spot Dianne. The smile dropped from her face when Dianne and Gail walked down the ramp together, no man in sight.

When they got to the car, Dianne's father was asleep in the driver's seat. As they pulled out of the parking lot, Dianne decided to beat her mother to the punch. She told her about the nice stockbroker who'd be calling her once she got back to the city. Her father nodded, her mother smiled and asked her if he had "potential." Gail gave a knowing look.

DISCERNING THE PATTERN

Dianne's *wish* is to land a husband. This is an all-pervasive feeling. Despite the intensity of this wish, despite its prominence in her life, what Dianne doesn't realize is that this wish is influenced by a *need*. Dianne's need is to find the care she lacked, the love her parents deprived her of. It is not a mature, mutually reciprocal relationship that she wants. Rather, Dianne is desperately, frantically searching for someone to care for her in a total and all-encompassing way, a way that makes up for a sense of past deprivation. What she really wants is a man who will take care of her and care about her in the same way that a parent acts as a protector to a helpless child, and the intensity of this longing for love denied drives her to any and every man who offers the slightest hope that he will provide it. This need results in

Dianne's poor judgment. Any man who pays the slightest bit of attention to her becomes attractive. Any man with any "come on," any "line," becomes her choice. These become her choice because they seem to have a "potential" to meet her need. Dianne's experience with men is a series of "revolving door" relationships: quickies, one-night stands, one short-lived affair after another. One disappointment follows quickly on the heels of the one before as she awakens (often in bed) to find herself with a man who shows none of the caring and caretaking she craves. Each fruitless encounter leaves her with mounting frustration. She never seems able to develop a relationship that could lead to marriage. The result is that time after time Dianne finds herself failing to satisfy her conscious wish to land a husband. Ungratified, as well, is her unconscious need to be cared for, to be mothered by a man. Unfulfilled in both her wish and her need, she is driven again to repeat her unsuccessful pattern. Once more Dianne finds herself desperately looking and reassuring herself (and her mother) that somewhere in the near future there is a man with "potential."

Why does Dianne have this desperate and driving need to find a man who will care for and mother her? Why does this pattern of being drawn to any and every man who seems the slightest bit attentive have such a grip on her? Why is her need so powerful?

Dianne would have to say that she was closer to her mother than to her father. It wasn't that she didn't like her father. On the contrary, she felt he was a good guy, but he was constantly off working and never had the time for her. Mother was another story. She was always around—perpetually running from hairdresser appointments to card games perhaps—but there.

Time together was devoted to one thing: shopping. They lived in suburbia mainly because her mother had wanted her brother and her to start school off "on the right foot." Father had succeeded in affording a home in East Hills by the time

DIANNE'S CYCLE

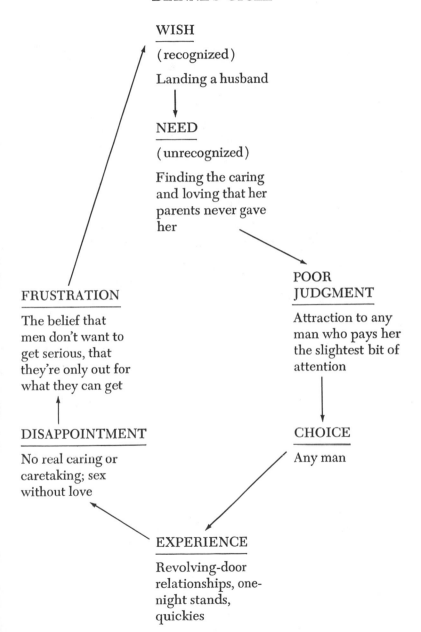

WISH

(recognized)

Landing a husband

NEED

(unrecognized)

Finding the caring
and loving that her
parents never gave
her

POOR
JUDGMENT

Attraction to any
man who pays her
the slightest bit of
attention

FRUSTRATION

The belief that
men don't want to
get serious, that
they're only out for
what they can get

DISAPPOINTMENT

No real caring or
caretaking; sex
without love

CHOICE

Any man

EXPERIENCE

Revolving-door
relationships, one-
night stands,
quickies

her brother, two years younger than she, was eight. The area's shopping malls were her mother's favorite place, second only to the country club. Dianne could not recall a single dress she hadn't bought with her mother. And every season, like clockwork, the old clothes were replaced by the latest fashions.

One shopping trip was unforgettable. As Dianne remembers, "Mother kept repeating that short skirts were in and insisted, despite my fuss, that my skirts be shortened inches above my knees. I died the first day I wore one to school. I kept tugging at it and finally tied a sweater around my waist to try and hide my legs."

Dianne hardly felt like "the best-dressed girl in East Hills" that her mother declared her to be. But Mother was always making pronouncements that made her cringe. The brassiere episode still made Dianne seethe. It was fifteen minutes before her date for the club's summer-end dance was to arrive. It was bad enough that she'd probably be the only fourteen-year-old at the dance, but now her mother was treating her as if she were merchandise going on display. Every detail, from nail polish to pantyhose, was reviewed, and after a final once-over her mother left the room, clicking her tongue and shaking her head. A minute later she was back.

"You need an uplift. I knew this dress wouldn't look right without a little cleavage. Put this on," she insisted, handing Dianne a bra she had purchased for this reason. Embarrassed to the point of tears and feeling humiliated, Dianne knew she had no choice but to do as her mother wished, and she's never forgiven her.

Looking back at her parents' relationship, Dianne could recall that while they stayed married, they were never close. Dad worked and was a good provider, but Mother had her own life. She always seemed more social than Father.

"Mother never really put Father down, but there was the sense that she was disappointed in her life with him. She'd always warn me to be very careful about whomever I finally 'landed.' 'I want you to be happy,' was her constant refrain."

Despite pushing, prodding, and priming, Dianne never felt her mother was really interested in her.

"I was the first girl my age to date. My mother encouraged it, and it was always as if my mother wanted to come along on my dates. She'd wait up for me and then insist on hearing every detail. Whenever I gave a party—and she always wanted me to give them—she stayed around, even when I was older. I think she used the excuse that we needed a parent to be close by. She even managed to dance with some of the boys. Mother would always make me show her the latest dance steps.

"Boy, did I envy my brother. His baseball, football, basketball, and tennis camp kept him busy every season of the year. I'm not even sure he needed those sports. I think he could have done anything and my mother would have given the okay. Only I was watched like a hawk."

Despite the watch Mother kept over her, the prying and questioning she carried on, Dianne never confided in her or told her any of her true feelings. "The only way to survive was to 'yes' her, give her the answers she wanted to hear. At least that way she'd get off my back for a while. Anyway, she didn't really care to hear anything I had to say. So it worked out just fine."

Dianne's childhood experiences affect her lovestyle. The need to be mothered by a man so as to compensate for a sense of acceptance she never felt has its roots in her family life, especially in her relationship with her mother. Dianne is a product of an emotionally absent father and a selfish and frustrated mother who wanted only to bask in her daughter's reflected glory. Mother was an unhappy woman who tried to use Dianne to make up for her own disappointments in life. Mother's interest in her daughter extended only to how much she could get out of it. Emotionally their relationship was barren. Without realizing it, Dianne was being used, yet somewhere in her heart she felt it. Mother's obsession with

Dianne's attractiveness, allure, charm, talent—all the *external* trappings that could "get" a man—left Dianne feeling she had no value for herself. She grew up to think that, like a piece of merchandise, she was only important if there was a demand for her. It left her with a hollow, empty feeling, a longing for someone to truly care for her and about her, to accept her for what she really was.

Despite all the effort put into Dianne, she is a young woman starved for love and affection and real acceptance. Feeling emotionally empty, she frenetically seeks, in every man, the caring she lacked. Any man who pays any attention to her arouses in her the sense that he might be "the one," that is, the one person who will want her, love her, care for her. The hugging and cuddling of the man in Guadeloupe, the two of them spending day and night together in bed, the instant intensity and intimacy—all make Dianne euphoric. It's the closest she gets to what she is looking for, the warmth and mothering that she seeks. So desperate is her search, so great is her longing, that it takes almost nothing to stimulate Dianne's hope that she has found in this man the love she missed, that she has found someone who will fill the emptiness.

But Dianne can't relax and be herself. She has been indoctrinated to believe that she can only get attention by packaging herself. It's what's up front that counts. So she cruises the bars and beaches, takes trips, goes on diets, buys designer jeans, and reads all the women's magazines in the hope that she will be at the right place and have the right look to catch someone's eye. Though she doesn't truly enjoy sex and doesn't believe that sleeping with a guy is going to get him, it is another asset that may help. So she jumps from one bed to another, she submits again and again against her better judgment, because maybe this time this "morning after" will be different. Maybe he'll wake up and ask her to stay forever. In this way her short-lived relationship is like a drug fix, a rush of possibilities, a false sense of euphoria followed by a bitter and disappointing crash. When Dianne wakes up in a strange bed and does not get that intense love and care she is seeking, she is disgusted and humiliated.

When one man, Fred, does ask her to stay to "cheer him at softball," she leaves. It's not enough. It's not the declaration of permanent love she is waiting for. Dianne isn't simply looking for the beginnings of a relationship Fred may be offering. She is looking for the mother love, the care, the acceptance, she never had. When it's not forthcoming, she cannot tolerate the disappointment and pain. She leaves to look frantically for the next person who holds out the hope of giving it to her. The chocolates are a kind of temporary relief, as if with enough sweets she could fill the painful void. Sadly they don't work. Her need to be cared for goes unsatisfied. It drives her on to the next man. This indiscriminate race makes Dianne appear to be promiscuous. Ironically it is her deep longing for one, and only one, man that drives her on. In her heart Dianne is emotionally monogamous. But this frenzy never permits her to develop an enduring relationship. Wish and need unsatisfied, Dianne resumes her frenetic and frantic lovestyle once more.

Learning from the Present

Where are you? Are you anything like Dianne? Is your need to find the mothering, the caring you lacked? What was your early experience that may have affected your lovestyle? Review these questions to help you know where you stand:

Have you dated so many men that you've lost track?

(Going through men—this is a hallmark of your need.)

Do you find yourself easily attracted to men, and easily disappointed by them?

(At first each man holds out hope, but your search is for a feeling that a man can never instantly provide.)

You date men against your better judgment (even though you know he doesn't date anyone twice).

(You ignore his track record, hoping without foundation that this time, with you, he will be different.)

Do you diet constantly?

(You're always trying to improve the packaging, hoping that will bring you what you lack.)

Do you try singles bars, tennis clubs, cruises, singles weekends—anything as a way of meeting guys?

(Your need pushes you in a restless pursuit of a man to fill the emotional void.)

Do you feel men use you?

(They do, because your craving for love allows it to happen; it impairs your judgment.)

Do you want to be able to leave a place; you don't like to stay the night? Is his place better because there you don't have to throw him out, you can just go?

(When you don't feel that rush of love you're after, you get depressed. You have to be able to run, as if you could leave the pain behind.)

Do you sleep with men you date even though it may not be what you really want?

(You hold out hope that sex will get him for you.)

Do you believe men never get serious about girls who are "easy"?

(You believe it but act otherwise. Your desperation to be wanted makes you act against your better judgment.)

Do you sometimes feel like merchandise, meat on a hook?

(Your need leaves you doubting there is something inside you that someone could love. You feel you cannot be loved for what you are but for what you appear to be.)

Would you rather cuddle, hug, and have your back scratched than have sex?

(This is your real hunger—for the basics, for the caring you somehow missed.)

Do you sometimes binge, whether it's eating, shopping, or running around?

(Sometimes a woman with your need will do anything to fill up the emptiness. Regrettably it is only your body, your closets, or your calendar that is filled.)

Do you never seem able to find a nice guy who wants to settle down and get serious?

(This takes time. When you're starving, how can you wait for things to develop?)

Is your tendency to get into a relationship quickly? To meet a guy and spend the next forty-eight hours with him?

(Intensity gives you the illusion of caring. Invariably it burns itself out.)

Would you rather be in a relationship, even a lousy

one, than waiting around for one? Is anything better
than sitting at home alone?

(Other people help ward off the anxiety, the panic. Being
alone makes you aware of the void in your life.)

Do you find it's very important for you to feel attractive
and desirable, and that sometimes going to bed with a
guy can make you feel that way?

(Unsure of yourself as a person, you try to reassure yourself
through desirability.)

Is your work or career just something to carry you over
until you're married?

(Your value as a person is only established by landing a
man.)

Do you feel you scare guys away? They pick up your
serious intentions and take off?

(With your need, what men pick up is your longing and its
intensity. It can frighten them.)

Learning from the Past

Would you describe your mother as frustrated? Was
your mother overinvolved in pushing you into things
you didn't want to do?

(When a mother disregards a child's feelings and uses her
as a means to an end, it can end with a child feeling worthless.)

Was your mother more concerned about your appearance than what was on your mind or in your heart?

(The message is it's what's up front that counts. The feeling
that never leaves is that there is no concern for what's
inside.)

Were you given music, dance, art, and tennis lessons? Were you being produced, packaged for a market?

(A lot of attention does not necessarily equal a lot of love.)

Did your mother ever give you the sense you should do something like lose at tennis or wear something special because "the boys will like you better"?

(Your worth was determined by your capacity to attract men—even if it meant manipulating them.)

Did you have early sex play?

(Even as a child you tried to use sex to gain friendship, caring.)

Did your mother seem to be living vicariously through you? Were you the one that could make her happy?

(This kind of mothering says, "You don't count as a person; only what you can do for me matters.")

Did your mother fill her life with various activities but never seem to find real satisfaction or be totally happy?

(You saw, felt, and identified with the emptiness your mother felt. She even tried to use you to fill in the spaces in her life. It continues to burden you.)

Did you keep things from your mother? (Do you still?) Could you only tell her the things she wanted to hear? Did you feel she wanted it that way? Was she not the sort of person you could tell what was on your mind, what you really felt?

(Once you recognized there was little concern for your feelings, you stopped trying to communicate them.)

Is the only time you can talk about a man to your parents when you can convey the feeling he has potential as a spouse?

(That's all they want to hear, so it's all you tell.)

Is seeing an engagement ring on your finger the only thing that would make your mother happy?

(Your mother doesn't know how to judge feelings. She can only measure success when it's tangible. You bring this confusion to your adult relationships. You don't know how to read your own emotions or anyone else's.)

Was your father okay but never been very involved with you?

(Your model was a barren relationship between emotional strangers. It's the same barrenness you feel within yourself.)

UNLEARNING THE PATTERN

If your need is akin to Dianne's search for caring, some of these questions will remind you of yourself, your lovers, your family. Answering them will help you confirm your lovestyle—how it developed, how it impairs your judgment, how your need controls the course of your love life.

Change. Start the process by reviewing the nature of your pattern. You are a woman whose need to find love pitches you into many ungratifying encounters with men. You have been involved with many, often for short periods of time, and you walk away longing for something more. Sex, physical closeness, is often a way to make yourself feel you are on the way to that something more, a way to forget the loneliness for a moment. When nothing develops, the shame and disappointment are wounding. Your *need* makes you so impatient, leaves you so hungry for love, that its intensity turns a man off. It prevents your *wish* to marry from being fulfilled.

The key to breaking out of this unsuccessful lovestyle is to interrupt the cycle. Becoming conscious of the driving force behind your behavior is the first step. It's not enough to think over your need from time to time. What is really required is a kind of self-indoctrination. Making an effort to memorize your need should be a continual process. Start by writing it down.

My need is to find the caring and love I lacked.

How can you use this as an effective reinforcer for your memory? Try and tie in these reminders to activities that are part of your lovecycle. For example, paste one on the back of your credit card case. Look at it the next time you take it out to pay for a singles weekend or the shopping binge you find yourself on after meeting another guy who doesn't want a serious relationship. Place another one in your wallet. Retrieve it when you pay for the 6:00 A.M. cab fare coming back from his place. And as soon as you buy your chocolates, put one inside the bag.

Which method of birth control do you use? Put one in your diaphragm or pill case. Perhaps it will remind you of how your sexual behavior fits into your cycle.

Attach one to the telephone and look at it when you talk to your mother. Analyze your own particular pattern and come up with other strategic places.

These reminders placed appropriately help in forcing you to be conscious of your pattern. Use them to begin to break its hold. Also analyze your relationships.

Your Relationship Analysis

The need operates in your present adult life and shows itself in other earlier relationships with men. Dianne's analy-

sis of the significant men in her life reveals continual interactions with men tinted by her need.

Uncle Bruce, her father's youngest brother, a bachelor
The brightest and happiest memories of Dianne's childhood involve her uncle. Flying in from Paris for her grandmother's
funeral, he spent a week at their house. Though she had been
only seven, she can still remember every detail vividly, the circus,
the stories he read, the games they played. The enormous pink
panda he bought her was something she still has not let her
mother discard. She didn't cry when he left. Instead she pretended he was a prince going on a special magical journey. Every
time he is in the States, Dianne spends as much time as she can
with him. He teasingly quips that she doesn't let him out of her
sight.

Mr. Chauncey, the family gardener
When she was ten years old, he came to work for her family.
Dianne loved to follow him around. He would spend time ex-
plaining the various plants to her. This relationship almost cost
him his job. Not wanting to leave him, Dianne went along to his
next assignment, saying her parents wouldn't mind. When she
returned home several hours later, her mother threatened to fire
Mr. Chauncey. Only when Dianne begged her father did her
parents refrain from dismissing him.

Jeffrey, a boy from the neighborhood
When they were about six years old, they played a "game" in his
garage with another little boy. Jeff made her pull down her
panties and sit on the cold concrete floor in front of them. Dianne,
knowing it was wrong, ran away crying. Feeling Jeff would stop
playing with her if she didn't comply, she swore not to tell her
mother. For about a year, until Jeff lost interest in this "game,"
they continued to play it together.

Peter, a fourth-grade classmate
Unlike Dianne, he was a very well liked child. Dianne was one
of many children who wanted to be his friend. He barely noticed
her. She started to bring him presents: comic books, cookies, gum.
When there was a good dessert at lunch, she would give hers to
him. Once, without telling her parents, she took a silver dollar
from her father's collection and gave it to Peter. At first she gave
him things openly. As classmates began to tease her, she tried to

do it secretly. Whenever they spotted her, she was taunted. After months of this Dianne was delighted to find that he wanted her to be his partner for the school science fair. However, he came to her house only once to work on it and left the rest up to her.

Larry, her only boyfriend in high school
Dianne had many boys after her in school; she was considered an easy make. "All you have to do is ask Dee for a blow job and you have it," she overheard someone say. Dianne always wanted to go steady, but none of the boys she dated were ever interested. Larry was a new boy, a transfer student from another school. Lockers were assigned alphabetically, so Dianne's was next to his. He was very shy and Dianne got friendly with him slowly. Even though she wasn't crazy about him, when he finally asked her to a big school dance, she was pleased. Only older college boys asked her out to country club or fraternity dances, and they were always family friends snared by her mother. This was one of the few times she'd been asked to her own high school dance. About a week before the dance Larry found a note in his locker giving him a list of boy's names with whom Dianne had "gone all the way." Without giving her an explanation Larry broke their date. He began sharing a locker with someone else just to avoid her.

The theme of real longing for love, attention and acceptance recurs throughout Dianne's interactions with men.

Uncle Bruce represents such a high point in Dianne's life because he was, even over the short run, totally involved and available to her. The panda bear is cherished into her adulthood as a warm, soft object that symbolizes her attachment to him and that important experience. Trying to cope with losing Uncle Bruce, his care, his love, she tries to transform the pain of separation from him into a positive magical fantasy. Commenting on Dianne's sticking so near to him, her uncle seems to be sensing her tremendous need for closeness, a need his short visits cannot satisfy.

Mr. Chauncey's attention is so precious that again Dianne can't let him out of her sight; she literally follows him. Her need for affection is so strong it prompts her to leave without recognition of the effect her behavior will have.

How does Dianne's need show up in her interactions with contemporaries? The hallmark of Dianne's relationship to her peers is her attempt to do anything to win their friendship. She submits to Jeff's sex play, play that makes him happy and Dianne uncomfortable, and she comes back for more in order not to lose his attentions.

Dianne attempts to buy Peter's affections, even if it puts her at risk with parents and peers. Keep in mind her choice: She tries to get affection from him despite the fact that he clearly isn't interested in her. During her adolescence she is desperate to be accepted, and her high school years become filled with a succession of boys, all of whom Dianne tries to get and to please by using sex. Larry, an adolescent himself, not recognizing Dianne's behavior as longing but only seeing it as "cheap," wants nothing to do with her. Rejection, once again, is the legacy of the need that drives Dianne to search for caring and love she has missed.

Though each of Dianne's experiences is different, an analysis provides an understanding of how each is often dramatically influenced by the need. Having understood this, try to review and evaluate your own past. Which friends, relations, and colleagues have been part of your life, part of your need? Once you begin to sense how these past relationships were influenced by your need, the next issue at hand is to concentrate on how it affects your adult love life.

Men You Should Be Alert To

Make yourself vigilant to any feelings that suggest your need. This heightened awareness is an important deterrent to being pulled inexorably into an unsuccessful lovestyle. Your acute sense of emotional deprivation leaves you with a desperate desire to find the love, care, and acceptance denied you. Be alert to any man who makes the slightest gesture indicating interest in you. This will stimulate a sense that there may be more to come, feelings that may make you try too hard, go too fast, give too much.

Be aware that your sense of desperation drives you to find even a momentary relief a man may provide, relief inevitably followed by a letdown and a bitter aftertaste.

You must be alert to men who

Come on strong, who are known to be or who are Don Juans

Know how to pitch a line

Are sure of themselves, smooth, aloof, slick

Are debonair, cool

Are sexually pushy, and expect you'll sleep with them the first time you meet

You know are exploiters

Are on the make, looking for a pick-up, are fixtures in a singles bar

Have reputations for never sleeping with the same woman twice

Are playboys

All the women run after

Make you feel insecure and whom you sense you have no hold on from the outset

Ignore you between dates

Call at the last minute for a date, after you haven't heard from them for a while

Collect telephone numbers, in a bar, at the beach, at a party

Starting in with men who fit your need must be avoided. Refuse to get trapped in your old pattern. Saying "no" to these men means saying "no" to your need, "no" to another trip through your old pattern. You can do it.

Patricia

Patricia was adamant. This party would be different. Maybe she and Sonia were sharing expenses, but it was her apartment and she had the final say on the guest list. That's a laugh, she thought. In Santa Barbara there weren't any guest lists. Everyone in the complex just assumed they were invited. Most would be gone by year's end.

This time Pat was going to make a real party. Good food, wine, her special brownies, a real party.

"Look," she said to Sonia. "I'm not interested in a black-tie affair. Those days of dinner for twelve were over when I left Dallas—eight rooms of wall-to-wall carpeting and a husband who thought the only really fine entertainment in Texas was Monday-night football. But I'm tired of meeting blond gymnasts on roller skates or forty-year-olds who still think they're in a fraternity. I'm also pretty fed up with struggling young artists who just need a place to crash for a few days. Remember the last artist you brought home from est? Once you two walked into this apartment, I don't think you kept your clothes on for more than fifteen minutes. I was thinking of calling the Guinness people to see if your sex marathon hadn't broken some record—longest screw in history for forty-five-year-old former suburban housewife." Sonia couldn't help laughing at that crack.

In a year of living together the two women had become close friends. Even though Pat had been divorced for eight years and Sonia for only two, they understood each other. In many ways Sonia was very much like Pat had been right after she left her husband—going in all directions at once, breaking loose, even a little wild, especially when it came to sex.

Pat saw herself as Sonia's mentor; she was going to try to help her avoid some of the pitfalls of the singles scene that she herself had fallen prey to. That's why she had insisted Sonia come to her women's group. Sonia needed help. She was still emotionally tied to the man she'd had an affair with in Montreal. "God," thought Pat, "I don't think there's a woman who's left home who doesn't first have an affair." If not for Ian, she herself would still be the PTA rep of Dallas's District 27. Ian was the instructor of her ceramics class at the Y, and a locally known artist. His British accent made him irresistible. He was sensational in bed, and with him Pat felt as if she were having sex for the first time. She still smiles remembering the first time he went down on her; until that moment she had thought multiple orgasms were something that only happened in porn novels.

Pat never regretted her affair. Her husband Peter's behavior left her no choice; she had tried to change things between them, but it didn't work. Looking back, she thought how ridiculous her efforts had been. At her women's group she'd gotten hold of a sex manual. Maybe sex could be better if Peter would be a little more thoughtful, imaginative. Her hope was short-lived. The only thing she could remember was Peter looking at the pictures as if it were a *Playboy* magazine and then rolling over to go to sleep. It was too much. She felt as if they were just two different people, except that it was she alone who noticed the difference.

That same week Pat found a condom in her daughter's dresser drawer, and that was it. All she could say to herself

was, "At fifteen, my daughter's probably had better sex than
I've had in my whole life."

An affair had to happen.

Pat couldn't believe how easy it was to hide her affair
from Peter. It shouldn't have really surprised her. They had
never really communicated. Maybe Peter never realized it
(he was always pretty insensitive), but they lived separate
lives. He wouldn't even notice that things were any different.
He just plodded along from work to golf club to Rotary
meetings as if nothing else existed. He was all business. She
couldn't talk to him about anything that seriously bothered
her.

Pat tried not to, but she found herself continually compar-
ing Peter with her new lover. She explained her feelings to
Sonia, knowing that she, of all people, could understand:
"Ian made me realize who I was for the first time in my life.
He validated me, gave credence to my mind, believed in me.
He was short, poor, brilliant, politically involved, a do-
gooder liberal. He slept around. He was everything at forty
that my parents didn't want for me when I was sixteen. And
I was madly in love. I owe a lot to him."

After two years Pat had to leave her husband. Her mother
was furious the second she got wind of the separation. Eight
years later she still hadn't accepted it. "You're going to
throw away a home, a family, just because you've had a little
fling and feel dissatisfied. You don't appreciate what you
have, you're ungrateful; your husband is hardworking, he's
wonderful. You're just selfish. How can you do this to me?"

These words echoed in Pat's ears. Yes, her mother was
right. She'd given up a lot. It wasn't that she regretted losing
her old way of life, but these days, with all the guys she had
been meeting, her mother's words took on a different meaning. Things were a million times better—especially sex—but
her relationships were dead ends. The men she met never
seemed to think about a joint future.

Money was also on Pat's mind. She had stopped thinking

poor is good, rich is bad, and realized that the life of a middle-aged hippie was not for her. Some money came in from her pottery work. However, she didn't try to fool herself: Alimony was her main form of support.

She wished she could meet a man with whom she could have a relationship as equals. She didn't want to go back to being totally dependent on someone else, especially for money.

Pat's thoughts were interrupted by Sonia's question: "Well, who do you want to invite anyway?" Sky was great at night, but he didn't have a thing to say once the sun was up. Beauty but no brains. Eric with the convertible—great, but how many malts and drive-ins could anyone endure once past puberty? Mack? The greatest blue eyes in Santa Barbara, and his poems aren't half-bad, but otherwise he was awful. Tony next door—the best man she had ever slept with. Where had he learned it all at age twenty-five? Sidney, the dentist—unfortunately, Sidney thinks he's still nineteen. He's got money, position, but there's no sense of commitment. He's really pretty nice, but she was tired of people who acted as if life were a dress rehearsal for the real thing. Pat was ready for something different.

DISCERNING THE PATTERN

Pat wants something different. Her *wish* is to find a man who will give her understanding and security: fun, pleasure, excitement, but with some element of stability. This is a conscious desire. Pat's *need* is to break away, to find identity as an adult, something she could not do as a young girl. She needs finally to go through a teenage rebellion that she was denied.

As this need overpowers her wish, it brings some trouble. Pat is unconsciously struggling to break away, and she is attracted to men who are the total opposite of her old values. If a man is romantic, poor, unconventional, antiestablishment, and fun loving, he automatically becomes attractive. A man farthest from what she has been is the man who can best help her separate and break away. He fits her need. This is why Ian, the struggling artist, becomes her choice. The men in Santa Barbara are also chosen because they make Pat feel she is different from her old self. She has a series of affairs and brief infatuations. But there is no stability, no maturity, nothing lasting about them, and they leave her with a feeling of disappointment.

After a while she has a growing sense of frustration— where is there a different kind of male, a man who is both stable and exciting? This man that cannot be found is one who would satisfy her conscious wish for security and understanding. Her wish goes unsatisfied. Once more the need overpowers the wish. As long as this need to break away remains obscured and unexplored, it will no doubt drive her on to repeat a pattern that does not bring happiness.

How did Pat's need to break away develop? Where did it come from and why does it determine how she responds to men?

Anyone who knew Pat as a young girl, and knows what she's doing now, is invariably shocked. Growing up, Pat was everyone's dream of a child: pretty, popular (even in grade school), and an "A" student. "I've only happy memories of my childhood parties, friends, family gatherings. I was always the best dressed. Nothing was spared. When I turned eighteen and started college, my father even bought me a magnificent fire-engine-red car."

Her father, a bank vice-president, enjoyed having his "girls" look good. "Dad thought Mother was beautiful and he liked to be seen with her. It was terribly important to my mother also. When we went to church, there was nothing that made them feel better than a comment on 'what a lovely-

PATRICIA'S CYCLE

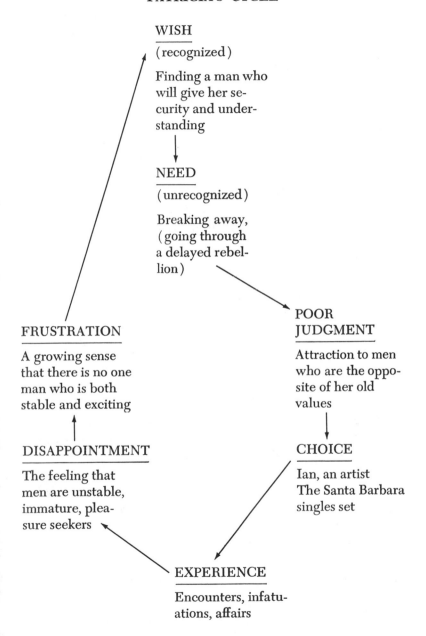

WISH

(recognized)

Finding a man who will give her security and understanding

NEED

(unrecognized)

Breaking away, (going through a delayed rebellion)

POOR JUDGMENT

Attraction to men who are the opposite of her old values

FRUSTRATION

A growing sense that there is no one man who is both stable and exciting

DISAPPOINTMENT

The feeling that men are unstable, immature, pleasure seekers

CHOICE

Ian, an artist
The Santa Barbara singles set

EXPERIENCE

Encounters, infatuations, affairs

looking family you have.' On Easter, Mother went all out. We looked as if we stepped off the cover of *Family* magazine." Pat could remember every Easter outfit in detail, especially since without fail year after year they went to a photography studio for the annual family portrait.

Yet there was a kind of contradiction in Pat's relationship with her mother. "On the one hand she was totally involved in my life. She told me not only how to dress but how to act. She was full of advice, especially about boys, so I was always hearing about how decent girls act, how terrible it was to be 'fast,' how only cheap girls had their ears pierced, that boys always want their wives to be virgins. She bought me falsies when she thought I needed them. When I got older, I know she watched for my sanitary napkins just to be sure I was still a 'good girl,' not skipping my periods. Her list of do's and don't's was endless. *Proper, nice, right, correct*, were her favorite words.

Despite her mother's involvement with her Pat never really communicated with her, never knew her as a person. Pat's own feelings were never talked about. As she recalled, "Frankly, I don't think I really had any ideas or feelings of my own. I just accepted everything at face value. What my parents said went. It never occurred to me to think otherwise. The few times I did anything she didn't care for, I felt like I was destroying her. She never yelled, she just looked so disappointed and sad that I never resisted."

Mother was effective: Pat was a "good girl." "When I started dating, I wouldn't let a guy get to 'first base' for the longest time. Even in college I hung on to the idea that I'm not the type to 'go all the way,' though by that time the fact that I was still a virgin was pretty much a technicality."

From her first date on, Pat made sure that any boy she brought home was someone her parents would like, ones with good manners. The boys who weren't up to her parents' standards simply never made it home; those relationships started and ended in the backseat of a car.

While Pat always knew that she'd go on to college, she never really thought in terms of a career. "My father always said that the most important degree you'll ever earn is an M-R-S."

Her father's comment was almost prophetic. In her second year of studying fine arts at George Washington University ("I had an artistic flair, and Mother thought I could use it to work in a gallery or museum") she met Peter, who was completing a master's degree in business at Georgetown University. Pat's plans to finish school were abandoned, since Peter got a job offer in Dallas. "As my mother said from the minute she met him, 'Don't let this one get away. He's any woman's dream.'"

"I was disappointed to leave school, but I was so excited about my June wedding. It didn't seem to matter. I spent my last semester reading brides' magazines and flying home to see the furniture Mother picked and to have gown fittings."

It was everything that Pat wanted, or so she thought.

How does this background influence Pat's current life?

Pat and her family are a product of the 1950s. They are people concerned with propriety, comfortable if they can conform and seeking acceptance in the world around them, people who look to and need well-defined roles and models as a way of structuring their lives. Feelings, ideas, and inner needs are never openly acknowledged.

Pat learned to be what was expected of her rather than to be what she wanted. The truth is she never even anticipated that she would want something. In fact the pressure on Pat to live up to expectations was so great that it drove out any sense of her own identity. It wasn't that she didn't have all the makings of her own person; she was intelligent, a good student, pretty, personable, artistic. Rather, she was programmed to feel that these qualities were worthwhile only if

they were used to help fulfill what was expected of her first
as a daughter, later as wife and mother. Her qualities were
good if they got her what was best from life, such as the
right husband.

In her teenage years, when most children make an attempt to break away, to find themselves, Pat remained the
compliant, good daughter. Marriage was a continuation of
this same life. With Peter she may have moved out physically from her home, but emotionally she never left. Her
marriage had all the conventional trappings of the good life,
but there was still no communication, no opportunity for Pat
to be a person in her own right.

For seventeen years she worked against permitting herself
to feel dissatisfied. But then a number of things happened to
create an atmosphere that made Pat evaluate her life. She
recognized that she wasn't getting any younger. She wit-
nessed with some envy her children's growing interest and
enjoyment of sex. She came to realize that she had something to offer. And she occasionally saw friends' lives radically changed, which confirmed the idea that things could
unexpectedly turn. The women's movement was critical as
well. It gave her an important opportunity to see that there
were other ways to live.

And so with a delay of twenty years she finally rebelled
and ran away with a man opposite to everything her parents
and ex-husband stood for. A series of men followed who
served the same purpose—to pull her away, to free her.

After several years of "freedom," however, her past caught
up with her. While she "found" herself and still wants freedom, fun, and meaning in her life, she is not comfortable
with an unstable, marginal existence. She wishes something
more substantial. Conflict arises. This is the problem of delayed rebellion: She needs both comfort and adventure.
Having taken so long to break away, Pat is afraid to go back
to anything that resembles the life she once knew. Her men
reaffirm her struggle for a personal identity, but they are

chosen only for this reason. Men who fit her need to break away are not men who can satisfy her wish to find security and understanding.

Learning from the Present

The following questions can help you isolate some of the basic elements in this pattern.

Has your taste in men changed dramatically in the last few years?

(This is a telltale sign of your need. Different men reflect a different you.)

Do you go with more flamboyant and fun-loving, rather than the good, and dutiful, type of man?

(You've finally had enough. You're rebelling.)

Were you (are you) married to a man while dreaming of someone entirely different?

(This is a warning sign. You first feel discontent and only later act on it.)

Would people you know from the past be surprised or even shocked to hear about the men in your life now?

(The hallmark of any rebellion is this swing of the pendulum.)

Was your marriage a copy of your parents'?

(If your marriage was a clone of that of your parents, rest assured you were never a teenage rebel.)

Were your parents perfectly happy with your choice of a husband?

(If you were never disapproved of—especially when it came to dating—you never had a chance to test your own values out against theirs.)

Even if your life was comfortable, did you feel something was missing, that just being wife and mother wasn't enough?

(What was missing was you. You had a role but no sense of your identity apart from it.)

Did you try to improve your marriage, work it out, give it a last try?

(Rejecting your old values isn't easy. You held on for as long as you could.)

Did you feel your husband had limited interests, was dull, didn't communicate?

(What you sensed was your own growth. You felt as if you were radically changing and he wasn't.)

Did your husband fail to take your attempts to communicate seriously.

(Like your parents, your husband encouraged the status quo.)

Did you suggest marital therapy and have it rejected on the grounds that he didn't have any problems?

(You were feeling like a different person, something he either couldn't or didn't want to feel.)

Did your husband never realize that your marriage was in serious trouble? Was he unable to understand why you threatened to leave?

(This is a common refrain in partnerships where one person goes through a delayed struggle for separation and identity.)

Was sex before you left disappointing, unimaginative? Did you think you were frigid?

(Since you never gave up being a good girl, it's no wonder you never allowed yourself to enjoy sex.)

Was it only with extramarital or postmarital lovers that you discovered you weren't frigid?

(Your rebellion was a release, both emotionally and sexually.)

Did you have an affair while you were married? Was it your lover who made you realize you had to get out of your marriage?

(A surefire mark of your need is that never having asserted your independence you need a man to reassure you, to validate you.)

If your mother saw the type of man you date now, would it "kill" her?

(Girls use boys to drive their mothers crazy. Women use men.)

Did you never really know or believe in your talents, skills, creativity until you met people who noticed them?

(You're a late bloomer—in all areas.)

Do you sometimes feel that the men you go with now are too young, too poor, too way out, or too different?

(Your need drives you to men who are very different. But being an adult rebel—not a teenager—you're self-conscious about their limitations.)

Occasionally when you think about how you're behaving these days, do you ask yourself, "Is this really me?"

(Unlike your adolescent counterpart, the thought of a permanent partner enters your thinking. It makes you look at these men in your life with a more critical eye.)

Do you feel ambivalent about your decision to leave? Do you wonder if it was too selfish? That you might have been unfair to your children, that you've gone too far?

(Guilt is the high price you pay for such a delay in development.)

Do you find you're more critical of the men you go out with now than you used to be, that you want something more?

(No matter how fiercely you struggle to rebel, the bottom line is that you are the product of two worlds.)

Do men who seem too stable make you nervous?

(This stability reminds you of your past. You're afraid of having to submerge yourself again, lose your separateness.)

Learning from the Past

Were you always a good girl? Never gave your parents any reason for upset, embarrassment?

(Somewhere in the personal history of a woman breaking loose there is always a "good girl.")

Were you pretty, popular, a good student?

(Doing everything right as a child means that you had no option to behave otherwise.)

Were you never one to disobey, stay out too late, run around?

(This is part of the teenage struggle for self-definition. If you didn't do it then, you may be grappling with self-determination now.)

If you did something your parents wouldn't approve of, did you make sure they didn't know about it?

(Only now can you feel the courage of your convictions; better late than never.)

Were you teacher's pet? Did adults always love you?

(As a child the more you sought approval, the less likely you were to rebel.)

Did you only date boys you could bring home, the ones with good manners?

(Boys like this were probably just another facet of your search for approval.)

Did you have a sibling with problems? Did your parents have difficulties you knew about (a battle against illness, impoverished childhoods)?

(Maybe you sensed that your parents had more than their share of problems. The root of compliance is sometimes an overwhelming sense of responsibility and guilt: You can't be bad, you just couldn't do it to them.)

Were you a Girl Scout? Sang in church? Were you a joiner?

(Perhaps as a child you needed to conform more than you needed to rebel.)

Were your parents proper, concerned about what other people thought? Were they always concerned with the way they looked, dressed, behaved, and so on?

(Your family message may have been that acceptance and love come through approval. Perhaps only as an adult can you chance rejection.)

The way your parents felt about sex, was it hard to imagine that they ever did it themselves?

(Straitlaced parents may contribute to why it's taken you so long to find out that sex is fun.)

Even if you had your own ideas about things, did you always defer to your parents?

(You worked at being good even if it meant giving up part of yourself.)

Were your creative talents encouraged only to the point that they made you more attractive or capable as a wife and mother?

(Your family value system may have encouraged the taking on of roles and not finding out who you really are.)

Although you didn't realize it then, looking back, do you feel that your parents (especially your mother) dominated or controlled your life?

(You failed to question it then and are only doing it now.)

When everyone else was getting married, did you too?

(Prevailing values are never questioned by good girls.)

UNLEARNING THE PATTERN

Are you becoming increasingly convinced that your need is to rebel and that it drives you into a lovestyle that you continually repeat? If you find that your pattern and past resembles Pat's, this may help.

Focus on your need to break away. Propriety has been replaced with abandon, but all the years have had their effect. You cannot simply shed your background. Even with its limitations, it's yours. You cannot be satisfied with the men whom you choose to help you rebel. They are too far from a major part of your personal history.

Write down your need.

My need is to break away.

The trick is to keep this need in view. Think of strategic spots where it will best remind you of your pattern, and put it there to intercept you.

The next time you draw up a list of "eligible" men for a party, write your need in bold letters at the top of it. Finish it off with your need on the bottom, too.

If you are artistically and creatively inclined, design a special way of presenting your need to yourself. You might paint or draw it. The next time you attend a ceramics class you can make this reminder your special project. If you smoke dope, put your need with the paraphernalia as a reminder of your drive to break away.

Put one in the frame with your children's picture. Do you have a memento, a special gift from your mother (the pearls she gave you when you were married)? Put a reminder of your need with this.

Keep it with your deposit slips when you bank your alimony; use it to jar your unconscious need into the foreground of your thinking. The more you think about your need, the more you can gain control of your emotional life.

Your Relationship Analysis

Are you beginning to sense that a need to break away may underlie your adult relationships? Give some thought to how it may have influenced your interactions with men all through your life. Here are the men in Pat's early years:

Evan, a younger brother
While schoolwork was never a problem for Pat, it was a source of difficulty for Evan. Mother would encourage Pat to help him by saying, "That's what big sisters are for." It was taken for

granted that though college was nice for everyone, a man really
needed it. In high school when Evan showed promise for football, the family went all out. They attended all of his home games
and frequently Father traveled to away games. Knowing how
important the team was to Evan, Pat would often help him with
homework so he wouldn't miss practice. Though she did resent
the extra chores, Pat never refused them. Since her divorce and
her move to Santa Barbara, her brother has been very cool toward
Pat, telling her directly that her behavior and life-style are a
disgrace to the family.

Clark, a fifth-grade classmate

At eleven Pat was enrolled in Madam Le Vrone's social dance
class for young ladies and gentlemen. When everyone was given
a chance to find a partner, Pat was always chosen by Clark. He
was the neatest boy in class, she remembered, and had blond
wavy hair, and used to say "yes, sir" whenever he spoke to the
teacher. Clark was her "date" for the final dance; he came to
"pick her up" at home. All four parents couldn't get over how
adorable they looked, and Pat still has an eight-by-ten photo-
graph—"I must have been wearing six crinolines"—that was
taken when they were crowned May Prince and Princess.

Chet, a junior from a school in the next district

Chet lived fairly close to Pat but, because of zoning, he went to
a different school. He was three years older than she and they
met through a mutual friend, Robin. They frequently hung out
together at Robin's house and after a time they started to neck
and pet heavily, sometimes in Robin's basement, other times in
Chet's car. Despite this relationship, Pat never invited Chet to a
school or church dance or brought him home. The following
year Chet attended Pat's school and she panicked. Terrified he
would tell people about her, she avoided him at all costs. When
she did finally see him, she went as white as a ghost; her hands
became clammy, her heart raced, and she acted as if she didn't
know him. Relief came only when he graduated at the end of the
school year and left town to go to college.

Reed, her "almost fiancé," a college junior

Pat's mother met Reed first, while he was working as a swim instructor during his summer break. She mentioned him at home
and arranged for him to meet Pat. She thought they'd make a
"nifty" couple, and although Pat was only a senior in high school,

before long they were dating each other exclusively and talking about their future. Toward the spring Pat's mother suggested they have dinner with Reed's family. The meeting did not go well. It started off with Reed's father declaring that religion was oppressive and ended with a growing realization that Reed's mother had a drinking problem. There was total silence in the car on the way home. Once home, Mother went to her room, closed the door, took some aspirin for a terrible headache, and only said, "Who would have believed Reed came from that family? It's a good thing you're not engaged to that boy. Anyway you're too young to get so serious." Within several weeks Pat was dating other people, she had decided she was too young to get married.

Mr. Rappaport, speech and drama teacher

Mr. Rappaport was different. He was really an actor, not a teacher at all, and Pat had a crush on him from the first class when he read poetry out loud. She chose all the classes he taught as her electives, and joined the clubs he served as faculty advisor. She never told anyone, not even her best friend, about her feelings. He was the most fascinating teacher she ever had. The greatest classes were those when he talked about his adventures working with a Broadway road company.

Pat's need to break away affects her earliest relationships with men in a number of different ways. Her brother, Evan, is an example of a relationship based on compliance and submission. As brother and sister they epitomize the style of their family, where female-male roles are well defined and Pat acted the way she was expected to. She never challenged, questioned, or got angry about, for example, the pre-eminence Evan's future success was accorded by her parents (even when it might have been at her expense). Carrying on in the style of his family, Evan self-righteously gets angry at Pat's efforts to assert herself.

Clark, even though only eleven, is her parents' ideal. What they want is to pair this "perfect little gentleman" with their princess. Pat offers no objection.

Experimenting sexually with Chet is an attempt by Pat to rebel. Despite all the prohibitions against sex, Pat manages, but only away from her home territory, to do something she wants. Later the fear that someone may find out she isn't "a good girl" is overwhelming.

And what of her "almost fiancé"? Pat becomes involved with Reed because he gets Mother's seal of approval; he makes a good impression and has a fine appearance. However, once it's clear his background doesn't fit her family's scheme of things, he's no longer acceptable. Typically, Pat accepts this rejection with barely a whimper of protest.

Finally there is actor-teacher Mr. Rappaport. He is attractive because at least in her dreams and fantasies he transports Pat away. But such romance is not permissible, so she can never even tell anyone her secret, and instead she turns her energies to become his best student.

Does your need emerge in your early experiences? Which cousin, uncle, friend, teacher, lover, or colleague may have been an expression of your need? What of your early relationships with men? Were they marked by compliance, submission, acceptance? When you did consider doing something that was different from the preconceived and permissible, did it have to happen only in your imagination? Did it make you unbearably guilty? Did you feel compelled to end or hide relationships that were unacceptable? Did you ignore any angry feelings you may have had or did you simply not permit them to surface? Were you the "good girl"?

Once you've clarified how your need has affected your past relationships, you can focus on the influence it has in your present experiences with men.

Men You Should Be Alert To

As important as the men in your life have been in helping you to find yourself, they are of limited value now. In fact, they are a liability. A hard declaration, but true. They cannot offer you your wish to have a lasting attachment. So you must be alert to men who

Don't talk about the future
Are impoverished artists or poets with creative blocks
Are boyish forty-year-olds
Don't own a suit
Stimulate you intellectually and emotionally but don't want to get serious
Are just good in bed, but—
Are only looking for an affair, a fling
Work just long enough to get on unemployment
Need a place to crash "for a few days"
Want to travel before they settle down
Wear T shirts with sayings (for example, "Chicken farmers raise better cocks")
Are young enough to be your son

Consciously avoid alliances with these men, or you will act out your unsuccessful lovestyle. They herald the re-enactment of your pattern.

You can diminish the power of your need. Remove it as a hidden force in your love life and you will be free to begin a mature relationship with a man.

13

Allison

Allison was arguing with her boyfriend in the back of the lobby. She had had arguments like this before in her life.

"Look, Allison, I am not going up there. It was a mistake to even come this far. I don't know how I let you talk me into this. Look, you told me your mother said, 'It's either me or him.' I'm not walking into another person's home if the people there hate me because I'm black. So what if you told her I'm coming? Believe me, I won't be missed. Just go up there and relax, but without me. If you want to see me tomorrow, I'll be at the ballet studio. If not, I'll . . . I'll understand."

Allison got into the elevator fuming. She wasn't so in love with Kariim that she worried about losing him, but the thought of walking into the party alone after she had given her parents an ultimatum about Kariim made her furious. "Damn it. My mother's gonna give me a knowing smile, like she won and I lost. But I'll set her straight."

Before Allison even walked through the door, she shot a glance at her mother and said through her teeth, "Don't you dare say one word to me about Kariim ever again. Just stay out of my life."

The look on Allison's face caught Cousin Roberta's eye. "At the risk of my own life I'll tell you, Allison, that you look

234

as if you might strike the next person who speaks to you. What's going on?"

"Just the usual crap."

"Let's talk about it."

Allison didn't refuse. It may have been her thirtieth birthday, but it was hardly her party; Mother had invited most of the guests. Instead of parading around to all of them, she'd close herself in a bedroom with Roberta and talk. Allison didn't care if she ruined the evening for her mother. In fact she felt her mother deserved it, since she had ruined hers.

Later in the evening Allison came downstairs with two huge shopping bags and Pat, the doorman, called a cab for her. Her father told her to call once she was home. He hated her loft, and his parting words were typical: "I don't care how many locks are on the door, it's not the sort of place for you to be living. And why can't you have a girl as a roommate instead of that carpenter and his little boy?" Allison left with barely a good-bye or thank you, even though her father slipped a ten-dollar bill into her hand.

On the ride downtown Allison thought about Kariim. At this point he was probably so insulted that he wouldn't want anything to do with her. Who could blame him? The one time Kariim came to the house her father barely said a word to him. Didn't Father realize she was not his sweet little girl anymore?

In the last few years not much that she had done met with his approval, even her work. Her jewelry cooperative didn't even rate as employment from his point of view. "And I'm doing the best work of my life. Luciano even said my titanium designs are some of the best he's ever seen. If I would finally have that one-woman show Luciano's been promising me, I'm sure I'd get reviewed. But Luciano probably isn't anxious for that to happen."

Allison had an on-again, off-again relationship with Luciano. It never amounted to anything serious, since he had a wife he was planning to bring over soon from Italy. It was

Luciano who had gotten her pregnant the first time. When in her fourth month she asked her mother for five hundred dollars for an abortion, her mother made her swear she wouldn't tell her father. Once over her initial shock, Mother questioned the amount needed. Allison told her, "I don't think I'm ever going to marry, so I toyed with the idea of having the child. When I finally decided I wasn't ready for that yet, it was too late for an inexpensive vacuum procedure. But if you want a little *bambino*, Grandma, you can keep your five hundred dollars."

It wasn't until months later, in one of their "on-again" moments, that Allison told Luciano she had even been pregnant. All this had little effect on their working relationship. Luciano kept praising her out of one side of his mouth and telling her she needed more training out of the other. It was infuriating. One minute, she felt as if she was ready to take off; another, she felt as if she couldn't make it without him.

"If only I had my degree in architecture. Then I wouldn't have to work for someone. I could be on my own."

Allison blamed the lack of a diploma on her parents; her father's fulfilling his threat to not pay for school if she didn't finish at the end of her fifth year had screwed her up. Her senior thesis had to be finished on time, "or else." That's why she had copied parts of an old thesis she had found in the library. How could she have guessed her professor would remember a paper from ten years ago? Plagiarism. They had forced her into doing the one and only thing for which you can get kicked out of school. Her parents were mortified, especially when they had to cancel the graduation party, for which the invitations were already in the mail.

With its meter reading six dollars, the taxi pulled up to Allison's loft. She handed the driver the ten still in her hand and told him to keep the change. Loaded down with the bags, she knocked on her front door with her foot. A sleepy little boy let her in.

"Christopher, don't ever grow up. Things just go from bad
to worse. No matter who you find in this world, there's always something that gets in the way. You're so cute now, but
once you're big, you'll give the girls grief, just like any man."

Christopher, hearing nothing of what she said, wandered
back to his loft bed. Dumping the presents in a corner and
knowing she wouldn't open them, Allison suddenly realized
she'd forgotten her pocketbook uptown. It was something
she needed, the keys for the studio were inside. Allison
didn't care how late it was, her father would just have to
bring it down tonight.

She called home. Her father, hearing her voice, said he'd
been waiting for her call.

"Sorry to disappoint you, but I haven't been raped on the
way upstairs. Actually, I'm not calling you to tuck you in. I
left my bag at your place and I need it. Tonight."

"Tonight?"

"Look, if you're not coming, there's always the subway. I'll
be there in fifteen minutes," Allison said, slamming down the
receiver.

Despite her threat Allison never moved to the front door.
She started to undress. The phone rang. She didn't rush to
pick it up. "Let it ring a few times," she thought. "He has it
coming to him."

DISCERNING THE PATTERN

If you could catch Allison in a quiet moment, she would
say that all she wanted was to be free to enjoy a man and
make a life on her own with him. To have a relationship
without anyone interfering. This is her acknowledged wish.
What Allison is not cognizant of is that underlying unconscious need to get back at her parents. The driving force in

her relationships is this need to retaliate and cause her parents pain.

She is attracted to men who are anathema to her parents. A man unbearable to them because of his social, moral, or religious values is one to whom she responds. Her parents are people who are acutely upset by the thought of their daughter's romantic involvements with these men.

Kariim, a black dancer, is sure to shock them. As is Luciano, a married designer, who exploits Allison at work and who shows no interest nor takes any responsibility for getting her pregnant. He especially is a parents' nightmare, the worst type of man they could envision for Allison. The striking feature of her pattern is that objectionable men are always brought to her parents' attention, and inevitably tension, aggravation, arguments, conflict, and misery follow.

Not understanding the role her need plays in her affair, Allison only registers disappointment. Something always interferes with her relationships and ruins them. This creates a deep sense of frustration; men are nothing but grief, and no relationship can ever go smoothly or work out. A life of her own with a man seems an impossibility. Need overpowers wish. It is even more important for her to hurt her parents than to be happy.

How did her past experiences generate this?

Friends and neighbors who knew Allison, even as a teenager, had a uniform reaction. Shaking their heads, they'd ask themselves, "What did her parents ever do to deserve a daughter like that?" They didn't and still don't know how to account for such a difficult child in such a nice family. What could it be?

"Mother was already a pediatrician when she married my father. He was just starting on his own in real estate. Even though my mother wasn't sure she wanted kids, they started a family right away. I guess they felt pressured because of their age. Keith was born ten months after their wedding. Justin came eighteen months later." Allison's

ALLISON'S CYCLE

WISH
___

(recognized)

Enjoying a man
and making a life
of her own with
him

NEED
___

(unrecognized)

Getting back at
and hurting her
parents

POOR
JUDGMENT
___

Attraction to a
man who is the
"wrong" race,
creed, color, class,
pedigree—a man
who is anathema
to her parents

FRUSTRATION
___

The conviction
that men always
mean grief, that no
relationship can
ever go smoothly

CHOICE
___

Kariim, a dancer
Luciano, a married
designer

DISAPPOINTMENT
___

Things interfering
with her relation-
ship; something
always coming up
to ruin things

EXPERIENCE
___

Relationships full
of tension, aggra-
vation, arguments,
hostility

mother would have stopped after two, but her father had really wanted a girl. Two years later Allison was conceived. "My mother always said the best way to have kids is one right after another so you can have everyone out of diapers right away. So I wondered why my brothers came so quickly and then things slowed down. I don't think her work was the reason. Even before Keith my mother had decided against private practice. Ever since I can remember, she's always worked from nine to three in a clinic. With three children she felt she couldn't handle full-time work. I think she was better off that way. Sometimes I wonder why she's a pediatrician; she's not really wild about kids. Her first love is research."

When Allison was born, her father was delighted, but this proved a mixed blessing, especially as she got older. Her father was attentive, but it was sometimes too much. It made her self-conscious. "When I was thirteen and came home from school with a friend, I'd try and avoid my father. I got embarrassed when he'd hug me in front of my friends and keep me for a half hour asking about school and telling me about his day. He always seemed to ask more questions than other parents did. I think my father talked to me even more than he did to my mother. Looking back, I can understand why my father wanted to talk. It wasn't that my parents never communicated, but my mother could put a pile of journals in front of her and spend an entire evening in another world. Only once did I hear them fight about it. Mother said something to the effect that, as a businessman, Dad just couldn't understand her professional interests. She sounded really bitter. I remember my father's words exactly: 'I'm sorry that I'm not what you want me to be, but I never pretended to be anything else.' "

Though Allison never knew exactly what was going on between her parents, she felt its effect. Her parents, especially her father, were overinvolved in her life. There was a double standard in the family. Her father let his sons do what they wanted but was extremely concerned about Allison's behavior. Her parents were overprotective. To her embarrassment, in grade school, Allison was still walked to school long after other children were allowed to go on their own. If it rained, she was the only one whose mother sent the baby-sitter to school with boots. "If I had trouble in class, my mother would go up to 'straighten things out.' Once I had a fight with a girl. Don't you think my mother got hold of the girl and 'told her a thing or two'!"

Allison's childhood remembrances were liberally sprinkled with these moments of embarrassment. She remembers them all too well. What she remembers too is that her feelings about her parents grew negative. "Since I turned thirteen, I've felt as if I wanted to burst every time my parents told me something. I can't explain it, but we're like oil and water."

What adds to Allison's confusion is the fact that whenever she was nasty to her parents, her father would soon after act as if nothing had happened. When she was small and had been "a bad girl" that morning, he would return home in the evening with a doll.

"When I was a teenager, my father hated to see me go to those huge rock concerts. He was livid about my friends, dope, sex, everything. But as I walked out the door, he'd always shove a bill in my pocket for a cab ride home."

Allison looked forward to college as a way of getting her parents off her back. When she got accepted to a school within commuting distance from home, she went only on the condition that she could live near the campus. It didn't last.

"My parents were always worried that I was smoking grass, having sex, carrying on. So when I came down with mono in my sophomore year, my father used it as the perfect excuse to get me home. I couldn't take care of myself, he said. So he wasn't going to pay for my apartment. I'd have to live home. What else could I do? Starting with the spring semester I commuted."

What does all this mean in Allison's adult life? How is she affected by these experiences?

Allison's parents never got what they wanted or expected from each other. Her mother found an outlet for her disappointment in work, and her father turned to Allison. Unwittingly he used her as a way of coping with his difficult situation. He was lonely; he needed his daughter. And he badly needed his daughter to need him. His overprotectiveness and overinvolvement, his willingness to forgive her no matter what, are to this day the only ways he knows of holding his daughter.

The sum total of this is that Allison feels trapped by her family, rejected by her mother, used by and dependent on her father. She can't live with them or without them. This is what Allison brings to her adult life, this terrible sense of being used, rejected, and enveloped at the same time. Her anger at this unbearable dilemma is such that it totally dominates her life. The need to retaliate for this untenable situation is the major component in her relationships. A man is chosen by her only as a vehicle, an object, a weapon, for her assault on her parents. Her choices are not based on what they are for her but rather what these relationships can do to her parents. Allison is so consumed by this pervasive anger that she unwittingly sacrifices her happiness in order to inflict pain.

Learning from the Present

Is Allison's lovestyle anything like yours? Does it strike you that the men in your life may be serving your need to hurt your parents? Do you end up completely vulnerable in relationships that drive your parents up a wall? Are your lovers objectionable—not just unacceptable—men who treat you in such a way that it can only bring your parents anguish?

Is there always a problem about your relationship, an insurmountable difference (you're white, he's black; you're black, he's white; you're Jewish, he's a practicing Catholic; you're heterosexual, he's bisexual; he's a great lover but he's got a wife in another city; your parents survived Auschwitz, he's German)?

(Differences between people, no matter how extreme, are not insurmountable. What is insurmountable, as long as you act from your need, is your inability to give up using these men to get at your parents.)

Is your life-style very different from your parents'? You don't live the way they'd want to see you? You don't have the kind of job they'd expect?

(With your need you evoke disapproval continually. It's not simply that you are different but that you want them to react, want them to be irritated. You rub it in.)

Do you live in a bad neighborhood, although you might be able to afford better?

(With your need this is not an economic decision but an emotional one. You do it for the impact it has on your parents.)

Do you take risks and your parents know about it (for example, taking the subway alone at night; waiting tables in a dive; hitchhiking; smuggling joints on your trip to Europe; driving after you drink)?

(The dead giveaway that your need is in operation: You make sure your parents get wind of your goings on.)

Do you find yourself stuck for money? You end up taking

money from your parents, even though you swore you wouldn't?

(This symbolizes the nature of your relationship to your parents; you're angrily dependent on them.)

Are your boyfriends reluctant to meet your parents? Do they resist or avoid it ("I'll just wait in the car")? Do you insist?

(Men try to steer clear of your parents because they know they're not approved of. Your insistence is a sure sign you're using them for just that reason.)

Do you tell men that they're the cause of discord with your parents?

(You do because with your need it's the turmoil around the relationship, not the man and his feelings, that's paramount.)

Do your parents die a thousand deaths when you bring a man home?

(Unconsciously that's what you want. Why else would you force things into such an open confrontation.)

Do you manage to let your parents know about the men in your life? Do they happen to see you with him, call when he's there, hear through a friend?

(If they always seem to find out accidentally, it's time you gave up believing it's an accident. It's your need at work!)

Does everyone (friends, neighbors, relatives, doormen) seem to get wind of your relationships and the difficulties it causes?

(You can't have a private life with your need. If your personal life were yours alone, your parents might not know enough to feel miserable.)

Have you told your parents you're not interested in marriage, children, and so on, even though you know they wouldn't like anything more than to see you settle down? Have you tossed around the idea of getting pregnant and being a single parent?

(Angry, empty threats are your trademark.)

Do you live or work near your parents? Do you have contact with people they know? Do you call or come around to their home? Do you ask them favors (for example, to borrow their car or their vacation house)?

(The boundaries between your parents' life and your life are never clearly drawn. You need to intrude into one another's lives.)

Learning from the Past

Did your mother take care of your needs but was never terribly warm or motherly? She wasn't wild about children?

(It hurts being dependent on a mother you sense feels stuck with you. Your revenge is to show her just how stuck with you she really is!)

Was your mother involved in her own pursuits (such as work, charity, church)?

(You may have understood her interest in her world as disinterest in you. Angry for giving you up, you don't allow her that calm retreat.)

Once you were older, did your mother take an active part in your life only when you had trouble or difficulty?

(At least you found one way to grab her attention. As an adult it's still the chief way you make contact with her.)

Have you heard the refrain "But you were such a good baby, such a sweet little girl"?

(You probably were. A need such as yours starts to surface only when you begin moving toward independence.)

Did your mother have a conflict over her career and her family?

(Perhaps the real core of her conflict was her limited capacity for mothering. As an adult, especially with men, you make it clear to her just how badly she failed at it.)

Was your father overinvolved and overprotective?

(His tacit message was "you can't do it—let me." You are full of rage because you believe deep down he was right, you can't.)

Were your father's affections and attentions sometimes too much, even to the point where they could become embarrassing?

(You were a kind of sacrificial lamb, a mother's offering to keep a father quiet. You felt it and hated it.)

Did you give your parents a lot of grief and they never said no (for example, when you wrecked the car, they gave you a new one)?

(Hostility is generally part of the struggle to separate from parents. But no one ever sets limits on you, called a halt to your abuse, so the struggle goes on ad infinitum.)

Did your father always do things for you (gave you gifts or money)? It never stopped no matter how difficult you were?

(This is a kind of emotional seduction: Your father will do anything, will endure anything, to keep you hooked on him.)

Did you argue a lot with your parents? You got along

like oil and water, but in a pinch you went to them to bail you out?

(The core of your problem rests in an intense love-hate relationship. You can't live with them, you can't live without them.)

Were you the "problem child" of the family? Although you might have had siblings, did the family action center on you?

(This family notoriety is a measure of parental overinvolvement in your life, an overinvolvement you still cannot shake.)

Did you sense your parents were disappointed in each other? Your parents weren't as close as they seemed to outsiders?

(Emotional disappointment is often the reason a parent uses a child as the central focus of life. Your anger at them may lie in feeling used by them.)

Did you feel your father was overinvested in you?

(Perhaps he needed you to feel good, to bring him happiness. It's an unfair burden for a child to carry. No wonder you fight so hard to shake it off.)

Bear in mind that these questions are not a test; there is no way to pass or fail. Instead they are designed to draw your attention to the behavior and feelings that are often associated with an unconscious need to hurt a parent.

UNLEARNING THE PATTERN

Once you have reviewed this pattern and feel ready to accept the nature of your need, you can begin to work on breaking the powerful hold it has over you.

You can begin this process by focusing on your lovestyle. Your need to hurt your parents has its roots in a deep and abiding rage against being trapped—of feeling unable to live with them or without them. Your men are unwittingly the vehicle for your revenge. You are not going to bring pleasure to your parents under any circumstances. In fact the men you respond to are always in some way objectionable, even abhorrent, to them. Often you get yourself involved with men who treat you shabbily, and without being aware you accept this treatment because you want your parents' reaction. ("You're destroying me. I can't stand to see this. I won't have him in my house. What did I ever do to deserve this?")

The anger controls and consumes your life. Ultimately your need to hurt them leads you to hurt yourself.

This pattern can be interrupted. It requires a major effort to keep the need conscious. Only when you are consciously thinking about your need can you prevent it from driving you on.

In order for your effort to be effective, you should use cards as a stimulus to jar you into actively thinking about this. Each should be tied into the activities typical of your pattern.

One should be kept in the pocket of your coat. The pocket into which your father invariably slips a twenty-dollar bill. When you reach for the money, read it. Think about how this "payoff" fits into your pattern. Keep one by the phone when you call your parents to ask for something. One can go in your checkbook. When you go to pay the rent, find yourself short and think about asking for help; use it to remind you of how your need keeps you dependent.

Put one on the door of your apartment, the one in the wrong neighborhood, shared with the wrong person. Think about what your living arrangements mean in light of your need to hurt your parents.

Sneak a copy into your old bedroom at your parents' home. The next time you're about to fight with your parents

at their place, go look at it. Force yourself to think about the
real nature of your anger toward them.

Think of other strategic spots for these reminders. Disrupt
your patterns. The more you consciously think about it, the
less likely you are to act it out unwittingly. *The more you
work on replacing thought with action, the greater is your
capacity for change.*

Your Relationship Analysis

While you are working on this, you can proceed to
another phase of the process of change: relationship analysis.

As you become aware of the role anger and retaliation
play in your lovestyle, try and apply this insight to a review
of your past relationships with men. This can help you appreciate how pervasive your need is.

Allison's relationship analysis follows.

Justin, her brother

Even as teenagers he and Allison fought. It often began with
Allison asking him for help with homework, since he was a math
whiz. They'd sit at the dining room table while Allison worked
on her problems. If Justin would interrupt her to ask how she
was doing, Allison got nasty. He got furious in return. Invariably,
her parents had to break things up because they'd end up hitting
each other. "Justin still can't stand me. He'd even told me if it
wasn't for me, my family wouldn't have any problems."

Bruce, the superintendent's son

When Allison was seven, she'd come home from school and play
with Bruce, who was nine. Often they'd play in the basement of
the apartment house until Allison's mother came home. One
afternoon Bruce's father found them playing doctor. He was
furious; he hit Bruce and brought Allison to her mother, asking
that she not play with his son anymore. Her parents were terribly embarrassed; every worker in the building would know by
the next day.

Tony, a fourteen-year-old high school classmate
Tony was Allison's boyfriend in ninth grade. Hanging out at his father's pizza parlor or closing themselves in Allison's bedroom were their main activities. She brought Tony home so often that her mother would snap, "Doesn't this boy have a home of his own?" Their going steady came to a dead stop after Allison was suspended from school for cutting classes and smoking cigarettes with Tony and several other boys in the boys' bathroom.

Mike, a young attendant in the garage where her father kept the family car
When Allison was seventeen, she ran away with Mike, making it all the way to Oregon. Stopped for speeding, the police found pills in the car and they were arrested. Only a desperate collect phone call to Father, the first since she had run off, got them the money needed for bail and an airline ticket for Allison to fly home.

Monsieur Packer
As a high school senior, Allison went on a foreign study program to live with a family in Lyons, France. She was reluctant to go, but after her disastrous trip to Oregon the year before, it was either working in Father's office during the summer and observing a strict curfew or France.

Right from the start things were not good; her hostess acted jealous every time her husband spoke to Allison. This made Allison very angry, and she decided to annoy the woman even more by deliberately flirting with her husband. Four weeks later Madame Packer caught Allison kissing Monsieur Packer in the orchard. The program leader was summoned, and after obtaining money from her parents for a plane ticket home, he escorted her personally to the Paris airport.

The need to hurt her parents also had repercussions in Allison's early relationships. With Justin, Allison has a relationship that parallels her parents'. She draws him into being involved with her, is dependent on him, then becomes terribly resentful—"fighting mad"—about it.

Bruce, in a way, is a forerunner of the men to come. As with Tony and Mike, she finds an unsuitable boy and manages to cause an embarrassing scene involving him.

Typically, everything happens right under her parents' noses and, predictably, her escapade ends with her parents "bailing her out" of whatever mess she has gotten into. Something they never refuse to do.

Monsieur Packer is a man with whom Allison creates one more disaster requiring parental intervention. Sex is a big part in all of these relationships, too.

Allison's relationship analysis suggests the pervasiveness of her need as the themes of anger, dependence, and retaliation emerge.

Men You Should Be Alert To

If you see yourself in Allison, you must be alert to men who are wildly objectionable to your parents because they

Are antiestablishment
Advocate causes that are anathema to your family
Seem to represent insurmountable differences in religious beliefs or status
Are twice your age
Mistreat you
Are dope heads
Are on the farthest borders of society
Are bums, drifters, leeches
Are of an ethnic background you know your parents cannot come to terms with
Are in the "wrong" line of work

Stop using men as weapons. It's something you must do in order to begin love responsibly and truly.

Jessica

When the phone at the other end rang for the fifth time, Jessica knew that Howard had fallen back to sleep. It was only 7:30 A.M., so she let it ring for another second. If he still didn't pick up, she'd board the plane and call him from D.C. Suddenly Jessica could hear Howard fumbling with the receiver.

"Hello, JJ," he mumbled, knowing that it could only be her. Jessica smiled. JJ was a nickname from her Vermont boarding school that had stuck with her over the years. She had known Howard even then. He was a junior at the boys' school nearest her girls' school. Even though they had only started dating years later in New York, he rarely called her anything but her old nickname. It was a sign of their common history.

"Howard, the plane's delayed a few minutes, so I called to tell you to have a good week. And don't forget, I'll be at Kennedy at six P.M. this Friday," she added.

"JJ, don't you think that after fourteen months of this routine you can trust me to remember your arrival time?"

Jessica felt the blood rising in her cheeks. She was embarrassed. But it was like her to double-check, not to leave anything in doubt. Most people thought of her as terribly efficient. At work it was a real asset; in the Federal Reserve there were always a million items to keep tabs on, a million people to get back to, and Jessica answered every letter and returned every call. She alone knew that her efficiency was actually motivated by her distrust. She could never bring herself to delegate anything because she could never be sure that anyone would follow through. She didn't like relying on people and she didn't like being taken by surprise. Often her concern seemed exaggerated. If Howard ever didn't come at the time he'd promised, she would become terribly anxious within a few minutes. "He's had an accident," she would think. Her fear would start to mount as she'd picture in her mind what could have happened. Thinking the worst was a habit Jessica couldn't break. She felt annoyed at herself for letting her imagination run wild, and at times like this she'd fight the fear by trying to be terribly rational.

The boarding call interrupted her phone conversation. A quick good-bye, and a moment later she was on the shuttle to Washington. When she looked up and spotted Scott coming down the aisle, she caught his attention and pointed to the empty seat next to her. Frankly, Jessica thought he was a bloody bore; the one and only thing he could talk about was banking, but she welcomed the chance to occupy her mind on the trip and get back into her work. Before she knew it, they were taxiing into Dulles Airport.

Scott's wife was waiting for him, so Jessica was alone in the limousine for the forty-minute ride to the office. Seated in the back as she was, the Lucite partition kept her from even chatting with the driver. Without knowing exactly when it started, Jessica found her heart begin to beat quickly. She found herself breathing rapidly and then she broke out in a cold sweat. Frightened by all these sensations, she thought she might be having a heart attack or going crazy. But she fought the panic. "I'll call the doctor from the office," she told herself. "If something's really wrong, he's nearby." The thought of going directly to the doctor was out of the question. She hadn't ever missed work on account of illness, and she wouldn't start now.

Her heart was still pounding as she rode up in the elevator. The minute she stepped through the door, Frieda, her secretary, announced that an emergency executive board meeting had been called. She had ten minutes to prepare for it. Only when Jessica entered the board room a quarter of an hour later did she realize that her "heart attack" syndrome had vanished.

The meeting broke at noon, and she went off to join Jim Courtney for lunch. Like her, he too was from Atlanta, and had been a friend of her oldest brother. He had come to Washington two years before she had, and Jessica was grateful for his company. They had a lot in common, and even though they were just friends, they often went out together. Besides, in Washington society you really needed an escort. When she walked into the restaurant, it gave Jessica a good feeling to see him sitting at their usual table. *The way I feel right now you'd think Court was my boyfriend. Well, there's a lot about him that's right for me. Maybe I just don't give my feelings for Court enough credence.*

At the table Jessica found herself going over a checklist of Court's qualities: handsome, bright, curious. "So much more to him than Howard," she mused. So much more interesting, fun, always there when she needed him. Jessica didn't really hear what Court was saying. She tried to look involved, responsive, but she was absorbed in her thoughts about him.

Her thoughts went back to her affair with Howard. In Court's presence her enthusiasm for her lover was quickly evaporating, and she found herself thankful she had never moved in with Howard. He just wasn't what she had expected; she had become bored by him. *Really,* she thought, *this affair is six months too long already. I wish I could wind things down with him. But I just can't dump someone. I'll do it gradually. This weekend I'm going to suggest we see other people. And next week I'm going to make up*

some excuse about a business trip. I hope he takes the hint.
Let him break off with me. That way I won't hurt him so
much.

A month passed. Alone in Washington and having lied to
Howard that she couldn't come to New York because of a
bad cold, Jessica's relationship with Court changed. Things
happened very naturally; they spent the entire weekend together as lovers. But lying near Court on that first Sunday
morning, she couldn't help feeling a little disappointed with
their lovemaking. Court was too polite, too stiff. Having
faked an orgasm, she hoped sex would get better once he felt
more relaxed.

With Court still asleep and things so quiet and still, Jessica knew she could really get caught up in an endless series
of doubts about their relationship. "I am simply not going to
get carried away," she swore to herself. *There are millions*
of other things I have to be concerned about. It's the end of
the quarter, and my report has to be filed in three days.
Now, if I get in early tomorrow, I can have Frieda start
typing by nine A.M. Yet trying hard to have work occupy
her thoughts didn't do the trick this time. Court's warm
sleeping body next to her made it impossible. Jessica was
beginning to feel terrible. There was no going back to being
just friends.

"No man seems to have all the qualities I want. I'm beginning to think no man exists out there for me."

As she contemplated the men in her life, Jessica stared at
Court and was suddenly struck by a thought: With his gray-
streaked hair, Court looked like he could be the older
brother of her one-time boyfriend, Paul.

It was a year ago, but she could vividly recall Paul the
first time she'd met him. Dressed in his formal riding outfit,
he had greeted her at the Southampton Summer Horse
Show. Recognizing her name, he explained that he had been
the Dartmouth roommate of her boarding-school friend,
Howard. "What an irony," Jessica told herself. "I meet Paul

because I know Howard. Then I get together with Howard again because of Paul."

The week of the horse show was glorious. There was a big barbecue at the estate of Paul's parents. Then they hosted a formal dance that was something out of a Scott Fitzgerald novel. The fact that Paul's horse won a ribbon made it all the more exciting. Jessica enjoyed Paul and his family. Although Paul seemed to talk only of his horses, she thought that once the show was over, his other interests would come out. Anyway there was something really solid about him, and that felt good.

The problem with Paul didn't take too long to surface. Once the show and the summer were over, Paul was a different person. Finishing his last year at Harvard Business School, he couldn't find anything to talk about but business, business, and more business. "How could anyone be so boring?" Jessica thought, remembering that more than once she had fallen asleep in the midst of his conversation. Thankfully, when the next semester started, she saw him only on weekends.

Christmas of that year Howard moved to New York. During the vacation the three of them spent time together; they were inseparable. Once Paul returned to Boston, Jessica started to spend her weeknights with Howard. In the course of time, without thinking much about it, Howard became the important man in her life.

Jessica's thoughts were interrupted. Court stirred. He was about to awaken. She'd get up and squeeze some fresh juice for him and grab an aspirin for herself.

DISCERNING THE PATTERN

If you asked Jessica about the men in her life, she'd probably say something very reasonable like, "I just want a man who can match me, not that I'm so smart or so talented or so good. But I have a lot of interests. I wonder if a man really exists out there for me." In short, Jessica's conscious *wish* is to have a man who can fit her exactly and totally. Yet underlying this consciously expressed wish, Jessica has an unrecognized *need* to avoid feeling abandoned, and it is a driving, dominant force in her life. She only allows men into her life who pose no risk. They are solid, reliable, predictable, and along with that unimaginative, rigid, and unexciting, especially when it comes to sex. In her unconscious attempt to avoid abandonment she is drawn to men who are known quantities: Court because he is a family friend, has come recommended by her brother, has an excellent reputation as a lawyer, and has come through for Jessica for a long period before becoming her lover. Howard has similar attributes. He has been a known quantity from her boarding-school days and is a close friend of her former lover. Paul comes with a perfect pedigree—wealthy Southampton family, Ivy League education and a solid character, a set of credentials that intimates a relationship in which Jessica would be safe, taken care of, not abandoned.

Experience with these men is marked by Jessica's rising boredom and waning interest. While feeling safe, she takes no pleasure or joy in her affairs. Although she quickly realizes that these men are not exciting, that they are no fun and no match for her, she holds on to them. Her need is to prevent separation and it keeps her tied to a man long after she senses her disappointment. Only after another man is on the scene for a while can she safely admit to her frustration, the feeling that this was not love and that the man did not have all the qualities she wants. Not feeling satisfied in her wish to find a man who suits her completely, Jessica is immediately ready to start the search again. Jessica's lovestyle is a continuous cycle in which the end of one relationship is the prelude to the next.

What accounts for Jessica's need to forestall separation

JESSICA'S CYCLE

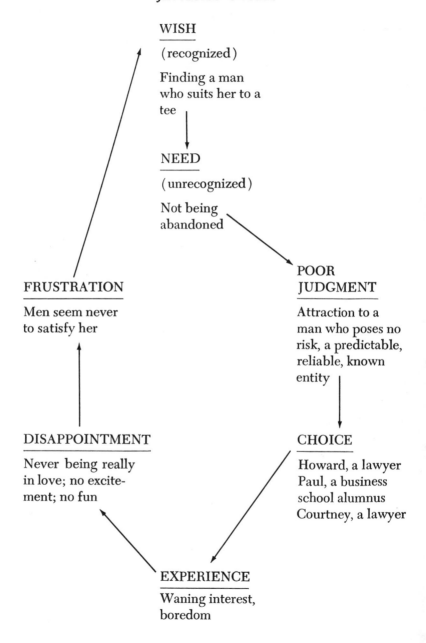

WISH

(recognized)

Finding a man
who suits her to a
tee

NEED

(unrecognized)

Not being
abandoned

FRUSTRATION

Men seem never
to satisfy her

POOR
JUDGMENT

Attraction to a
man who poses no
risk, a predictable,
reliable, known
entity

DISAPPOINTMENT

Never being really
in love; no excite-
ment; no fun

CHOICE

Howard, a lawyer
Paul, a business
school alumnus
Courtney, a lawyer

EXPERIENCE

Waning interest,
boredom

and her fear of being abandoned? How did her early experiences create this need?

When Jessica talks about her childhood, one of the first experiences that comes to her mind is sleep-away camp: "I started at seven and went back every summer till I was sixteen. Once I got over my homesickness that first year, I really loved it. I came home with a duffel bag full of trophies. After that I went back voluntarily."

Jessica remembers her first trip vividly. "Only Dad went with me. He took me as far as Tallahassee, where I stayed at his friend's house overnight. I cried, begging Dad not to leave, but he 'wouldn't have any of it.' I had to go. I was so frightened that night that I didn't close my eyes for one minute. Their daughter was also going to camp. The two of us took a plane to Key West. Once I got there, I ended up being the only one from Atlanta. I cried for a week. Eventually, somehow, I fit in." As planned, Dad picked Jessica up in August, but she sensed something was very wrong. He was too quiet. Back home, when she saw her brother John, it was written on his face—divorce. At dinner her worst fears were confirmed. Jessica's father cleared his throat and said, "Jessica, your mom and I have decided to get a divorce. It has nothing to do with you or your brother. We just find we do not make each other happy. We think it's best this way. I've moved out, but I just live nearby, in Greenfield. We'll still spend plenty of time together." Jessica cried but didn't offer a word of protest. Now she understood why they had insisted she go to camp.

Thinking back on her parents, Jessica describes her mother as unhappy. Although her mother had tried hard to have children (there were several miscarriages between the seven years that separated her and John), Jessica felt that she was never really interested in caring for her. More often than not she was left in a housekeeper's care. Added to this was the fact that her mother was sickly. It was not unusual

for noises to wake Jessica at midnight and to find Mother
gone, admitted to the local hospital.

"Then there was Mother's sleeping problem. She was always taking something to help her through the night. At one
point things really got bad. In fact, when I was in college,
she went for a rest cure at a spa. I'm sure it was a cover for a
detoxification program. I don't really blame her; she was
bored and unhappy. I think her sickness was a way of getting attention. It's a shame about my mother; no one now
would believe she was Phi Beta Kappa."

Jessica had always felt good about her father. "My father
is really nice. He's always treated me like a grown-up, always taken my opinions seriously. We went through some
hard times. He remarried fairly quickly, and my stepmother
is not wild about me. For a long time it hurt me that he
didn't do anything about it."

When Jessica thinks of her family life before the divorce,
she remembers feeling that all the members of her family
were unusual. "We never went camping or on trips together.
We weren't close-knit. My parents weren't like other parents." At fifteen she was shipped off to boarding school. "I
didn't want to do it. I hardly saw my father, plus I had tons
of friends and I was a straight-A student. What was the
point of going away? I guess they felt a girls' school would
be good for me, the right kind of experience, the best girls'
school in the East. It wasn't that Mother wanted to get rid of
me. I was petrified. I wrote home all the time, but I didn't
say that I wanted to come home. I had to stick it out. After a
while I started to like it. Anyway my mother had been
pulled out of boarding school by her mother when she was
homesick, and I think it made her feel strongly about not
pulling me out."

The nearby prep school was full of boys eager to be
friends. Fairly soon Jessica was one of the crowd. Having so
many friends helped her feel more comfortable away from
home. "Some of my best friends are still those boys."

How does this background affect Jessica's adult relationships? Jessica's childhood was filled with separations from important people, separations that were made more difficult by the fact that these important people were not people she felt sure of or close to. Unbeknown to them, their lack of involvement created a sense of insecurity, a feeling that perhaps they would leave her or get rid of her. In some important way this fear was realized in the awkward manner in which they handled her first camp trip and their divorce. It left her feeling tricked and it further undermined her trust in them.

Another source of Jessica's insecurity was her mother's illness and preoccupation with herself. It was as if her mother were there physically but not emotionally. The midnight trips to the hospital only served to frighten an already mistrustful child still further. Only now does Jessica understand that these sudden departures were due to miscarriages and must have been particularly harrowing experiences for her as a small child.

Jessica's feelings of abandonment were intensified when her stepmother became a wedge between her and her father. His unavailability was painful. It left her feeling hurt, vulnerable, unprotected, and lonely. These feelings are brought into her intimate relations with men. Jessica never allows herself to get into a situation where she will be pushed away or left behind. She structures things so that she can handle them. She makes it so that no man is too important or matters too much, that she's never too reliant and cannot get along without someone. Security, continuity, and predictability come first. All lovers are approached rationally. Jessica never dives into a relationship, never risks the unknown. A man must be a known quantity. If he is an old school chum, like Howard, or is first a friend, like Courtney, then a relationship is possible. A good reputation or good family stock like Paul's are the things that allow Jessica to respond to a man, to feel secure. She is attracted to men whose style assures her that they will pull no surprises, that she will not be cast away. To improve on her security system, Jessica never lets go of one man before she has another. What's more, breaking off with a man is not acceptable. Instead she just creates situations where she gradually phases them out.

These feelings carry over into other areas of her life. Jessica learned early that achievement reduces or blocks the pain. The trophies in camp, the straight A's in school, and the executive position in the Federal Reserve, unlike personal relationships, give her a feeling that she is in control.

Is Jessica's lovestyle similar to yours? Is there any resemblance to the way your love life proceeds? Do you end up with solid, reliable men, only to end up feeling bored?

Learning from the Present

Are you on very friendly terms with many men? Is there generally more than one man in your life at one time?

(For you there is security in numbers. If one man drops out, there's always another. It's part of your emotional insurance policy.)

Do you maintain ties to friends from home, camp, boarding school, college?

(You work on keeping connected to people. You're not comfortable severing ties. Being cut off frightens you.)

When you move to a new place, do you look for old faces rather than starting right off with new acquaintances?

(Familiarity makes transitions easier, less unpredictable.)

Do you like to meet men only with an introduction or through a friend?

(You can only handle men in your life who are a known quantity.)

Would you never go to a singles bar, weekend, and so on? Would you never date a stranger?

(These situations are too risky for you. There are too many unknowns.)

Do you never get swept off your feet? Is it more as if a man has to meet your standards, match your interests?

(Evaluation, assessment, comes before involvement. You've got to be careful with men; you can't afford to lose control. Letting go makes you feel too vulnerable to the possibility of loss.)

Do you begin a new relationship while the old one is winding down?

(For you a relationship is a high-risk venture. Like a mountain climber, you don't leave your footing until you know the next step is absolutely sure.)

Do you keep men in a kind of cold storage, on the side, available for a relationship?

(You're never without a possible man near at hand. It helps allay your anxiety about being left high and dry.)

Do you have important relationships that are limited to time or geography? You see them on weekends only, or fly in four times a year?

(You protect yourself by putting limitations on your involvements; you build separations into the relationships. This way you control the separations; they don't just happen to you.)

Do you end up testing men to see how dependable they are, calling them to check and see if they really are home?

(This is the crux of your need: You are never, ever sure of anyone.)

Do you sometimes make a friend into a lover and then, when you find you're not in love, wish you could go back to the way you were?

(Progressing from friend to lover reduces your risk, for you know what to expect. Unfortunately you gain predictability but sacrifice intensity, excitement.)

Do you never break off with a man directly but rather phase him out, giving hints until he just gives up on you?

(Dumping a man makes you feel guilty. Knowing what rejection feels like, you can't bring yourself to do it.)

Can you be affectionate but not generally feel passionate about a man?

(Passion means a loss of control. You can't chance it.)

Do your relationships start gradually?

(You don't negotiate surprises well. Slow but steady is your motto with men.)

If someone doesn't show up or is late, do you think the worst, that something bad has happened, that they've forgotten, and so on?

(You become overwhelmed by the unexpected. You're frightened because even seemingly minor separations cause you to anticipate the worst: abandonment.)

Do you decide whether or not you love a man, that is, it's not a feeling that just comes over you? Do you feel that a relationship with a man is too serious to lose your head over?

(You lead with your head not your heart. It's safer.)

Would you be unlikely to move in with a man or give up your apartment?

(With a man you have to know exactly where you stand. You always leave yourself a way to bail out. Being comfortable means letting down your guard, something you don't allow. At the heart of every relationship lurks distrust.)

For you should a serious relationship come only once— "till death do us part"?

(Marriage means putting yourself in someone else's hands. You can't even think about it unless you were assured it's forever.)

Is your career very important? Do you like to work, not wanting to depend on any man?

(Being independent, you need trust only yourself. Your life is directed by you. Things are certain, reliable.)

Even if everything else in your life goes bust, do you feel that you can always make it on your skill and talent?

(This is your survival tactic. You anticipate the worst and want to be able to cope with it.)

Learning from the Past

Did you experience separation from important people in your life?

(A separation is often part of the emotional history of a woman with your need.)

Did someone important die—a parent, grandparent, caretaker, pet?

(Often a child's mind isn't equipped to comprehend the complexities of death. Rather it is felt to be the ultimate abandonment.)

Were you sent away as a child to camp, relatives, or boarding school when you weren't ready or despite your protests?

(It doesn't always matter who leaves whom, the feeling of rejection can persist.)

Did your parents leave you for prolonged periods of time (for example, for vacations, business, illness)?

(For a young child separation can feel like loss, rejection, abandonment. The reasons for it, though comprehensible to the adult mind, do little to relieve a child's pain.)

Were your parents separated or divorced?

(You learn that even in the face of love declared, the ground can give out from under you.)

Do you have a cool or even bad relationship with your stepparent?

(When a stepparent becomes a wedge between parent and child, the feelings of estrangement and distrust can worsen.)

Would you consider your mother sad, self-involved, leaning toward depression? Were your parents detached or uninvolved?

(Distrust is not the inevitable consequence of separation. But if you lacked emotional support from your parents, it makes trusting that much harder.)

Did you feel that your family wasn't close-knit? Compared with the way others lived, did it seem that you didn't do things together?

(If you don't feel close to the most important people in your life, it is difficult as an adult to let men become important by letting them be close.)

Did your parents make you do things you might not have wanted—"for your own good"?

(You sensed things were done to you. You felt powerless. Resenting this, as an adult, you work toward keeping things under your control.)

Are the good memories in your life related to your achievements in sports or scholarships?

(Doing well meant mastery, control over your fate, independence. No wonder success in work is so important to you.)

Do you recall unexpected or unexplained events in your childhood? Did you worry about accidents, death?

(As a child you sensed that if you weren't in charge, anything could happen. With men you're out to protect yourself from the unexpected.)

Did you sleep with a favorite stuffed animal or a special blanket, suck your thumb?

(Children who have felt the pain of separation sometimes turn to objects for solace.)

If Jessica's lovestyle is like yours, some of these questions have made you nod in agreement. Keep in mind that it's not the number of questions you answer yes to that's critical. What's important is if these questions enable you to see your pattern and the early experiences that contributed to its creation.

UNLEARNING THE PATTERN

Start the process of change by reviewing your lovestyle. You are a woman whose need to prevent separation and feelings of abandonment means that you are guarded, rational, and logical in your approach to men. You don't move too quickly or deeply and never get too carried away. Keeping two feet on the ground is your style. Risk taking is not.

Your personal history has left its mark. You can't permit a man to have the emotional upperhand. Instead, you evaluate men and then decide to start something. You begin only if you read unflagging stability, not passion. Where does this lead? The real difficulty is that along with stability comes boredom as its predictable consequence. Eventually you realize that something is missing and that you want something more.

Print your need on a card:

My need is to avoid separation and block feelings of abandonment.

For a person with this pattern work may play an important role, so attempts to reinforce their need should be tied in with the workplace. Perhaps you could put one card in an envelope marked "Personal." Instruct your secretary to bring it to you whenever you work overtime. Use one as a marker in your personal appointment book. Reduce the declaration to an acronym and place it beside your desk clock. You might keep one near your list of emergency telephone numbers, near the name of the doctor you call when you have an anxiety attack, another one wrapped around the vial of Valium or the painkiller you may take for headaches. Your stationery box may be a good place; whenever you write to "keep in touch," let it surface to remind you of your need to keep connected to people.

Other strategic spots can be left to your own imagination. (Borrow suggestions from other chapters if they're useful.) The more you deduce the details of your own pattern, the easier it will be to find effective places.

Work on bringing your need out into the open. Once you are convinced of the reality of your need, you can attempt the next step toward change: relationship analysis.

Your Relationship Analysis

Since you are becoming conscious of the role separation and abandonment play in your lovestyle, try to apply this insight to other significant relationships in your past. In this way you may begin to see how pervasive your need is and how often it has played a decisive role in your personal life.

Jessica's relationship analysis follows:

Grandfather Conrad, Mother's father

Grandfather retired before Jessica was born. As Jessica grew older and was able to do things he enjoyed, they became closer. At five they started riding together. Checkers and chess followed. By the time she was a teenager, she was his favorite first mate when they went sailing. She was notified at boarding school when he died, but didn't go home for the funeral. It bothered Jessica that she didn't cry, that she was able to go on as if it were just another day. During spring break she made a point of going to his grave; she wanted to cry, but she just couldn't.

Dwight, Jim, and Chester, three camp friends

As a child, whenever she thought of her camp, Jessica immediately thought of the brother camp across the lake and these three male friends. During the winter they didn't see one another, but during the summer they were inseparable. Everyone knew that if you went to look for one of them, you'd find all four. They were always on the same team, were "blood brothers," had a secret code, and swore that under no conditions would they ever go to another camp.

Donald and George, Jessica's "main" boyfriends
Donald was the boy she left in Atlanta. Despite her youth at the time, Jessica considered her relationship with Donald very serious. She wrote to him every single day, even though she saw him only over Thanksgiving and Christmas holiday recesses. Both of them understood that they could date other people. George was her "school" boyfriend, but it was strictly platonic.

Dr. Emanuel Gold, the family physician
Everyone, including Jessica, has always been treated by him. "He's one of the most busy and respected physicians in the country and he still has time for everyone. He really cares. I always tease him and call him the Marcus Welby of Atlanta." Even though she spent a number of years in Washington and New York, Jessica still regards him as her doctor. If she needs medical attention outside of Atlanta, it's always someone he knows and approves of. When they leave his office, Jessica's mother invariably tells her, "You need a man like Dr. Gold."

Throughout Jessica's life the theme of her need to avoid separation and the feeling of abandonment emerges in several ways.

With Grandfather it has two aspects. Jessica makes an effort to achieve, to master skills. She learns riding, checkers, chess, and sailing as a way of cementing her relationship with him. His death, the ultimate and permanent separation, is so painful that she must block it out completely; she misses him, but she can't mourn.

Her camp buddies are another example of her need to remain continuously attached to the same people. Remember that camp is the scene of her first painful separation from home. It is almost as if she must transform this symbol of separation into a symbol of unflagging continuity.

The boyfriends of her adolescent years are again an example of her effort to keep things uninterrupted. Keep in mind her constant correspondence and the presence of one boy at home and one at school—no gaps.

Dr. Gold is a dream come true. Caring, dependable, respected, solid, knowledgeable, always available, the kind of person you can trust.

Men You Should Be Alert To

For you these men are a mismatch. What makes your cycle particularly difficult to break is that you hang on to nice men, not exploiters. It may seem almost ridiculous to you, but good guys are your bad guys.

So watch out for men who

Are flawlessly respectable
Have immaculate credentials and/or pedigrees
Could be called a "mother's dream"
Have known you for a long time
Accept long-term platonic relationships
Are old family friends or former roommates
Tolerate another man in your life
Accept long-distance or part-time relationships
Are stolid, solid citizens
Are sexually unimaginative, you'd guess (you'll find your guess is right)

These are men who by their qualities send you a sub-liminal message that they will not bail out and leave you high and dry. These Rocks of Gibraltar unfortunately make for a lifeless relationship that can never bring you satisfaction.

When to Be Alone

Although intimacy, love, and commitment are central to each person's well-being, there are moments in life when attachments are neither possible nor appropriate. Life events may be so demanding or disruptive that they create a situation in which a woman is simply not emotionally available.

A woman who finds herself alone, having lost an intimate partner through death, is someone who needs time to absorb that loss. Though the feeling of loneliness may be acute, a woman should understand that this is an inevitable consequence of such loss. She should neither expect nor demand that she will be able to erase these feelings. Closeness requires reaching into one's deepest nature. It can only happen when there has been time for healing.

Other major life events may call for an emotional hiatus as well. Following separation, divorce, or breakup of a long-standing relationship, it may be appropriate for a woman to give herself time before she begins to consider the question of new emotional attachments.

There are other stresses of life that can act to divert your emotional resources and energy and make sharing your innermost self with a man impossible. The important thing to recognize is that although these moments may be part of your experience, they do not eliminate your capacity for intimacy. This means that the work involved in creating important bonds between people is emotionally demanding; it requires emotional resources within you that are sometimes, for reasons outside of your control, in short supply.

This is a book about women. Confining the focus to women is not to say that men are without problems in their love lives. On the contrary, men who fail to achieve intimacy with women are also often repeating old, unsuccessful patterns of relating.

However, women are usually more willing and able to be self-critical and to question themselves. They tend to be more reflective. You can probably corroborate this by your own experience. Think about the way women discuss problems with one another as compared with the way men do it. Think of how many more women's groups there are than men's. Mental-health professionals can further attest to the fact that the ratio of women to men in therapy is about three to one.

One can speculate that these may be cultural differences. Perhaps in our society men are not permitted to deal openly with emotions, whereas women are encouraged to do so. Perhaps women, feeling less valued than men, are more likely to be unsure of and question their behavior. Doubtless there is no single reason for this difference. Yet the fact remains that women approach their life problems in their own special ways. Ultimately it is out of respect for such differences that this book has been created. Why? Because although there are problems, needs, and problematic patterns in our lives, there are also answers. And hope. Life is change, and change is hope. You are worth it.

THE MARSHALL FIELD & COMPANY IDEA

TO DO THE RIGHT THING AT THE RIGHT TIME, IN THE RIGHT WAY;

TO DO SOME THINGS BETTER THAN THEY WERE EVER DONE BEFORE;

TO ELIMINATE ERRORS;

TO KNOW BOTH SIDES OF THE QUESTION;

TO BE COURTEOUS,

TO BE AN EXAMPLE,

TO LOVE OUR WORK;

TO ANTICIPATE REQUIREMENTS;

TO DEVELOP RESOURCES;

TO RECOGNIZE NO IMPEDIMENTS;

TO MASTER CIRCUMSTANCES;

TO ACT FROM REASON RATHER THAN RULE;

TO BE SATISFIED WITH NOTHING SHORT OF PERFECTION.

01	State Street, Chicago, 60690	• (312) 781-1000
	Personal Shopping Service	• (312) 781-1050
02	Oak Park, Oak Park 60301	• (312) 386-3600
03	Evanston, Evanston 60201	• (312) 475-6600
04	Lake Forest, Lake Forest 60045	• (312) 234-2340
05	Park Forest, Park Forest 60466	• (312) 748-2500
06	Old Orchard, Skokie 60076	• (312) 674-1234
07	Mayfair, Wauwatosa, WI. 53226	• (414) 771-2121
08	Oakbrook, Oak Brook 60521	• (312) 654-1234
09	River Oaks, Calumet City 60409	• (312) 868-1234
10	Woodfield, Schaumburg 60172	• (312) 882-1234
11	Hawthorn, Vernon Hills 60061	• (312) 367-1234
12	CherryVale, Rockford 61112	• (815) 332-2424
13	Fox Valley, Aurora 60505	• (312) 851-7234
14	Water Tower, Chicago 60611	• (312) 781-1234
15	Orland Square, Orland Park 60462	• (312) 349-1234
16	Louis Joliet, Joliet 60435	• (815) 439-1234
17	Spring Hill, West Dundee 60118	• (312) 428-1234
18	Stratford Square, Bloomingdale 60108	• (312) 980-1234
25	The Galleria, Houston, TX. 77056	• (713) 840-0440

ENTRY
DESCRIPTIONS ▶

MDS	• MERCHANDISE	ATD	• AMOUNT TENDERED	CHG	• CHARGE
STL	• SUB TOTAL	CDU	• CHANGE DUE YOU	COD	• COLLECT ON DELIVERY
ATX	• TAX	TTL	• TOTAL	RTN	• MERCH RET'D
MTX	• TAX	CSH	• CASH	FEE	• COD OR SHIPPING CHARGE

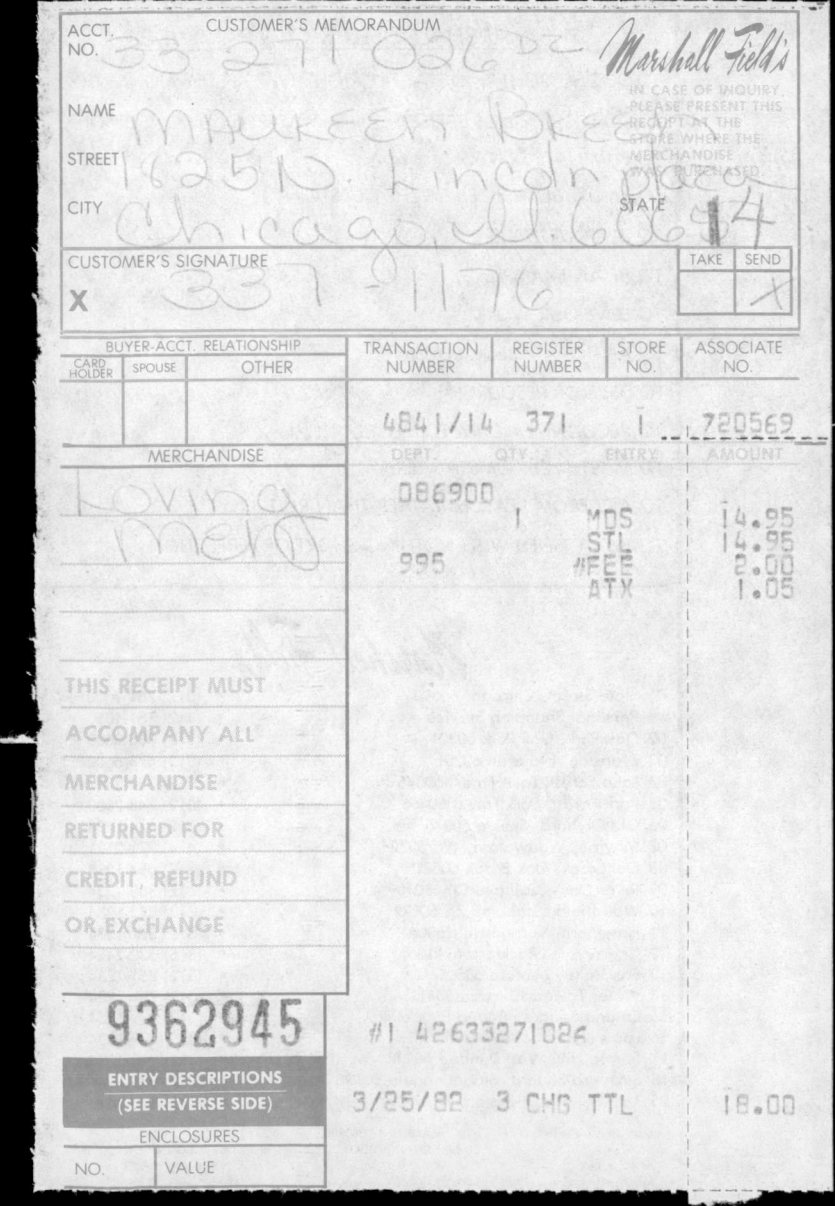

ACCT. NO. 33 271 026 DC

CUSTOMER'S MEMORANDUM

Marshall Field's

IN CASE OF INQUIRY, PLEASE PRESENT THIS RECEIPT AT THE STORE WHERE THE MERCHANDISE WAS PURCHASED

NAME MAUREEN BEE

STREET 16251 N. Lincoln place

CITY Chicago, Ill. 60614   STATE

CUSTOMER'S SIGNATURE

X 337-1176

TAKE	SEND
	X

BUYER-ACCT. RELATIONSHIP			TRANSACTION NUMBER	REGISTER NUMBER	STORE NO.	ASSOCIATE NO.
CARD HOLDER	SPOUSE	OTHER	4841/14	371	1	720569

MERCHANDISE	DEPT.	QTY.	ENTRY	AMOUNT
Loving mem	086900	1	MDS	14.95
			STL	14.95
	995		#FEE	2.00
			ATX	1.05

THIS RECEIPT MUST

ACCOMPANY ALL

MERCHANDISE

RETURNED FOR

CREDIT, REFUND

OR EXCHANGE

9362945

ENTRY DESCRIPTIONS
(SEE REVERSE SIDE)

ENCLOSURES

NO.	VALUE

#1 42633271026

3/25/82 3 CHG TTL   18.00

Acknowledgments

The completion of this book leaves us with many people to thank. More than anyone else it is Juris Jurjevics, our editor, who is responsible for bringing this book to fruition. He is a man of great talent, sensitivity, and humor—all of which he brought in abundance to this work. For this, and for his friendship, we thank him.

We also wish to acknowledge the help of Barbara Sanders, who provided not only enthusiasm and support, but the title for this book; and Themis Dimon, our first reader and critic, who was a constant source of ideas.

Our grateful thanks are also extended to Laura Cantales, Jennifer Wright, Freida Maslin, and Nechama Maslinsky for their technical assistance on the manuscript. To all our colleagues who gave us their time and their thoughts, we are similarly indebted.

And finally we of course thank the many women who shared their private selves with us and in so doing reached out to countless others.